WHEN KINGDOM LIGHT SHINES

Stories that inspire faith

MARK ELLIS

WHEN KINGDOM LIGHT SHINES
Copyright © 2024 Mark Ellis
ISBN: 978-1-964359-00-7
LCCN: 2024914077

All rights reserved. No part of this book may be reproduced, stored in a retrieval system, or transmitted in any form or by any means--electronic, mechanical, digital, photocopy, or any other---without prior permission from the publisher and author, except as provided by the United States of America copyright law.

Unless otherwise noted, all scriptures are from THE HOLY BIBLE, NEW INTERNATIONAL VERSION®. Copyright © 1973, 1978, 1984, 2011 by Biblica, Inc.™. Used by permission of Zondervan.

Scripture quotations marked (ESV) are taken from THE HOLY BIBLE, ENGLISH STANDARD VERSION®, Copyright © 2001 by Crossway, a publishing ministry of Good News Publishers. Used by permission.

Scripture quotations marked (KJV) are taken from the KING JAMES VERSION, public domain.

Scripture quotations marked (NASB) are taken from the NEW AMERICAN STANDARD BIBLE®, Copyright © 1960, 1962, 1963, 1968, 1971, 1972, 1973, 1975, 1977, 1995 by The Lockman Foundation. Used by permission.

Scripture quotations marked (NKJV) are taken from the NEW KING JAMES VERSION®. Copyright © 1982 by Thomas Nelson, Inc. Used by permission. All rights reserved.

Address all personal correspondence to:
Mark Ellis
P.O. Box 7022
Capistrano Beach, CA, 92624
www.godreports.com
mark@godreports.com

Individuals and church groups may order books from Mark Ellis or God Reports directly, or from the publisher. All proceeds from the sale of this book will go to Christian Writers & Artists Ministries, a non-profit 501c3, DBA God Reports and Assist News.Retailers and wholesalers should order from our distributors. Refer to the Deeper Revelation Books website for distribution information, as well as an online catalog of all our books.

Published by:
Deeper Revelation Books
Revealing "the deep things of God" (1 Cor. 2:10)
P.O. Box 4260
Cleveland, TN 37320 423-478-2843
Website: www.deeperrevelationbooks.org
Email: info@deeperrevelationbooks.org

Deeper Revelation Books and its divisions assist Christian writers in publishing and distributing their works. Our authors are the ultimate decision-makers in the process. Final responsibility for the creative design, content, permissions, editorial accuracy, stories and doctrinal views, either expressed or implied, belongs to the author. What you hold in your hand is an expression of this author's passion to publish the truth to this generation with a spirit of excellence. It was a blessing and an honor to assist in this process.

TABLE OF CONTENTS

Introduction 10

CHAPTER 1
Dream Led to Hidden Tribe 12

CHAPTER 2
9/11 Remembrance 22

CHAPTER 3
Idaho Boy Sent Shoebox to 'Christmas Child'
in the Philippines 30

CHAPTER 4
Atheist Art Professor's Near-Death
Experience in Hell 33

CHAPTER 5
A Migraine Headache Saved Her Life 40

CHAPTER 6
North Korean Woman's Prison Story 46

CHAPTER 7
His Encounter with Jesus Began in the Mosque ... 55

CHAPTER 8
She Did the Unimaginable to Save Jews 59

CHAPTER 9
Movement He Founded Changed His Own Life ... 66

CHAPTER 10
Missionary Died Thinking He Was a Failure 71

CHAPTER 11
Fastest Growing Church Has No Walls 74

CHAPTER 12
How Islam Progressively Takes Over Countries ... 78

CHAPTER 13
Woman's Near-Death Vision of Heaven
Confirms Other Accounts 82

CHAPTER 14
Airline Pilot Prompted by Holy Spirit to
Speed Departure Before Disaster Struck 85

Chapter 15
Good Book Survived Nashville Tornado 88

Chapter 16
Top Female Porn Star Found Jesus 89

Chapter 17
Winston Churchill Warned
About the Dangers of Radical Islam 93

Chapter 18
They Called Themselves Christians,
But Refused to Forgive 95

Chapter 19
Encounter with Jesus on the Moon
Left Astronaut Changed 98

Chapter 20
How God Answered Francis Chan's
Ridiculous Prayer for a Son-In-Law 102

Chapter 21
Jesus Appeared to Muslim Family, Said
He Was Sending a Man to Tell Them More 105

Chapter 22
D-Day Chaplain Carried No Weapons,
Led Men off Landing Craft 108

Chapter 23
The Early Roots of the Jesus Movement 111

Chapter 24
The Communal Hippie House That Became
Ground Zero for Jesus Movement 120

Chapter 25
The Untold Story of Pastor Ray Ortlund's
Homegoing 127

Chapter 26
Anne Ortlund's Valentine Remembrance 132

Chapter 27
Jesus Movement Prodigal Slid into Sin 136

Chapter 28
A Mechanic's Cry for Help 142

CHAPTER 29
Researcher Finds True Location of
Jewish Temple 148

CHAPTER 30
Born with a Hole in Her Heart 152

CHAPTER 31
Businessman's Near-Death Experience of Hell 155

CHAPTER 32
Vincent Van Gogh's Unappreciated Journey
with Christ 160

CHAPTER 33
For the Burpo Family, Heaven Is for Real 165

CHAPTER 34
Lost Forty-Seven Days at Sea 169

CHAPTER 35
Mysterious 'Jesus Photo' Stirs Faith,
Brings Comfort and Peace to Many 176

CHAPTER 36
Satanist Plotted to Kill Prominent Pastor 180

CHAPTER 37
Noted Physicist Says String Theory
Suggests We're All Living in God's Matrix 186

CHAPTER 38
Hostile Tribe's Chief Found Resurrection 188

CHAPTER 39
Atheist Pilot Mocked God, until He Ran
Out of Fuel in a Snowstorm 193

CHAPTER 40
Emma's Guardian Angels 196

CHAPTER 41
Muslim Struggled with Life-Threatening
Shingles 199

CHAPTER 42
Raised by Gay Parents, He Shocked Them
by Coming Out as a Christian 203

CHAPTER 43
Explosion and Fire Burned 95% of His Body 206

CHAPTER 44
Muslim Husband Locked Christian Wife
Out of the House 211

CHAPTER 45
Identical Twin Studies Prove Homosexuality
Is Not Genetic 213

CHAPTER 46
What Book Was Actor Steve McQueen
Holding When He Left Us? 216

CHAPTER 47
The Day Jesus Invaded a Buddhist Monastery
in the Himalayas 220

CHAPTER 48
Gay Hollywood Insider Experienced
'Change of Affection' 223

CHAPTER 49
Church Caught a Vision to Free
Modern-Day Slaves 230

CHAPTER 50
Former Muslim Raised from the Dead
Shocked Her Neighbors 240

CHAPTER 51
Heavy Metal Satanist Rescued by Christ 243

CHAPTER 52
The Kundalini Yoga Instructor
Who Found Jesus 250

CHAPTER 53
Stage Four Lung Cancer Went into Her Brain 254

CHAPTER 54
Computer Scientist-Engineer Experienced
Vision of Hell 257

CHAPTER 55
Mickey Rooney's Encounter with
Unusual Busboy 264

CHAPTER 56
Paul Harvey's Amazing Prediction
About the Future of America 266

CHAPTER 57
Jesus Miraculously Healed Woman's
'Incurable' Cancer 268

CHAPTER 58
He Preached the Gospel as Hijacked Plane
Hit the Water 272

CHAPTER 59
When God Sends Signs in the Natural World
after the Death of a Loved One 275

CHAPTER 60
Dying Farmer Left Civil War Bible
Behind for New Age Homebuyer 278

INTRODUCTION

I took my first overseas mission trip to the southern Philippines in 2004 to visit two Wycliffe Bible Translators. Carl and Lauretta DuBois had spent over forty years translating the Scripture and had recently completed their second translation of the Bible.

Their house was the size of my two-car garage in Orange County, California. I learned they had been evacuated twice from their home: once under threat from communists and once when endangered by radical Islamists.

There were also other challenges they endured. Lauretta fought breast cancer during their term of service. As well as when they began their second Bible translation, one of their two sons fell from a tree and was paralyzed from the waist down.

As I flew home from the island of Mindanao, I reflected on the sacrifices they made to bring a precious gift to the Tagabawa—God's living Word. Even after their retirement a few years later, the gift of God's eternal Word would keep on giving.

As an assistant pastor at a small church in Laguna Beach, California, I had been writing on the side, contributing stories to ASSIST News Service about the church around the world. My first assignment in October 2000 was to cover a Promise Keepers event in Los Angeles.

I was excited to write a story about the DuBois' missionary efforts in the Philippines, but I wondered how many other missionaries serving overseas had their own compelling stories to share.

I thought about developing a website to share stories and testimonies from believers living out their faith around the world. Five years later, the God Reports website was birthed, with a mission to support and encourage Christian missions, by sharing stories and testimonies from believers around the world.

It remains my conviction that God's stories are the best stories, and that He is doing even greater things in the world today than He did in the first century. The following pages are filled with my favorite stories over the last twenty-five years—stories I trust will inspire and enlarge your faith in the great God we serve.

Chapter 1

Dream Led to Hidden Tribe

In 2013, Caleb Byerly woke up with a start and began to furiously write in his journal everything he saw in a rather unusual dream. For the previous five years, the small-town North Carolina resident had been engaged in mission outreach to indigenous people and tribal areas in Southeast Asia and the Pacific Islands.

"In the dream, I was standing on top of this mountain. I was looking out across the mountain, and I saw a tribe of people," he recounted. Caleb and his wife, Gladys, live in Moravian Falls, a town of 1400, in the foothills of the Brushy Mountains.

He had never seen the tribe before and felt drawn to them, so he asked, "What tribe are you? What people are you?"

"We're the Tinananon tribe," they replied. Caleb had never heard of this people group, and he began to carefully observe their actions in his dream.

A tribal chief walked to the front carrying a musical instrument. Caleb happened to be an instrument maker by profession, so his eyes "zoomed in" to study the distinctive design of an instrument unlike anything he had ever seen before.

It had thirty strings going all the way around the top of a golden bowl, from the outside, crisscrossing in the middle of the instrument. "I suddenly got a full download of everything about this instrument, what dimensions the instrument was, what material it was made out of, even like how it was tuned and how it was played. After that, I kind of zoomed back out."

"This tribal chief, he took the instrument, and he put it on the table. He took two small sticks, and he began to play this instrument. As he played, the whole tribe started to dance, and they started to worship. This kind of sound of worship just filled the place. It was as if heaven and earth just collided. After that, I woke up from the dream."

God had spoken to Caleb through dreams previously, so he meticulously recorded in his journal the name of the Tinananon tribe. He made detailed drawings of the bowl, its dimensions and materials, a wooden ring that goes around the bowl, the strings connected by wooden pegs, and the two sticks used to play the instrument.

"I feel like when God speaks to you, it's an invitation to partner and walk with God. It's not just God commanding you to do things or God just saying, 'Do this, do that.' But it's the Holy Spirit inviting you into some new journey that he's calling you into, and it's connected to you, it's connected to your DNA, and your calling. I really value that a lot. I really thought that this would be a really exciting thing to follow with the Lord."

Caleb began to search online for any reference to a Tinananon people group but came up short. "I contacted different organizations like Wycliffe Bible Translators and Summer Institute of Linguistics to see if they knew anything about this tribe. But everywhere I searched, I could not find that word. I tried the different spellings, but just couldn't find anything there. So, I kind of gave up on that." [Summer Institute of Linguistics is now known as SIL International.]

But as an instrument maker, he was intrigued by the idea of recreating the instrument he saw in the dream. "At that time, I was doing full-time missions work, and I was also doing some instrument making on the side, and instrument making was a passion of mine. And I was making flutes and some drums, basic instruments. This instrument I saw in my dream was a lot more difficult than what I was used to."

"I'm gonna make this thing!" he decided. Even though he had not put metal and wood together in that way, he was up for the challenge.

"I got into my shop, and I just kept breaking this thing. I kept breaking things and snapping things. I could not figure out this one process. I got really frustrated. I was like, 'I'm just gonna put this thing to the side.' I just couldn't figure it out."

"So, I kind of gave up on the whole dream. I felt like I had done my part. I wasn't getting anywhere. So, I just kind of gave it up."

About six months later, he took a mission trip to the island of Mindanao in the southern Philippines, an area where he had previously been involved in ministry.

"I was on a Jeepney, which is like a public transportation. There was this man that was sitting on the other side of me. I could tell this guy was staring at me. I was like, *What's this guy doing?* Every time that I would look at him, he would like look away."

Caleb knows the national language of the Philippines, Tagalog, because his wife is from the northern Philippines. During the first two years of their marriage, she patiently taught him the language.

So, Caleb addressed the man. "As I was talking to him, it turns out that he's a believer! So, we're chatting and then right in the middle of our conversation, I heard the Lord speak to me. It wasn't an audible voice or anything. It was just felt."

The Lord spoke to Caleb's heart and said, *I want you to ask that man about the Tinananon.*

Inside, Caleb resisted. *No, I'm not going to ask this man about the Tinananon,* he thought, *I've already tried to do all my research.*

A second time, the Lord nudged his heart, *Ask this man about the Tinananon.*

Caleb built up his courage and said meekly, "Sir, do you happen to know Tinananon?"

As soon as he said the word Tinananon, the man's eyes got really big.

He leaned in and said, "Hey, that's my people—that's my tribe! How do you know my people?"

Caleb was rendered speechless for a moment but eventually said, "Tell me everything you know about your tribe."

Manigos began to explain that his tribe lived in a deep mountainous region of Mindanao. "This area is a really dangerous place," he said, "No one from outside goes to this place." Manigos estimated his people group numbers between 70,000 and 100,000 people, scattered throughout the mountainous region in pockets.

Caleb invited Manigos to follow him to the place he was staying and showed him his journal entry with the word "Tinananon."

Manigos began shaking his head, and tears streamed down his face.

He said, "Remember earlier on the bus, I kept looking at you."

"Yes, what was that all about?"

"I kept looking at you, and the reason why is because I've seen you before ... I just realized where I saw you; I also saw you in a dream three years ago."

Manigos explained that he was born in the Tinananon tribe. He left as a young man and went to Davao City, the largest city on the island of Mindanao, with around 1.9 million people. He came to know Jesus while he lived in the city, then God called him back to his tribe through a dream.

In the dream, Manigos had gone back to evangelize his people—with Caleb! "He saw me in his dream," Caleb said, "and I came and joined him. He and I began to minister and bring the Good News of Jesus to his people."

They were filled with wonder and awe at the way God brought them together. "This is certainly the Lord. This is the leadership of the Holy Spirit!" Caleb exclaimed.

The two men stayed together for several days. "We all worshipped together and prayed together for a few days." Manigos invited Caleb to visit his tribe.

"Yeah, I would love to go to your tribe," Caleb replied, "but I need to ask my wife first." His wife, Gladys, was eight months pregnant at the time. Going on a potentially dangerous journey, immediately before the birth of their first child was a big decision they had to make.

After Caleb flew home to North Carolina, he and his wife sought the Lord's direction. "We felt like the Lord's hand was on it," he said. "And if the Lord showed this, up to this point, then He would continue to be with us. So, I decided I was going to go, but I wanted to get back in the shop and try to make this instrument again."

Caleb got very focused and asked the Holy Spirit to help him. "The Lord gave me divine wisdom, gave me insight, on the process of what to do ... with the help of the Holy Spirit and my wife, we were able to get it. I finally made this instrument!"

He put the strings on it for the first time. "I tuned it up the way I heard it in the dream. I got the two little sticks, and I started to play it. It was that same sound I heard in the dream."

He and his wife sought the Lord once more about the timing of his return to the Philippines. With Gladys eight months pregnant, they were wondering if he should wait until after the baby's arrival. They felt the Lord was impressing on their hearts— go now!

Caleb bought a plane ticket and left the next day for the Philippines, taking the instrument with him.

He met a tribal friend named Ansulao and his new friend, Manigos, at the border of the mountain range closest to the tribe. "All three of us, we got on this one little motorbike. It was like 120 cc, a little motorbike."

A large storm had passed through the steep, undeveloped mountainous area the day before. "It was really muddy, very hard to get through there. And then, while we were on this motorbike, another storm came. I was trying to hold this instrument, and I couldn't hold it to my left or my right, so I had to put it above my head (wrapped in a cloth)."

"Imagine three people on a little motorcycle. I was holding this musical instrument above my head trying to balance."

As they entered the area of the Tinananon tribal group, Caleb heard the still small voice of the Lord once more, *Caleb, I want you to take the instrument to the chief.*

They started asking about how to find the chief's house, which they learned was another three and a half hours away, on the other side of the mountain.

By the time they reached the chief's house, it was almost evening. Mud covered their clothing as they approached a small, wooden house and knocked on the door.

When the chief opened the door, he had a shocked expression on his face—especially to see an American in this remote area.

"We are—I am—coming to your tribe for the first time," Caleb said. "It's such a joy to be here. But before we go to any other parts of your tribe, we just want to honor you, and give this as a gift to you," he said, holding the instrument in his outstretched arms, still covered by a cloth.

The chief placed the instrument on a table and took the cloth off. "He saw this instrument and he started staring at it. He kept looking at this instrument over and over again. He kept asking me, 'Where did you get that from?'"

"Well, I just kind of made it," Caleb replied.

"No, no, I'm serious. Where did you get that from?"

"Well, if you really want to know. Last year, I had this dream. In the dream, I heard the name of your tribe, the Tinananon, for the first time. I'd never heard that word before. I also saw this musical instrument in the dream. I felt like my God has given this dream to me."

"After that I met this man, Manigos, who is from your tribe, and he helped lead me to your house today. I was able to make this instrument. I just felt like I wanted to give this instrument to you today."

The chief continued shaking his head in disbelief, examining the instrument carefully, asking questions about it. He summoned other elders from the Tinananon tribe and they walked around it incredulously, pointing at it, saying "Salimbaa."

"They have their own native tongue," Caleb notes. "And I don't totally understand their language. So, I was pretty lost about what they were talking about."

Finally, the chief motioned to them and said, "I need to show you something." They left his house and went down a small pathway over to another structure.

"They call the house, 'Paluvaran,' which means House of Prayer in their language. This is the place where they worship. But it's also sort of a storehouse of all their kind of ancient articles of their tribes. They have pottery work, metalwork, weaving, all these different things that are tangible evidence that their tribe has been living and existing for hundreds of years."

"I was amazed by this place. They had all these musical instruments on the side of the wall." As a professional instrument maker, Caleb found it fascinating and incredible. "It was kind of like the holy of holies of their tribe. It was the most sacred spot of their tribe, and they took me inside there."

The chief informed him there were different musical instruments for each of their gods. "They have the god of the tree, the god of the stone, god of the river. And they're not necessarily gods, but they believe that the one true God or the Creator has sent down angels to guard these different things like the angel of the river, the angel of the stone."

"Instead of praying and worshiping directly to God, they pray and worship to these different angels; the angels would be the ones to connect them to God. And so, it's a little bit different, but it's not completely like they believe in many different gods. They believe in the one true God."

Caleb noticed there was one spot that was blank on the wall between the other instruments. "They said that somewhere between 100 and 150 years ago, there was a tribal war. During this war, their most valuable musical instrument that worshiped the God of all gods was taken away from them."

In response, they lamented for a time and created a song that goes something like this:

The Salimbaa was taken away from us,

God is going to redeem it back to us one day.

"And when that instrument is redeemed back to them, that is going to be the sign that God is coming back again. Because God is going to come down from heaven, and He's going to call all the righteous people to Him."

"It was a prophecy. This instrument is the instrument that

worships the God of all gods. They said, 'Today, you brought the Salimbaa to us!'"

Caleb was blown away. "Oh, my goodness!" he exclaimed.

After that, there was a small gathering of tribal leaders. "This is it! This is the Salimbaa!" they cried. Everyone knew what it was when they saw it and heard it played.

Caleb learned the Salimbaa's golden bowl, with strings stretching from side to side around the bowl, has a convergence in the middle that is the place where the Tinananon believe the Salimbaa connects heaven and earth.

"They said, in the last days, God is going to be coming down from heaven. When God comes down from heaven, God is going to be riding on the inside of the Salimbaa, as if the Salimbaa was an aircraft that connects heaven and earth."

"Salimbaa is the aircraft from heaven. He's going to ride down from heaven, and He's going to call all the righteous people to Him. So, I mean, the way that I interpret that is the Salimbaa is Jesus—Jesus is the Way, and the Truth, and the Life, and He is the only way to heaven."

"I really believe that Jesus is the only salvation way to heaven. That's been my prayer for this tribe ever since."

Their name for the God above all gods is Manama. "They started praying to Manama, and they dedicated this instrument back to God."

As a sign of special honor, the chief placed a tribal leader's headpiece on Caleb's shoulder. "We now consider you a chief of the Tinananon tribe," he said. "Whatever you believe God is calling us or leading us into, we're going to follow you."

Reeling from the whole experience, Caleb was humbled by the gesture. They stayed with the chief, Datu Lipatuan Suhat, for three days.

"There wasn't a lot that manifested with him giving his life to Jesus," Caleb told God Reports. "I did pray with him a lot and prophesied over him. But after we left, we didn't return for a few months, but during that time, within a month or two, the chief had an encounter with Jesus, and the Lord spoke to him and he wrote everything out. That is when he gave his heart to Jesus."

On the second visit, Caleb asked Chief Suhat how he could help the tribe. The chief pondered the question for over thirty minutes, then he said, "Well, if you can help us with one thing, I want you to help us translate the Bible into our language."

In January 2015, Caleb arranged for the Translators Association of the Philippines to meet with all fifty chiefs of the Tinananon tribe.

"Some of the chiefs didn't want the Bible to be translated and others did," Caleb told God Reports. "There was tension in the room. None of us as foreigners felt led to speak up. The chief came up to the front and opened up the Cebuano Bible, from Genesis."

Caleb learned the Tinananon believe that God came down and took the soil of Mindanao and put it in His hands and blew on it and that is when the first man came alive.

"We believe God made man from His breath," Chief Suhat said, "by taking the dust of the earth and breathing on it."

Chief Suhat proceeded to read the biblical account of the creation of man and said, "It's only the first few pages, imagine what it would be to have the whole Bible translated."

The other chiefs nodded their heads in agreement. "That's true," they said, and all fifty agreed to let the translators begin their project.

Chief Suhat passed away in 2015, after the translation project began, only a year after Caleb arrived with the Salimbaa.

"It was amazing to see that the last year of his life, that he got to see this, and that he led a lot of his people to a place of receiving Jesus ... I saw that he was a lover of Jesus. And he led his tribe to receive Jesus. And he gave us the complete open door to bring the Gospel."

Since then, there have been many churches planted among the Tinananon. "It's just amazing, the open doors that the chiefs have given us for this tribe."

"It was mostly through Manigos," Caleb says. "He and

some of his companions have just been able to take it and run with it. And it has been absolutely incredible to see the Gospel spread and grow."

"And a lot of people have come to know Jesus, hundreds of people, it could be in the thousands. We took another team there in December, and there were fifteen communities (church plants)."

"Manigos could speak the language and knew the culture. He has such a heart for his people. He has a God-given call to his people."

"I felt like the Lord had arranged everything," Caleb says, "in such a perfect way of organizing everything, just perfect timing. It was such an amazing series of events that took place that I couldn't take any kind of claim for it."

"The best way I guess I could explain is like I was right there in the middle of the journey with God. I felt like He was there in the moment. I was like, yeah, yeah, this is Him. This is Him; this is what He did!"

To see the article on God Reports with photos, go here:

Caleb and Gladys Byerly are the founders of Evergreen Missions. Their focus is to partner with God in bringing His kingdom to the earth. Caleb and Gladys focus mostly on mentoring and discipling indigenous leaders, who will go to their own people and bring them life from Christ Jesus.

Adam Fish and his wife, Brooke, started The Unseen Story, a podcast featuring firsthand accounts that reveal the reality of God's love. They brought Caleb's story to the attention of God Reports.

CHAPTER 2

9/11 Remembrance

Stanley Praimnath, born in Guyana, came to America with little money in his pockets in 1981. When he arrived, Praimnath landed a job in the garment industry in Jersey City, New Jersey, where he earned $125 a week. Then he got a job as a file clerk for a bank in downtown Manhattan.

Growing up in Guyana, his mother insisted he attend church, but he rebelled and drifted away during high school. "I woke up one day in America and decided I wanted to be a good guy, whatever 'good' means," he recalls. Then a friend called and invited him to church. "The more I went, the more I liked what I saw," Praimnath says. He was born again in 1983.

A few years later, he married a pastor's daughter and started a new career with Fuji Bank. On the side, he helped his father-in-law plant a church in a rough neighborhood of Queens, New York.

Within five years, Praimnath advanced to asst. vice-president, running all of Fuji Bank's operations on the 81st floor of the World Trade Center, Tower 2. That floor was immense—approximately one acre square, and almost completely soundproof from the outside.

Praimnath thought he was on top of the world, even planes flew at the same level. When he looked down, everything looked small. Praimnath says most of the people he worked with at Fuji Bank were Buddhists or Shinto; there were only a handful of Christians.

When most people went to lunch, Praimnath sat at his desk with a salad or soup, reading his Bible. He tried to share about Christ when he had opportunities, but most didn't want to hear.

On the morning of September 11, he was riding up the elevator to his office at 8:45 a.m. when Tower One was hit by the first plane. Riding in the elevator, Praimnath didn't see or hear a thing.

As soon as he laid his briefcase down, he began to receive a barrage of phone calls, first from his mother, then his wife and brothers. "Stan, are you okay?" they asked. He said, "Yes, yes, I'm fine," but none of them told him what happened. He wondered why his family was checking up on him.

When he hung up, he glanced out his window for the first time. He was stunned to see huge chunks of fiery debris, "fireballs," falling from Tower One. The other half of Fuji Bank's operations were in that tower, so he called there to try to reach his boss. There was no answer.

Praimnath decided it was time to get out, so he jumped in an elevator and headed down to the lobby. He was about to go through the turnstile exit when a security guard stopped him. "Where are you going?" the man asked.

"I'm going home," Stanley said.

The security guard said, "No, the building is safe and secure, go back to your office." Soon, an intercom was piping in the same message: "Your attention please, ladies and gentlemen, Building 2 is secure. There is no need to evacuate Building 2."

Praimnath got into the express elevator and in less than a minute was back up to the 81st floor. Several of his co-workers rode in the same elevator. They were laughing and exchanging pleasantries. When he got off that elevator, it was the last time he would see them again.

He walked into his office and the phone rang immediately. It was a woman from Chicago saying, "Stan, Stan, get out, get out of the building." He assured the woman he was fine. "But you're not logged on to the computer," she said. Stanley still didn't know a plane had hit the first building.

As he assured the woman he was safe, he stood up near his desk, while he held the phone in his hand, and just happened to look toward the Statue of Liberty. Suddenly, he saw a huge plane, gray in color, that flew straight at him. "It was coming at me at eye-level contact," he notes. Praimnath could make out the letter U on the tail. It was United Flight 175.

"As the plane was getting nearer, I could hear a revving sound the engine was making, like the sound a plane makes when it's about to take off," Praimnath says. "Quadruple that sound, and that's the sound I could hear, even in this soundproof building. I can still hear that sound in my head," he says. "That sound will never go away."

"I'm standing up looking at this plane getting bigger and nearer," Praimnath says. "You don't know how fast your mind is reacting."

In desperation, he cried out to God, "Lord, I can't do this—You take over," and he dove under his desk. Praimnath's Bible still sat on top of the desk. The plane slammed into the building with immense force. The bottom of the wing sliced through his office and stuck in his office door, twenty feet away from where he huddled.

"There was a massive fireball as the major part of the plane blew up," Praimnath says. "The only desk that stood firm was the one I was hiding under because my Bible was on top of that desk!"

Every wall was flattened as if a demolition crew had passed through. Other than his desk, every other piece of office furniture was smashed like matchboxes. Part of the floor above his head collapsed downward, and all the cables in the ceiling were dangling, falling, and short-circuiting, because the sprinklers came on.

"I thought if the floor doesn't completely collapse and kill me, I'll be electrocuted, or the plane's wing is going to blow up, and I'm going to die." Above Praimnath, a fiery inferno was raging. Fire had also broken out on his floor, some distance away. But in Praimnath's office, there was no fire. "That is a miracle," he says. "I was covered under the shadow of the Lord."

Praimnath had no way of knowing the clock was ticking, and his building would completely collapse within an hour's time.

He pushed debris away that was up to his shoulders. He couldn't completely stand up because the roof had collapsed downward. There was no way out of his office, because the plane's wing blocked the only exit door.

Praimnath let out an anguished cry to the Lord with every fiber of his being: "Lord, send somebody to help me, I don't want to die. What will happen to my wife and two kids?"

At that moment, Brian Clark, an executive vice-president with Euro Brokers, was walking down the only passable staircase from the 84th floor with six other people. Clark happened to be the fire warden on his floor, so he had a flashlight. When the group reached the 81st floor, they ran into a woman who told them to turn around and go back up.

But at that moment, Clark heard somebody far away who screamed and banged on a wall: "Help, help! I'm buried. Is anyone there? Help, I can't breathe." The voice in the distance was Praimnath's, and Clark decided he would stop to help. The others turned around and went up toward the top of the building, thinking they could escape to the roof.

Clark said later there was something in Praimnath's scream that impelled him to stay. His feet felt glued to the 81st floor. While the others in his group complained about the smoke and fumes, Clark said he felt like there was a bubble of protective oxygen around his head; the smoke never affected him. Those who went upward all perished. They didn't know the exit doors to the roof were locked after the 1993 terrorist bombing of the World Trade Center parking garage.

Through the rubble, Praimnath saw Brian Clark's flashlight in the distance. Clark called out in the direction of the screams, but Praimnath couldn't hear because he was temporarily deaf.

"I started crawling as fast as possible toward the light, because I knew if that man left me, I would die," Praimnath recalls. Praimnath could hear the air pressure sucking papers and other objects out of the shattered windows, probably due to a vortex created by the inferno. It was pitch-dark other than the darting flashlight he could see intermittently through the debris.

After he crawled through the wreckage of three departments, he finally reached a ten-foot sheetrock wall that was still intact. There was no way to get through it. His entire body was swollen, black and blue, by now.

Clark shouted at Praimnath through the wall, "Jump over it and I'll catch you on the other side."

"I can't do it," Praimnath shouted back.

"Think about your family," Clark retorted.

Praimnath tried to jump, but he missed and part of the ceiling caved in. As he reached up to prevent the ceiling from hitting him, a two-inch metal screw went through the palm of his hand. He cried out in pain; his body pierced in the same place as his Savior.

"What happened?" Clark called out.

"A metal screw went through my palm," he winced.

"Bite it out and try again," Clark said. Praimnath couldn't do that, so he hit the piece of wood attached to the screw and it came out of his hand. Immediately, his hand ballooned outward like a puffer fish.

"I began to plead with the invisible God," Praimnath recalls. "Lord, if you wanted me to die, why did you bring me all the way here? Who is going to walk my daughters down the aisle when they get married? What will befall my wife? Who will take care of my children? I want to see my family. Lord, just give me the strength one time more." Praimnath prayed aloud, and Clark could hear him through the wall.

Because of the fumes and smoke, Praimnath could barely breathe. He was at the end of his rope. He started to look at the wall and caress it gingerly with his good hand. Then he wound up and punched the wall as hard as he could. Miraculously, his hand passed through two layers of sheetrock to the other side and missed the supporting studs within the wall. "That is the grace of God," Praimnath says. "I couldn't do that now," he says.

Clark grabbed his hand momentarily, then Praimnath pulled it back through. Praimnath began to punch wildly at the hole until he could get his entire head through it, then his shoulders. Clark grabbed his head in a headlock and began to pull. Finally, Clark pulled with such force that Praimnath shot through the hole; they both landed on top of rubble and began to roll.

"He grabbed me and, around and round, we rolled together," Praimnath says. "We landed on the 80th floor."

When they both got up, Clark slapped him and said, "You could have died, do you know that. You're crazy." Then he extended his hand and introduced himself, "Brian Clark."

"Stanley Praimnath."

Clark grabbed Praimnath's hand gently and inspected his wound. They both had blood on their hands.

Then Clark looked Praimnath in the eyes and said, "All my life, I was an only child. I always wanted a brother. I found one today." They rubbed the blood on their hands together. Then Clark took his hand and put it around Stanley's shoulder. "Today, you're my blood brother. Come on buddy, let's go home."

As they worked their way down eighty flights, they saw some terrible sights. One man laid there with a broken back, bleeding from massive head injuries. "Please tell my wife and baby I love them. We just got married."

They saw a security guard watching over another injured man as they waited for help to arrive. Praimnath and Clark offered to carry the injured man down. "Don't touch him," the security guard said, believing paramedics would arrive shortly. Sadly, help never arrived. The security guard could have escaped but made the ultimate sacrifice.

When they made it to the lobby, they saw cops, emergency workers, and firefighters barking out orders. They yelled to the two men, "Run, run, run to Liberty." Liberty Street ran next to the World Trade Center.

"I'm going to Trinity Church," Praimnath said.

"I'm going with you," Clark replied.

As they left, people shouted at them, "Don't look up, don't look around, just run. Go, go, go." They jumped over fallen debris and giant shards of glass on their way out. Broken glass fell from the sky like confetti. "Not one piece touched us," Stanley recalls. As they ran away from the building, firefighters ran in with heavy gear on their backs to help others trapped above.

Praimnath heard loud thuds as jumpers from the upper stories hit the pavement. When he glanced up, he could see Tower 2 rock and sway.

They kept running until they reached Trinity Church. Both men grabbed hold of the iron fence surrounding the church as if their lives depended on it. As they looked back, panting from exhaustion, they could see Tower 2 sway and then stop.

"I could feel the vibration in the ground," Praimnath says. He turned to Brian and said, "It's going down."

At that instant, the building started to implode, one floor smashing on top of another. A giant tsunami of smoke, ash, dust, and debris began to rush toward them. Praimnath and Clark disappeared into the cloud and were separated for the rest of the day.

Praimnath made his way through the thick haze until he found a truck driver who gave him a lift to the Brooklyn Bridge. He finally found his wife's office, but she wasn't there. She had already gone home.

When the second plane hit the building, Praimnath's wife, Jennifer, assumed the worst. She waited at home, hoping and praying, but she thought he was gone. She started to go into shock.

When Praimnath called from her office she said, "Who is this?"

"It's me, Stan," he said.

There was a pause. "Don't do this to me," Jennifer said, convinced it was a cruel hoax. "Why are you doing this to me? My husband is dead."

"It's me, Stan. The Lord took care of me ... I'm coming home to you, girl."

Praimnath's story reminds his wife of the three Hebrew boys in the fiery furnace from the book of Daniel. "Those boys in the fiery furnace were unscathed and unharmed," Jennifer says. "Stan, you were in a towering inferno. Now all the impurities have been burned out of you and you're well done."

As they watched news accounts on television in the days that followed, Praimnath saw a replay of the second plane hit his tower. "If you look at the video," Praimnath says, "the plane is coming straight in toward the building, and at the last minute, it makes a tilt." Praimnath believes God pushed the plane away from him at the last second, in response to his heart cry to the Lord.

For weeks, he struggled with survivor's guilt. "Why did I live and why did so many good people die?" he asked God.

Then he heard a commentator talking about the significance of the numbers 9-1-1. Praimnath grabbed his Bible, and madly flipped through the scriptures, not even sure what he was looking for until he landed on Psalm 91:1 (ESV): *He who dwells in the shelter of the Most High will abide in the shadow of the Almighty.*

"My survival is all about God and His grace, because I'm not a hero," Praimnath says. "The Lord is the hero. If you call on Him with all your heart and soul, He will intervene on your behalf and deliver you," he says.

"I may never know why some people prayed and God didn't answer them or why I prayed and He answered me at the same time," he adds. "But I can tell you this, my God lives!"

The 9/11 Commission credits Praimnath as the only known survivor from the impact zone at the World Trade Center towers on September 11, 2001.

"The Lord saw fit for me to live," he says.

Praimnath's riveting tale of survival is chronicled in "Plucked from the Fire" (Rosedog Books), coauthored with William Hennessey.

CHAPTER 3

Idaho Boy Sent Shoebox to 'Christmas Child' in the Philippines

Many believers have stuffed a shoebox full of goodies for Operation Christmas Child, a project to bless children around the world run by Samaritan's Purse. But for one seven-year-old boy in Idaho, it led to a surprising outcome many years later.

In 2000, Tyrel Wolfe packed a shoebox for a young girl his age and added a photo of himself wearing cowboy attire, holding a lariat.

After he turned in his shoebox at church, he never gave much thought to the girl who received it 7,000 miles away.

Joana Marchan received the shoebox at a vacation Bible school in a suburb of Manila, Philippines. Not only was a photo of Tyrel included, but also his address.

She wrote a thank-you letter to express her appreciation, but it got lost in the mail.

Eleven years later, Joana decided to use Facebook to see if she could find the boy who packed her box. She searched for his name and got one hit in Idaho. She took a chance and submitted a friend request.

But Tyrel had never heard of Joana Marchan, so he ignored the request.

Two years later, Joana sent another friend request.

This time, Tyrel sent Joana a message asking how she knew him. She replied, telling him that he was the one who sent her a shoebox in 2000.

As the two got to know each other online, they discovered they shared a common faith in Christ and even enjoyed some of the same music.

Tyrel decided he wanted to meet Joana but had to work to save money for a plane ticket. After his graduation from high school, he flew to Manila a month later. He had been on Christian mission trips before but had never been to Asia and had never traveled by himself.

It was an emotional meeting. When Joana first saw Tyrel, she burst into tears.

"When I finally got there and saw her, I had to punch myself a couple times because I thought it was a dream," he told *People* magazine. "I was immediately attracted to her."

Tyrel instantly noticed a gap between his way of life and the more modest lifestyle of Joana's family in the Philippines. All eight members of her family slept on the floor of their 10×19-foot house.

Prior to the trip, they had agreed not to officially date until Tyrel had asked her father's permission in person. Midway through his visit, he asked her dad, who happened to be a pastor. He quickly agreed.

"I wanted to spend every moment I could with Joana while I was there, because once I left, I didn't know what would happen next," Tyrel told *People*.

Tyrel sensed that Joana was the one for him. After he got back to Idaho, he began to work and save so he could go back to visit.

They stayed in touch via Facebook and Skyped with each other often before Tyrel returned to the Philippines again in November. This time, he stayed for a month.

On his second trip, he asked her father for permission to marry Joana.

The couple held an engagement party in the Philippines and obtained a fiancée visa for Joana.

On October 5, 2014, they got married outdoors on Tyrel's parents' 400-acre cattle ranch in Midvale, Idaho. The groom wore a traditional shirt often worn by Filipino grooms.

As a special touch, wedding guests were asked if they would pack an Operation Christmas Child shoebox and bring it to the wedding.

The couple decided to live full time in the U.S. because the job prospects were better for Tyrel.

"It was a big change and adjustment for me," Joana told *People*. "I was raised in the city, and now I'm living in the country with much less people and more space, but it's a beautiful place."

In 2019, they were blessed with the birth of a baby boy.

CHAPTER 4

Atheist Art Professor's Near-Death Experience in Hell

In some near-death experiences, people report they were drawn toward "the light." But in this horrifying near-death experience for an atheist art professor, he was drawn into the darkness of hell, which dramatically altered the course of his life.

"I was a double atheist," says Howard Storm, who became a tenured art professor at Northern Kentucky University by age twenty-seven. "I was a know-it-all college professor, and universities are some of the most closed-minded places there are," he notes.

On the last day of a three-week European art tour he led, his group had returned to their hotel in Paris after a visit to the artist Delacroix's home and studio. As Howard stood in his room with his wife and another student, suddenly he screamed and dropped to the floor in agony.

"I had a perforation of the small stomach, known as the duodenum," he recalls. At first, Howard thought he was shot, and he glanced around the room to see if he could spot a smoking gun. As he writhed in pain on the ground, kicking and screaming, his wife called for a doctor.

"They said I needed surgery immediately," Howard says. "It's like having a burst appendix. I was told that if they don't get to it within five hours, you're probably going to die."

Howard had the misfortune of falling ill on Saturday in a country with socialized medicine, and no doctor could be found. "French doctors do seven surgeries a week, and after they do the seven surgeries, they take the weekend off," he discovered.

They placed him on a bed without sheets or a pillow and offered no pain medication. He waited in the room for ten hours. "I was just lying there going south," Howard says.

Meanwhile, intestinal contents were leaking into his abdominal cavity, which would soon lead to peritonitis, septic shock, and certain death.

At 8:30 p.m., a nurse came in and said they were still unable to find a doctor, but they would try to find one the next day, Sunday.

"I had been struggling very hard to stay alive, but when she said there was no doctor, I knew it was time to stop fighting," Howard says.

Yet the thought of death scared him. "I was terrified of dying because it meant lights out, the end of the story," he notes. "It seemed horrible that at thirty-eight years old, when I felt powerful and successful in my life, it would all come to an end in such a ridiculously pitiful way."

Howard made an impassioned farewell to his wife and told her to tell their friends and the rest of his family goodbye, then he lost consciousness.

It wasn't long after he lost consciousness that he had a very unusual out-of-body experience, and found himself standing next to his bed, looking at himself lying there. As he stood there, he noticed he didn't feel the pain in his stomach. He felt more alive than ever, and his senses seemed more heightened than usual.

He tried to communicate with his wife and another man in the room, but they didn't respond, which frustrated him. "I was glad I didn't have the pain, but also I was very confused and disturbed by the situation."

"I saw my body lying on the bed, but I refused to believe it was me. How could that be me if I was standing there," he wondered.

Suddenly, he heard people outside the room calling him by name. They spoke English, without a French accent, which seemed strange, because everyone in the hospital either spoke French or heavily accented English.

"Come with us," they said. "Hurry up, let's go."

Howard went to the doorway. "Are you from the doctor?"

he asked. "I need to have surgery. I'm sick, and I've been waiting a long time."

"We know all about you," one said. "We've been waiting for you. It's time for you to go. Hurry up."

Howard left the room and started to walk with them down a long hallway, which was very dimly lit—almost dingy. "They took me on a very long journey through a grey space that got increasingly darker and darker," he recalls.

They walked a long time, and Howard wondered why he was not tired when he had just suffered the worst day of his life.

"Where are we going?" Howard asked. "How come it's taking so long? What is the doctor's name?"

"Shut up," one said. "Be quiet," another said. "Don't ask questions."

Howard's fear and apprehension grew at the same time he lost trust in his guides. "Finally, it was so dark I was terrified, and I said, 'I'm not going any farther. I want to go back.'"

"You're almost there," one replied.

Howard dug in his heels. "I'm not going any farther," he said firmly.

His guides began to push and pull at him. Howard fought back, but he was horribly outnumbered.

"We had a big fight, and the fight turned into them annihilating me, which they did slowly and with much relish," he says. "Mostly they were biting and tearing at me. This went on for a long time. They did other things to humiliate and violate me which I don't talk about."

When Howard was no longer "amusing" to them, he collapsed on the ground, ripped apart, unable to move.

He laid there motionless for a few moments, completely spent. Then, he was surprised by a small voice inside his head that said, *Pray to God.*

He thought, *I don't pray. I don't even believe in God.*

Then he heard the voice a second time: *Pray to God.*

But I wouldn't know how to pray even if I wanted to pray,

he thought. Whose voice was this? he wondered. It sounded like his voice, but the words were completely foreign to his own thinking.

Then he heard the voice a third time repeat the same message. His mind drifted back to his days in Sunday school as a child. "I tried to remember things I memorized when I was very young," he says. He struggled to think of something he could pray.

He managed to blurt out, "The Lord is my shepherd, and I shall not want ..."

When the people around him heard his attempt to pray, they became enraged. "There is no God and nobody can hear you," they cried, along with other obscenities. "If you keep praying, we will really hurt you."

But Howard noticed something curious. The more he prayed and began to mention God, the more they backed away from him.

Emboldened, he began to shout out bits and pieces of "The Lord's Prayer," "The Battle Hymn of the Republic," and "God Bless America." Finally, he was screaming any fragments of God's truth he could muster from the moldy recesses of his memory bank.

It seemed to work! Even in the darkness, he could tell they fled, but not too far away.

As he lay there, Howard began to review his life. "I came to the conclusion I led a crummy life, and I had gone down the sewer pipe of the universe. I had gone into the septic tank with other human garbage. I was being processed by the garbage people into garbage like them."

Whatever life was supposed to be about, I missed it, he thought. "What I received was what I deserved, and the people who attacked me were people like me. They were my kindred spirits. Now I will be stuck with them forever." Feelings of self-loathing and hopelessness filled his mind.

His thoughts floated back again to himself as a nine-year-old in Sunday school. "I remembered myself singing "Jesus Loves Me," and I could feel it inside me. As a child, I thought

Jesus was really cool, and He was my buddy, and He would take care of me."

But even if Jesus is real, why would He care about me? he thought. *He probably hates my guts. I'm not going to think anymore; I'm going to ask Him. I've got nothing else to lose. I'll give Jesus a try.*

Then he yelled into the darkness, "Jesus, please save me!"

Within an instant, a brilliant light appeared that came closer and closer. He found himself bathed in a beautiful light, and for the first time, he could clearly see his own body's miserable condition, ghastly for his own eyes to behold. "I was almost all gore."

Immediately, he recognized Jesus, the King of Kings, the Rescuer, the Deliverer. "His arms reached down and touched me, and everything healed up and came back together," he recalls. "He filled me with a love I never knew existed."

Then He picked up Howard, like one football player picking up a fallen teammate on the field, put His arms around him, and Howard cried like a baby in His arms. "He carried me out of there, and we headed to where God lives."

In his mind, Howard began to think that Jesus made a terrible mistake. *I'm garbage and I don't belong in heaven*, he thought.

They stopped moving, and both Howard and Jesus were hanging in space, somewhere between heaven and hell. "We don't make mistakes," Jesus said tenderly.

"He could read everything in my mind and put His voice into my head," Howard recalls. "We had very rapid, instantaneous conversations."

Then Jesus told Howard He had angels who would show him his life. "It was a terrible experience because my life deteriorated after adolescence. I saw I became a selfish, unloving person. I was successful, a full tenured art professor at twenty-seven, the department head, but I was a jerk."

In this replay, he saw his heavy drinking and adultery. "I cheated on my wife proudly. It was horrible."

For the first time, he realized the way he lived his life hurt

Jesus. "I was in the arms of the most wonderful, holy, loving, kind person and we're looking at this stuff. Embarrassing doesn't even begin to describe it."

As they watched together, Howard could see the pain and disappointment on the face of Jesus. "When I did these things, it was like sticking a knife into His heart."

"Do you have any questions?" Jesus asked.

"I have a million questions," Howard replied, and proceeded to unburden himself of anything and everything he could imagine asking an omniscient being. Jesus answered Howard's questions kindly and patiently.

When Howard couldn't think of anything else to ask, he said, "I'm ready to go to heaven now."

"You're not going to heaven. You're going back to the world," Jesus replied.

Howard began to argue, but it was to no avail. Jesus told him to go back and live his life differently.

At 9:00 p.m., Howard was back in his hospital room in Paris. Less than thirty minutes had elapsed since he lost consciousness. As Howard opened his eyes, he heard the nurse say, "The doctor arrived at the hospital, and you're going to have the surgery."

As they wheeled him out of his room on a gurney, he saw his wife in the hallway. "Everything is going to be really good now," he said to her. When she heard him, she cried, thinking they were brave words.

When Howard emerged from surgery, with the effects of the anesthesia wearing off, he spoke to his wife. "It's all love," he told her. "You don't have to suffer anymore."

"You need to sleep," she replied, thinking he was slightly addled from the drugs. Then he awakened again and began to tell her about Jesus and the angels and heaven and hell.

"She was an atheist, and she didn't like it. She thought I lost my mind." Sadly, Howard's marriage ended in divorce after she left him many years later.

When his strength returned, Howard began to devour the Bible. "Since none of my atheist friends believed me, I started memorizing verses, and I would give them Bible lectures, but that didn't go over very well," he recalls.

He grew "desperate" for fellowship in a church and began to attend Christ Church in Fort Thomas, Kentucky, part of United Church of Christ. Howard's pastor worked with him patiently, and after three years, Howard was ordained as a lay minister in his church.

Sensing a deeper call into ministry, he attended United Theological Seminary in Dayton, Ohio and later pastored a church in Covington, Ohio.

He also wrote a book about his experience, *My Descent Into Death*, which he says was written primarily to non-believers.

Howard and his second wife, Marcia, a strong Christian, are both involved in missionary work in Belize. He maintains a passion for painting, with much of his art devoted to spiritual themes.

If you want to know more about a personal relationship with God, go here:

CHAPTER 5

A Migraine Headache Saved Her Life

"I was a super-groupie," says Jozy Pollock, a blonde, middle-aged woman, who dresses conservatively, and lets a prominent silver cross dangle from her neck. "Sometimes it seems like I've lived three or four separate lives," she says.

Born in England, she became the "Hula-Hoop Queen" in her youth. She married American magician, Channing Pollock, and moved to the United States, where they performed in Las Vegas and twice on the Ed Sullivan Show. Then the two of them went on the road with the flamboyant pianist, Liberace.

After divorcing her husband in 1968, she entered a fast-paced world of elite rock-and-roll musicians and dated several famous men. She was engaged to Nigel Olsson, the drummer for Elton John as John's career began to enter the stratosphere.

"We went from tour buses to private jets," she says, recalling the years 1972-1975. "Elton John is an amazing talent. The similarities between Elton and Liberace are unbelievable," she says. "They were both total showmen, both very generous to a fault, both loved to shop, and they were both gay."

Once she was touring with John in Italy when an article appeared in a local newspaper mentioning John's homosexuality, before this was widely known. "I was reading the article and told him, 'They're talking about you being a homosexual.'"

"How would they know?" he asked Pollock.

"Come over to the mirror," she beckoned. John was wearing silver platform boots and an outrageous outfit. "Look in the mirror. How do you think they know?"

Through Pollock's travels with Elton John, she met John Lennon at the Caribou Ranch in Nederland, Colorado. Jim Guercio, who produced many early Chicago albums, owned the ranch and its in-house recording studios.

"Elton was recording, and Lennon came up there to do "Lucy in the Sky with Diamonds," she says. This was during a period when John Lennon was not with Yoko Ono, but was seeing an assistant, May Pang.

"May and I were doing laundry for Nigel, Elton, and John Lennon," she says. "I said, 'May, do you realize we could cut up these sheets and sell them?'"

Pollock has mostly pleasant memories of John Lennon, if he was not under the influence of drugs. "When he was sober, he was wonderful," she says, "but when he was loaded, he was an idiot, like most people." Pollock experimented lightly with drugs herself but managed to avoid being drawn into heavy usage. "I was living in the fast lane, but I always had my foot on the break," she says.

Shortly afterward, Lennon reunited with Yoko Ono after she came to the concert at Madison Square Garden where John appeared on stage with Elton. "May was totally smitten with him," Pollock says, "but Yoko came back into the picture, and May was out. It was like May never existed. I don't understand the control Yoko had over John, but she had total control."

Pollock taught Elton John how to play backgammon and found him to be fiercely competitive. "He hates to lose," she says.

When the AIDS epidemic began to reach alarming proportions, Pollock spoke with John's manager about the frightening subject. "He said, 'It can only be the grace of God that saved me—and Elton too.'" Pollock notes that John was somewhat shy and would ask her to approach men for him. "Elton wanted to go to gay bars and none of the band would go, so I went with him. It made me sad to see all these fabulous looking men who weren't available to my girlfriends hoping to find a husband."

One night, Pollock went to a large gay bar in West Hollywood with Elton John, Bette Midler, Cher, and Richard Chamberlain. "Richard grabbed ahold of me and said, 'Don't leave my side.' He was totally terrified. He's gay, but it was not his scene—it was too overwhelming, all the men fawning over him."

"If Cher was bored, she would call me for excitement," Pollock says. "Cher was really down to earth and quite naive. She was not the swinger people thought she was. It was mostly hype."

Pollock had a series of run-ins with actress Sharon Tate. They first met in Italy while Pollock's husband was filming a movie. Tate was only sixteen at the time. "She was incredibly beautiful then," she says, recalling the first time Tate's father brought her to the movie set. Tate was put into the movie as an extra. Many years later, she ran into Tate in L.A. just before tragedy struck.

"I went to a club called The Daisy in Beverly Hills and ran into Sharon and Jay Sebring. Sharon says, 'When are you coming over to the house? Try to come this weekend because Roman's still in Europe, and I'll probably be on my own.'" Tate was married to director Roman Polanski, who was in London at the time.

On Thursday, Pollock traveled to Las Vegas with her boss to catch the opening of Anthony Newley's show, but she contracted a migraine headache. Friends persuaded Pollock to spend the night in Las Vegas. They booked a flight home for Pollock on Friday, in the late afternoon.

When Pollock arrived in L.A., she tried to call Tate, but couldn't find her phone number. Pollock's roommate wrote down the number, but because of the migraine headache and the resulting delay, the roommate had already left town for the weekend. "I looked everywhere for Sharon's number; I couldn't find it, and it was getting later and later. Then Judy Carne called with an extra ticket for the theatre, so I thought, *I'll drive over tomorrow.*"

The next morning, as Pollock prepared to drive over to Sharon Tate's house, she was stunned by news reports about the murders. Tate, Sebring, and three others were slaughtered Friday night by cult figure Charles Manson's followers. Tate was eight-and-a-half-months pregnant when she was murdered, and the gruesome manner of the killings, later chronicled in the book *Helter Skelter*, sickened Pollock and the rest of the world.

"After the killings, I was unable to read anything about the case, and it wasn't until I read *Helter Skelter* that I realized the maid had found the bodies Saturday morning when she came into work. It is quite usual in Beverly Hills for maids to be off on Saturday. If she hadn't come in, I probably would have been the one to discover the massacre. God protected me once again."

Reeling from her brush with death, it wasn't until much later when she could come to terms with it. Pollock now believes God spared her life for future ministry. "A migraine saved my life," she says. "God protects you when He has a purpose for you."

"A man of God in the will of God is immortal, until His work is done." – David Jeremiah

That quote includes women too. Several years after the killings, Pollock spoke at the California Institute of Women in a church service. As she left the service, she ran into Susan Atkins, one of the cultists who took part in the crime. "She was the one who actually cut the baby out of Sharon's body. I had all this rage and emotion rise up, and I wanted to get in her face, but the Holy Spirit prevented me."

"It was like God said, 'You teach others to forgive. Where is your forgiveness?' I recognized I have to forgive and was able to just walk away without the confrontation."

After a failed relationship with a man Pollock found through a psychic's predictions, she was at the end of her rope. She called a friend named Mike whose life had been transformed by Jesus Christ.

"I've had enough torment," she told Mike.

"Jozy, what do you really want?" he asked.

"All I want is peace."

"With Jesus, you can have peace, but you have to pray the sinner's prayer," Mike said.

"Wait a minute, I'm not a sinner, I'm a good person. I'm always helping people," she protested.

"No Jozy, you're a sinner."

All have sinned and fall short of the glory of God. (Romans 3:23)

"So, I prayed the sinner's prayer through gritted teeth. For six months, I rebelled against everything. I said, 'Lord, don't turn me into a Jesus freak. I just want to do this a little bit.'"

But after six months, Pollock sensed she was missing something. "I went to a Chi Coltrane Christian concert, and she was talking about being 'born again' and not feeling it, which was exactly where I was in my walk. I found out she had a Bible study at her home, so I went. I told her how I was feeling, and she prayed with me and laid hands on me," Pollock recalls. "I started speaking in tongues. Suddenly, I had a huge hunger and thirst for God."

"It was hard giving up my will," Pollock says. "But after I gave up my will, I had peace." After Pollock's water baptism, she says she had a "feeling of falling in love with Jesus."

"I always had a man in my life, and one waiting in the wings," she says. "After I was saved, I became invisible to men, which is just as well, so I could build my relationship with Jesus. I've been celibate since I've been saved."

"This was God's shield. God knew me better than I knew myself."

Her friends in the fast lane openly mocked her new faith. "They said, 'Jozy used to be so much fun, but now she's the kiss of death—all she talks about is Jesus.'" Pollock admits she "could clear a room."

"After I got saved, I went to an Elton John concert, and we all went over to Bernie Taupin's house afterward." Taupin is Elton John's famous lyricist, who collaborated with John on most of their important pieces. "We ordered burgers, and when they arrived, I said, 'Which one's mine?'"

"Elton says, 'The one with the cross on it.'"

"Another time, I went to another concert, and I was wearing cross earrings and a cross necklace, and he noticed all the crosses I was wearing."

"He said, 'What are you afraid of, vampires?'"

Slowly, Pollock's old friends began to drift away, as she

stopped going to the parties, and she was drawn more deeply into Christian ministry. One by one, she sold the pieces of jewelry given to her by famous men.

Today, Pollock lives in modest circumstances, far removed from the lifestyle of the rich and famous.

"I don't want to live in a mansion, but I would like a cozy home with enough space to take in lost women I can mentor," Pollock says. "I was once a glamour girl, but the fact that I'm not now is no big deal. They have all the fame, but I would love for them to have the peace I have."

Called into ministry, Pollock became the first Protestant female chaplain at L.A. Men's Central Jail. "I never thought I would be in ministry," Pollock says. But contrary to her original thinking, she has ministered to convicted murderers and has confronted and won over Satanists during her prison ministry.

CHAPTER 6

North Korean Woman's Prison Story

She entered Kaechon Prison a loyal communist, but lost her faith in the godless ideology of North Korea under horrifying conditions.

"I saw something so unimaginable and so terrible that I wanted to let the world know," says Soon Ok Lee, one of the rare human beings to survive and offer an eyewitness account of conditions inside North Korea's political prisons. Lee has testified before the U.S. Congress and published a book about her experiences, *Eyes of the Tailless Animals, Prison Memoirs of a North Korean Woman.*

She was falsely charged and sent to prison because of the wounded pride of one of her superiors at the material distribution center, where she worked. It seems a certain casual jacket style worn by Kim Jong ll caused a sensation among lower party figures, who all wanted to be seen in the stylish attire. Unfortunately, the material for the jackets were available only in China, and party officers began pressuring her for more than their share.

"The security bureau chief asked to have two jackets made out of the fabric while everyone else received only one," she writes. "Without raising my voice, I explained to him that I could not give him more than his share. Suddenly, he turned around and spit out, 'All right, Soon Ok. You will regret this,' and he left my office."

On a peaceful Sunday morning, a few weeks later, Lee was arrested for violating the commercial policies of the communist party and taking bribes. "It didn't make any sense to me; I was as pure as snow," she notes. "It was all the security bureau chief's cunning scheme for revenge."

Without a moment to say goodbye to her husband, who she would never see again, or her son, she was placed on a seven-hour train ride to her first cell. "For three days, they did not let me close my eyes," she writes about her first interrogation. "They kept beating me and demanding that I answer their questions. I just kept repeating, 'What do you want from me? I don't really understand.'"

Lee's tormentors seem demonic, by her account. She describes them having eyes "like ravenous animals, shining with an unearthly light. It scared me to look into their eyes." Their voices were "evil."

They used a variety of diabolical techniques to extract a confession from the slender, young woman. Once she was placed inside a furnace where bricks were baked. When she lost consciousness due to the intense heat, they dragged her out and poured cold water on her head to revive her, while intensifying their demands for confession.

She recalls being lashed by a leather whip while chained to a chair. "Even worse than the pain of the torture was being totally naked in front of all these men," she writes in her book. "The shame of it pounds in my ears. I was so angry I fought them."

As winter arrived and Lee had still not signed her confession, her interrogator commanded one of the guards to "let this woman freeze." Then she was forced to remain outdoors at night in her undergarments for extended periods until she was close to freezing to death. "For the first twenty or thirty minutes, my hands and feet were so cold that I felt kind of crazy. After that came the pain. But soon the pain disappeared, and my body became numb," she writes. The prison guards referred to this as the "frozen fish torture."

Lee was shocked to discover that most of the people she met in the prison yard were arrested for refusing to give bribes to their superiors, so they were all there because of "someone's revenge." Still a loyal communist, she wondered "how the law could allow this."

Seven months after her arrest, she was transferred to a province interrogation center. "At this point, I lost my right of citizenship in North Korea," she writes. "I was also expelled from the Party. This meant that I lost all my rights as a human being."

Her new interrogator tortured her for days to extract a confession. "After they released me from the fetters, I could not stand or walk straight because of my weakened condition, and I lost consciousness from time to time," she writes. "Once as I regained consciousness, my back itched." As Lee reached back to scratch, she caught sight of something crawling.

"Through swollen eyes, I saw maggots all over my back. Flies had landed on my deadened flesh and laid their eggs as I was unconscious for hours." Her new cell had no heat in the winter, and her interrogator insisted that her window be left open at night. "Cold wind and snowflakes blew into my cell and froze my body. It was too cold to sleep."

Lee survived on meager food rations that were typically a crust of dried corn with a few beans. "The food was supposed to have thirty percent beans and seventy percent corn; however, the jailers took most of the beans to eat themselves," she writes. The jailers warned them if they told anyone they didn't get their beans, their ribs would be broken.

Finally, the time arrived for Lee's public trial, held in an auditorium. A police officer met with her and warned her to say "yes" to every question she was asked in court.

"You have a choice," he said. "One is to do what I told you. The other is to be rebellious and then be secretly killed by us. If you die, I will cancel the trial, and you will be listed as a missing prisoner."

"Throughout the whole trial, my attorney did not say a word to defend me," she notes. "He came only to formally occupy a seat. No one told my son or husband about the trial. I did not even have a witness to speak up for me." As the trial ended, Lee was sentenced to thirteen years in prison for embezzling public funds.

In the book, Lee vividly describes her new home, Kaechon prison, filled with 6,000 political prisoners. As she arrived, a lieutenant introduced her to her new reality. "You are not a human being anymore," he said. "If you want to survive here, you'd better give up the idea that you are human." She was assigned number 832, her new identity.

New prisoners had to memorize a set of commandments,

which began with the first commandment: 'Adore the authorities of Kim Il Sung and Kim Jong Il with all your heart.' Both leaders are deified in North Korean society, and citizens are required to wear the image of 'The Great Leader' on their clothing at all times. Even visitors to the capital are required to visit a giant statue of the deceased dictator and pay homage to him by bowing down.

In her newcomer's cell, Lee met a thirty-nine-year-old woman who stole two pounds of sugar. She was sentenced to three years in prison and all her property was confiscated by the state. When she appealed to a higher court, her action upset the public prosecutor, who extended her sentence to twenty years.

Initially, Lee's food rations were eighty grams per meal, less than one mouthful; the regular ration was one hundred grams per meal of corn and a salty cabbage soup.

In her book, Lee describes prisoners awakened at 5 a.m., who then spent the entire day working in prison factories making clothing and shoes for export to western countries. "They survived every minute with fear," she notes. "After a day of heavy labor (which lasted until after midnight), they only had four hours of sleep from 1 to 5 a.m.; however, they could not relax even during these four hours," she writes. "Every night, two prisoners were assigned to watch the others who slept. The next morning, the prisoners who stayed awake had to report what the other prisoners said in their sleep."

Lee describes workers who faced demanding quotas and severe treatment if they made mistakes on the job. "When I was dyeing clothes, I had to be very alert," she writes. "If I would put the clothes into the dye in the wrong order, the color would come out wrong, and I would be put into solitary confinement."

"The solitary confinement cell was only high enough to allow a person to sit on the floor," she recalls. "Concrete thorns stuck out of the walls so the prisoner could not lean against them. The person could only sit and not move for many days." Many prisoners' legs became paralyzed as a result of such treatment and could never walk normally again.

Lee reports her factory sent 900,000 brassieres to Russia and tens of thousands of sweaters to Japan. The Japanese returned many of the sweaters, complaining they were unclean. "One time, France ordered paper roses," she writes. "Each prisoner had a quota of 1,000 roses per day. After rolling that many roses, their fingertips were worn out and blood oozed from the skin."

Even though Lee was raised an atheist, she first began to wonder about God's existence during her prison experience. "I thought about humans," she writes. "Sometimes they were extinguished so easily; sometimes they survived so incredibly. Based on man's miraculous survival, I could not deny the existence of God."

Sadly, Lee also witnessed forced abortion at Kaechon prison. While being transferred from one cell to another, she saw six pregnant women lying on a concrete floor giving birth to babies that were supposed to be stillborn. "Poison was injected into the babies," she recalls. "After the injection, the pregnant women suffered tremendous pain until the babies were stillborn about twenty-four hours later."

"Miraculously, some of the babies were born alive. They cried like normal babies do. When a live baby was born, a medical officer said to the medical prisoners, 'Kill it! These criminals don't have any right to have babies. What are you doing? Kill it right now!'"

"The mothers of these newborn babies just laid on the floor and sobbed so helplessly while a medical prisoner's shaking hands twisted the baby's neck. Male prisoners wrapped the babies in rags and dumped them into a basket."

Christian prisoners were known as "superstition believers." Because of their belief in heaven, they were never allowed to look up during their confinement and were forced to keep their eyes to the ground. "Once a month, the believers were placed in the yard in front of all the prisoners and asked to deny their faith," she writes. "Since they would not deny their faith, they were given the most difficult work assignments such as cleaning the toilets and removing human excrement."

Other dangerous assignments for Christians included work in the rubber factory, smelting factory, and the mine.

One day, she witnessed six Christian prisoners transferring over a ton of human excrement from the toilets to a large tank. It was the monsoon season, and these prisoners were working in the pouring rain.

A woman named Ok Dan Lee climbed up on the tank to open it, but slipped on the slick surface and fell into the noxious mixture.

"Sister, can you come out," one of her friends shouted to her.

"I'm having a difficult time," she gasped, as she struggled to keep her head above the waste.

"Let me come up and help," her friend said. An officer tried to stop her, but she climbed up the tank and jumped in to save her friend. Then another woman climbed up the tank and then another.

"In all, four women jumped into the tank to help their friends," Lee recalls. "Each of them tried to push the others up first." Then the officer below ordered the tank door be shut, cruelly sealing their fate. "The door was closed, and the women were left in the tank. No one ever tried to take the bodies out."

The actions of these women left Lee searching for answers. "When I saw their love, it raised questions in my mind that I could not erase," she writes. "How could they die for someone else? What was it about heaven that was worth the cost?"

Lee saw more evidence the Christians received greater abuse than other prisoners, yet she was struck by their attitude. "In some instances, while believers were being beaten, they would stand up halfway and begin to sing hymns and say 'Amen.' The guards thought they were crazy and took them back to the electric torture room. I never saw any of the believers return from that room."

"They did not only not falsely accuse others but were willing to take the blame for another. They even died for other prisoners."

On one occasion, she saw the warden launch into a tirade because a Christian would not deny his faith. His fury was so intense, Lee thought it looked like "he had been taking drugs to make him high." He began to stomp on the Christian, reminding the other prisoners, "This is going to happen to you if you ever believe in heaven."

Then the warden ordered all 6,000 prisoners in the camp to walk over the body of the Christian. "It was unimaginable how he died."

Lee also testifies to biochemical weapons experimentation on prisoners, including Christian prisoners. "Every morning, I had to call out those names," she says. "Many had just been added to the prison camp, so they were much healthier than the rest of us."

"They were taking them to the biological weapons laboratory. They would put them in rooms, release different biological agents, and see how quickly the people died," Lee says. "They would take others, strap them to beds, and inject them with things, and watch them die over days and weeks."

One day, the emergency bell rang in the camp, which usually signaled a prisoner was about to be executed. "I ran outside wondering who would be executed this time," Lee recalls. When everyone had gathered, an officer called out Soon Ok Lee's name.

"My heart dropped," Lee writes. "I couldn't understand what I had done to deserve a public execution."

Two soldiers led her in front of everyone and announced: "Soon Ok Lee has faithfully worked for Kim Il Sung, so we decided to reward her work. She will be returned to society. I am telling all of you, if you work as hard as she did, you can also go home."

Lee immediately noticed 140 Christians in the front row raise their heads to look at her, violating prison policy. "Their eyes were glowing with a heavenly light," she writes. She felt their eyes imploring her to testify about what she saw in the camp. "I will never forget the sight of those pleading eyes."

On the day of her release, she ran out the iron gates of the prison with "unbelievable joy" into the arms of her son.

"I saw my son running toward me. My son cried, 'Now everything is fine with life again!'" Her son was a university student who was forced to leave school after her arrest and spent a brief period in a labor camp. Lee's husband, a school principal, was also taken to a labor camp and perished there.

Lee estimates there are 200,000 prisoners in North Korea, and believes she is one of the very few who got out. "I was the first one in thirty years who was given the special privilege of a release from Kim Il Sung."

The book chronicles Lee's daring escape from North Korea, which she now viewed as a "den of evil." She and her son climbed over a mountain at night, then ran across a frozen river into China, made their way to Hong Kong, and finally South Korea. The entire journey took almost two years.

After their arrival, they were debriefed by South Korean officials. One day, an inspector came in to meet with them and said, "If you want to adjust quickly to living in South Korea by forgetting all your suffering, you should read this book." He handed them a Bible, which Lee had never seen before. Then he began to sing "Amazing Grace" to Lee.

"I knew the tune and joined him in singing," she writes, although she didn't remember where she learned the song. Later, memories began to return to her from when she was very young. She began to remember her mother and her friends gathering at night to "do embroidery" and sing about going to heaven. She remembered her mother singing hymns to her as she went to sleep.

"I realized my grandmother and my mother had been telling me about the Word of God in a safe way," she writes. "When children go to school, the teachers ask them if their parents ever secretly read out of a black book. The children are promised honor if they report their parents. But when the children tell on their parents, the parents are taken away."

After Lee's debriefing, she attended church for the first time, and began reading the Bible because she "wanted to have a good life." When she read John 8:32, that "the truth will set you free," she committed her life to Jesus Christ and began to experience "real freedom," she says. "Soon, my son also accepted Jesus and began to come to church with me."

For a long time after her release, Lee suffered nightmares about being tortured and thought she would live with her "sad heart forever." But God began to cleanse and heal her painful memories.

"I have been healed with the love of God and His comfort. I no longer dream dreadful dreams. I am free."

Lee's body still bears the marks of the torture she endured. Some of her teeth are broken, the left side of her face is partially paralyzed, and she carries a scar over her left eye. She still suffers headaches from being kicked in the head, her eyesight blurs from time to time, and her shoulders are uneven. Yet, she is grateful to God.

"Today, all the things I hoped and dreamed have come true," she says. "It's really a miracle."

CHAPTER 7

His Encounter with Jesus Began in the Mosque

Like other boys in his Pashtun tribe along the Pakistan-Afghan border, he was sent to a madrasa at age four, where he was compelled to read, recite, and memorize the Koran.

"The children mimic or copy the mullah, who is very heavy-handed. You have to memorize out of fear," says John Taimoor, founder of The Crossbearers, a ministry devoted to presenting biblical Christianity within an Islamic context.

By age fourteen, when he was reading Shakespeare and searching for heroes, he stumbled across the name 'Isa,' the Arabic name for Jesus in the Koran. "I read the name of Jesus and became curious," he says. "The Lord reached me right in the mosque."

When he asked the priest about Jesus, he was told that Moses and Jesus were brothers. When he inquired about how to find out more, they told him to find, 'The Book of Isa.' "Nobody had ever heard of a Bible."

Taimoor searched for a 'Book of Isa' for two years. When he asked his teacher or inquired at the library, he was met with suspicion. "What are you up to boy? Do you want to become a Christian?" they asked.

He met a young man at school rumored to be a Christian. "I begged him to get me a Book of Isa," he says. "He got so scared, he never returned to school again. He thought they would stone him or kill him." There were times Taimoor rode his motorbike thirty to forty miles because he heard about a gathering of Christians. "No one was willing to give me a Bible; they were so scared."

"Being strong-willed, the more people stopped me, the more determined I became," Taimoor adds.

One day, he happened to meet a missionary passing through the area north of Islamabad handing out small New Testaments. Taimoor spied on the man from a distance and hurriedly rode his motorbike toward him. "He looked at me and greeted me like a Muslim and said, 'This is the Book of Isa.'"

"It hit me like a bullet," Taimoor says. "I was almost paralyzed." Hesitantly, he asked the missionary the cost of the book.

"Nobody can pay the price for it," he said. "If you want it, you can give me whatever you would like to give." Taimoor fished into his pocket and pulled out the U.S. equivalent of twenty cents.

Racing home, Taimoor underwent a ritualistic cleansing, deciding this would be appropriate before reading such a book. "I didn't understand it in the beginning," he says. "But when I got to the fifth chapter of Matthew, something supernatural and unusual happened in my mind."

He read: *"Blessed are they which do hunger and thirst after righteousness: for they shall be filled."* (Matthew 5:6, KJV) After reading this verse, he believes the Holy Spirit fell upon him—and filled him—as his heart and mind were regenerated.

"I got saved without the help of any individual," Taimoor recalls. "I didn't say the sinner's prayer or go to any altar call. Within six months, I discovered Jesus Christ is God in human flesh."

It would be five years before Taimoor had any meaningful contact with other Christians or saw the entire Bible. In the meantime, he set out to memorize the New Testament. "As a Muslim, I thought every good Muslim memorizes the Koran," he recalls. "Naturally, Christians must be memorizing their books." He thought he should memorize the books before meeting other Christians. He also feared the book might be taken away from him at any time.

When his mother found out about his new faith, she told him, "If I had known you would become a Christian, I would have strangled you as a baby." Several years later, Taimoor's mother and brother both became believers.

Because Taimoor's faith developed outside of mainstream Christendom, some of his views would be considered provocative to Christians. "I respect Muhammad and use him next to the Bible and the church as the third great witness of the glory of Christ," Taimoor says. "I am proving to the Muslims the God they worship is the same God as ours," he says. He believes Muslims are like Jews—they worship the same God as Christians—but reject Jesus as Messiah.

Taimoor finds common ground with Muslims in their approach to eschatology, the study of "the last things." Many Muslims are waiting for 'Jesus, Son of Mary,' to return as a sign the Day of Judgment has come, according to Taimoor.

"Some Christians are uptight because I show them the term 'Allah' is legitimate," he says. He faults scholars who attempt to prove Muslims are worshipping the moon god. "Muslims don't worship the moon at all," he says. He notes the Bible Society has a Bible that uses the name Allah for God.

Many Christians will not understand John's strategy because it sounds like compromise. "To some degree it is," he admits. At the same time, he emphasizes his main thrust is to prove that Jesus Christ is God in human flesh. "We worship Him as the Creator and the Savior."

Taimoor believes more people with "guts" will be needed to carry out the Great Commission. "Jesus told us to go, but we don't go," he says. "There is too much education in America and not enough deployment." At the same time, he confesses it is difficult to leave the comforts of the U.S. behind for the ever-present risks in the Middle East.

One of Taimoor's ministry objectives is to establish new communities of 'messianic Muslims' throughout the Middle East based on the book of Ephesians. He likes to say his travel style is patterned after John Wesley. "I work in a circuit and then move on. I move fast," he says. "Some will follow along."

"If I had not become a Christian, I would have been a Taliban," Taimoor says. His houses near the border of Afghanistan and Pakistan are lined with prayer rugs and have the feel of an Eastern worship center. They're completely filled with Islamic books except for one—the Bible.

People can stay there for extended periods while they read and memorize the Scriptures. "When people come here, they want to know what this black book is all about," Taimoor says. "If they're serious, I tell them they can stay." Group meetings in his homes can last up to six hours, but he refuses to call this 'church,' instead preferring the term 'Jaamat Rabaani'—which means 'gathering of the people of God.' "If it looks like a church, they will burn it," he says.

"There are a lot of people in the Middle East who are really hungry and seeking," he notes. "They only fear Western missionaries because they think they are cultural terrorists. We need to be one of them and go in on their level."

CHAPTER 8

She Did the Unimaginable to Save Jews

She was only a teenager when Hitler's Panzer divisions overran her beloved Poland, separating the young nursing student from her family, and launching her on a mission a Catholic girl with Aryan features might never have imagined—rescuing Jews from certain death.

"God blessed my hands to save many lives," said Irene Gut Opdyke, shortly before her passing in 2003. (This author was the last to interview her before she died.)

Opdyke was honored by the Israeli Holocaust Commission in 1982 as one of the 'Righteous Among the Nations,' a title given to non-Jews who risked their lives by aiding and saving Jews during the Holocaust. She wrote a book about her ordeal, *In My Hands* (Random House), a riveting tale of heroism and survival under perilous conditions.

When Hitler invaded Poland in the year 1939, the seventeen-year-old was several hundred miles from her home, at nursing school in Radom, and could not return because her family lived close to the German border. "My little country was really bombarded," Opdyke said. "Hitler knocked everything down," she said. "The sky was black with them: row after row of German bombers, flying in formation over Radom."

The bombardment threw the hospital where she studied into chaos. "We were out of food, we were out of sulfa drugs, we had no clean sheets, the electricity was out, and the wounded kept arriving," she noted in her book. As the Polish army retreated from Radom, Opdyke volunteered to travel with them and assist with their medical needs. "I joined the Polish army to fight Hitler and send him back to Berlin," she said.

"Unfortunately, Russia and Germany made a pact, and they took my country from both sides," Opdyke explained.

Facing overwhelming opposition, she found herself hiding in the Ukrainian forest with ten Polish soldiers and several nurses. "We needed clothing and food because it was bitter cold," she said. One night, Opdyke went into the town of Lvov on a bartering mission.

As Opdyke walked down the road on a clear, moonless night, she heard a low, rumbling sound she didn't want to hear. It was the sound of a Russian patrol approaching, so she bolted for the woods. "I ran for my life to the forest, but I was captured by three Russian soldiers and brutally violated, beaten, and left in the snow to die," she said. "But I did not die."

Found by another Russian patrol the next morning, her lifeless body was thrown in the back of a military transport vehicle and hauled to a prison hospital controlled by the Russians. As she slowly recovered her strength over the ensuing weeks, her prayers intensified. "I wondered if the heavenly Father saw me, alone and defeated."

Opdyke gradually regained her strength in the hospital, only to face another harrowing incident. A Russian doctor in the hospital crept into her bed in the middle of the night and attempted to rape her as she slept. After this ordeal, she determined she would escape from the hospital.

"A Polish doctor from the Ukraine helped me to escape," she said. Opdyke slipped through a loose board in the fence surrounding the hospital grounds, and slowly made her way back toward her home in Radom. As a train she was riding crossed from Russian-controlled areas of Poland into the German sector, everyone was pulled off the train and placed under quarantine, supposedly to prevent the spread of "Russian diseases."

"The men, who had been separated from the women upon arrival, were being examined for circumcision; the circumcised men, the Jews, were taken away," she recounted. "To where? Why? Would they be back? No one knew."

Two years after the start of the war, Opdyke finally reached her family in Radom for a joyous homecoming. But everything about life in Radom had changed. All the streets had German names. All Polish intellectuals and professionals had been taken away to prison camps, and many other men in the town had simply disappeared, never to be heard from again.

The restaurant where Opdyke once worked served only Germans now. Posters covered the city mocking the Jews, falsely accusing them of every sort of crime. Jews from Radom, as well as the surrounding countryside, had been forced into two ghetto areas, surrounded by barbed wire. "Some said that Hitler was planning to exterminate the Jews, but we thought that was simply too preposterous to believe."

"Now we are like slaves, or worse," her father told her. "We must step off the sidewalk and remove our hats if a German approaches," he said. "And the death penalty is automatic for anyone helping the Jews." Opdyke was baffled by this hostility toward the Jews, wondering why the Germans didn't simply let them leave.

One night, after Opdyke's sisters went off to bed, she tearfully recounted the full story of her two-year ordeal to her parents, her voice dropping to a whisper as she told them of her rape. Then Opdyke's father gently put his hand on her shoulder. "War makes men animals," he said. "You must not let this ruin your life. God has plans for you. He did not let you die. He has plans for you."

Only a few weeks later, the Germans came for Opdyke's father. A ceramics factory her father designed was considered important for the war effort, and they wanted his expertise to make it function, so they took him away.

Then on a Sunday morning, while Opdyke worshipped in church, she heard the sound of heavy vehicles pull up in the square outside the church, doors slamming, and boots pounding up to the front doors. "Raus! Zum Strasse!" soldiers shouted as the people were herded outside into the square. The parishioners were surrounded by Wehrmacht soldiers with their guns drawn.

"You will be transported to Germany to work for the Reich," an officer shouted. "You Poles have been idle long enough."

Opdyke found herself working in a munitions factory and spent long hours on her feet packing ammunition into boxes. Due to exhaustion, malnutrition, and anemia, she fainted one day at her station. Because she spoke fluent German, she was transferred to the officer's mess, serving three meals a day to German officers who gathered from all over the city. Occasionally, she overheard officers talking at meals about "the Jewish problem."

One day, as Opdyke was setting tables for a formal dinner, she happened to look out an upper-story window, which looked down on the Glinice ghetto. "I had forgotten the Jews, driven from their homes," she recounted. Just then, she heard the sound of gunfire, and was startled to see men, women, and children running in the streets below her. Then there was the sound of police dogs barking and bodies lying in the snow, darkened with blood.

A German officer came up behind Opdyke and could see she was visibly shaken. "Don't speak of this to anyone," he warned. "Bad things happen to Jew-lovers. Do you understand me? Very bad."

In addition to her kitchen duties, Opdyke was placed in charge of the laundry facility, washing and mending officer's clothes. The laundry used a dozen Jewish workers from a local work camp who were trucked in daily to complete their wash assignments. One of the Jewish workers had been a successful businessman, one was a former medical student, one a lawyer, another a dressmaker, and one had been a nurse. "They worked in the laundry room as slave laborers, and I started taking care of them," Opdyke recalled.

"At least we are better off here than in the ghetto," one confided to Opdyke. "We are the strong ones, the ones who can work."

"I'll bring you food when I can," Opdyke told them. "I can hide it in laundry baskets," she said. "I'll look after you."

Their faces registered surprise. "You're only a girl. What can you do?"

After Opdyke left them with her promise, she began to experience inner doubts. She was "only a girl," but she reflected on the core of her inner beliefs. "I believe very strongly in God," Opdyke said, as she recalled her feelings. "My father insisted we are not born for ourselves. We have to help when help is needed."

Opdyke began smuggling food to her Jewish coworkers; later, she arranged to hide six Jews in a wagon and transport them secretly to the forest where many Jews were choosing to hide. "Better to live like wild beasts in the forest than wait for death in the ghetto," one confided to her.

One night, her boss, Major Rugemer, was having dinner with Sturmbannfuhrer Rokita, the head of the SS in Ternopol. As Opdyke worked around their table, she was startled to hear the direction their conversation was taking.

"You must know by now," Rokita told her boss, "the Fuhrer wants all the Jews exterminated. Once we finish with them, we'll eliminate the Poles and their tiresome Catholic church."

"Of course, the Aryan types, like Irene, we'll make good Germans out of them. But we must cleanse this land once and for all. We're scheduled to finish with the Jews soon. By the end of July," he said.

Stunned by the admission, Opdyke felt compelled to warn her Jewish friends. "I took it to the laundry room and shared with the Jewish 'slaves' and told them to warn the others," she said.

Only days later, Opdyke's boss was transferred to a villa in the surrounding countryside that became his headquarters, and when Opdyke surveyed her new workplace, she discovered a secret underground passage from the cellar of the villa, under the backyard, to a gazebo. She decided this would be the perfect place to hide her twelve Jewish friends from the day of disaster. Ironically, the rightful owner of the house before the war had been a wealthy Jewish architect.

"These slaves were my friends," Opdyke recalled. "I had to help them," she said, knowing the penalties for helping Jews. "The sentence was death if you helped them."

She followed a routine every day that allowed her hidden friends to come into the villa and shower, eat, and listen to news on the radio while her boss, Major Rugemer, was away supervising a weapons factory.

But one day, he came home earlier than expected and caught Irene and her two Jewish friends in the kitchen.

"Clara and Fanka and I stood facing Major Rugemer like statues, and the major stared at us in utter astonishment. His face began to tremble with emotion, but without a word, he turned on his heel and walked out."

Irene ran after him. "Herr Major!" she cried out.

"What in God's name have you done to me?" he shouted at her.

"They are innocent people; they've done nothing. Do not turn them in, I beg you!"

The major's face was red with fury. "Enough! How could you deceive me, Irene?"

"Punish me, Herr Major. I take all the blame—but let them escape!" she sobbed, collapsing at his feet.

"Let me think; I must have time to think."

The following night after dinner, Major Rugemer came home drunk.

"When he opened the library door, he stood swaying slightly, looking at me for a long time without speaking," Irene recounted.

She asked if he wanted coffee and he said no.

Then the major grabbed her and pulled her close. "I'll keep your God****ed secret, Irene," he snarled. "I've wanted you for so long, Irene. Do you think I'll keep your secret for nothing?"

Tears began to flow as he led her up to his bed chamber and she was violated.

The next morning, she took a bath in water so hot, it made her cry. *This was worse than rape*, she thought. *I know I have to bear this shame alone. I can never tell my friends how I bought their safety.*

As the Russians advanced on Poland and the Germans retreated, Irene was able to smuggle her friends into the forest, where they escaped. Irene also ran away and joined a group of partisans living in the forest outside Kielce.

Finally, Hitler and the Nazis were vanquished. "Poland was free, but I was tired," she noted. "I had no more strength left for fighting. It was time for me to start looking for my family."

Much later, as Irene reflected on her war experience, she said, "The war was a series of choices made by many people. Some of those choices were as wicked and shameful to humanity as anything in history."

Opdyke recognized she found help from above in her daring efforts. Throughout her ordeal, she said she "prayed and I pleaded with God. I knew I couldn't do it all by myself." "Somehow, with God's help, I helped them."

"This is my will: to do right, to tell you, and to remember. *Z Bogiem*. Go with God."

CHAPTER 9

Movement He Founded Changed His Own Life

The founder and president of Promise Keepers, award winning football coach Bill McCartney, was in Los Angeles recently. He sat down to discuss the overall condition of the men's movement he founded and ways his own personal life has been impacted by its teachings.

Since Promise Keepers convened a gathering of over a million men on the National Mall in Washington D.C. in 1997, there have been signs of a decline in numbers at recent events. This has caused Promise Keepers to shift from larger outdoor stadiums, holding as many as 50,000 men, to smaller arenas, holding 10,000 to 20,000.

"We've had exponential growth," McCartney says. "We peaked out with over a million men in one year (1997). So, now we are approaching 200,000 men this year. We're at seventy-five percent capacity overall in these arenas."

McCartney explained the shift as partially strategic. "You can hold a man's attention by doing it indoors. It's a captive setting. There is no question that the Lord shows up at these things, and so you watch what God's doing."

"In a very short time, we could fill stadiums again," he says. "If you bring men and boys together in the name of Jesus of Nazareth, the Holy Spirit will come. There's something in God's heart for men stepping up to the plate. That's what we've tapped into, and I don't think it will go away."

McCartney began to ruminate aloud about his own spiritual journey, from football coaching to leading a movement which would ultimately affect his own character. "My last year as a coach was in 1994," he says. "My team was undefeated and was ranked third in the nation—we had a great team. The pastor in our church said, 'We're going to have a visiting preacher next week. And he's coming with the single-most important thing he's learned in forty-one years of preaching.'" And I wondered, *what could be the single-most important thing?*

"So, here's what this preacher said: 'Do you want to know whether a man has character or not? All you have to do is look at his wife's countenance, and everything that he's invested or withheld will be in her face.'"

"I turned and looked at my wife, Lyndi. I didn't see splendor. I saw torment. I didn't see contentment—I saw anguish. And I tried to defend myself to myself but I couldn't. That's really the reason I stepped out of coaching. I realized that before God, I was a man without character."

Prior to the 1993 Fiesta Bowl, McCartney confessed to his wife that he had been unfaithful in their marriage, twenty years earlier, according to a profile in the *New York Times*. She later suffered from bulimia and contemplated suicide, all of which factored into his decision to quit coaching.

"So, you ask what Promise Keepers has done? For the last six years, I've been changing. I still need a lot of changing. I wish I could tell you I've arrived. Promise Keepers has had a radical impact on my own life at every level."

McCartney stepped away from coaching at the pinnacle of his career. "Coaching is compelling—it's intoxicating. But it's just a game. This is really where my heart is. I was in coaching for thirty-two years, and I was right there, ready to hit my prime. And the Lord says, *Let's go into this other arena.*"

"God's got me right where He wants me. I don't have a chance. I can't depend on anything. I've just gotta go to Him every day."

The former coach finds strength and accountability in a small group of men he meets with regularly. "I'm in a small group with three black guys. I feel more comfortable in that environment than I do in an environment with three white guys. And it's stretched me and enriched me. These guys believe in me, care about my family. I share the innermost secrets of my heart with them. I don't hold back because I believe these guys love me."

God's love continues to sustain McCartney, as well as

refine the rough edges in his character. "Two weeks ago, I was going to speak to 300 black preachers on being a peacemaker. And the Lord said, 'If you're going to preach on this then you'd better be living it. There's a couple in your life you're not right with, so go visit them.'"

"So, my wife and I went over to their house, and I said, 'I've come here to ask your forgiveness. I can tell there's some hurt here and there's some tension so I'm here to resolve it.' So, the two of them told me how I had hurt them. Then I started telling them how they'd hurt me. But as I walked out the door, I was downcast, I was sad."

Now tears began to well up in the coach's eyes as he recounted his mistake in handling their meeting. "The Lord showed me that you don't make peace by defending yourself. You make peace by being willing to suffer and take on somebody else's pain. Well ... I had to go back."

"When I went back, I was humiliated. It is humiliating to go back and say, 'I'm back and I'm sorry. This time it's not going to be about me. It's just going to be about you.' I guess I do struggle with pride—that's what got me there. I always want to protect myself."

McCartney has received important biblical insights by studying the beatitudes. "In the first two beatitudes, you look at yourself. Are you poor in spirit, are you mourning with Godly sorrow? The third beatitude is meekness. You let somebody else put the spotlight on you and you won't try to defend yourself.

"To hunger and thirst for righteousness means that as soon as the Holy Spirit says you've sinned, you say yes, and you surrender. Then the flow of God's spirit will come through. Who are the pure in heart? It is those who mourn the impurity in their hearts. The person who is pure in heart longs to see God.

"When you would really rather die and be with the Lord, you're ready to be a peacemaker. The peacemaker is the one who has totally forgotten about himself. Then he's the one who will get persecuted."

McCartney believes one of the reasons men do not return

to Promise Keepers, is that the church has not been making disciples. "The problem today is the church is indifferent, apathetic. The church is running on fumes. The church is not discipling men to the point where men are ready to disciple others. Billy Graham himself says that only four percent of the men who have received Christ at his events have gone on and been discipled.

"They don't come back to Promise Keepers because they get challenged and they come under conviction. They leave here real excited and then, a month later, they're not following through on what they thought they would do. What we have to do is change everything about the way the local church connects with men.

"If a pastor will take four consecutive weeks in the pulpit and preach to the men as if no one else were there, the church will get excited. The apostle Paul put all the men in front. He went right at the men; he didn't preach to the ladies. Sadly, ninety-five percent of men will hear an inspired message, and they are truly stirred by it, but when they walk out of the church, they will forget it."

McCartney explained this is one of the reasons he urges men to become accountable to one another. "This is why one of the speakers at the Los Angeles event urged men to give their telephone number to men sitting near them—even if they were strangers, so they would have someone to hold them accountable for their promises," he says.

The former coach recently turned sixty (August 22, 2000) and admits to being tired after some of the events. "When I leave here, I am physically spent, I will be just exhausted. When I get home, it's like I've just run a marathon, and I just want to go off by myself and hide. Part of this may be a sinful reaction. I think there's a lot of spiritual warfare, and I do think that it's strategic.

"If your motive is to give it up for the kingdom of God, I know you'll get refreshed. I know that I need rest and refreshing. Thankfully, God's mercies are fresh every morning."

McCartney continues to explore new directions for the movement he created under the Lord's inspiration. "We have an idea we're exploring that I don't care to talk about today because it's too premature. But I honestly believe you're going to see large stadiums filled again. We are casting a vision for men—that I don't think will go away."

Sadly, McCartney never saw large stadiums filled as they once were in the 1990s. This author believes the rise of the internet during the same period killed the men's movement, because of the easy availability of internet pornography, which captured men's hearts and led them astray.

Chapter 10

Missionary Died Thinking He Was a Failure

In 1912, medical missionary Dr. William Leslie went to live and minister to tribal people in a remote corner of the Democratic Republic of the Congo. After seventeen years, he returned to the U.S. a discouraged man—believing he failed to make an impact for Christ. He died nine years after his return.

But in 2010, a team led by Eric Ramsey with Tom Cox World Ministries made a shocking and sensational discovery. They found a network of reproducing churches hidden like glittering diamonds in the dense jungle, across the Kwilu River from Vanga, where Dr. Leslie was stationed.

With the help of a Mission Aviation Fellowship pilot, Ramsey and his team flew east from Kinshasa to Vanga, a two-and-a-half-hour flight in a Cessna Caravan. After they reached Vanga, they hiked a mile to the Kwilu River and used dugout canoes to cross the half-mile-wide expanse. Then they hiked with backpacks another ten miles into the jungle before they reached the first village of the Yansi people.

Based on his previous research, Ramsey thought the Yansi in this remote area might have some exposure to the name of Jesus, but no real understanding of who He is. They were unprepared for their remarkable find.

"When we got in there, we found a network of reproducing churches throughout the jungle," Ramsey reports. "Each village had its own Gospel choir, although they wouldn't call it that," he notes. "They wrote their own songs and would have sing-offs from village to village."

They found a church in each of the eight villages they visited scattered across thirty-four miles. Ramsey and his team even found a 1,000-seat stone "cathedral" in one of the villages. He learned that this church got so crowded in the 1980s, with many walking miles to attend, that a church planting movement began in the surrounding villages.

"There is no Bible in the Yansi language," Ramsey says. "They used a French Bible, so those who taught had to be fluent in French."

Apparently, Dr. Leslie crossed the Kwilu River once a year from Vanga and spent a month traveling through the jungle, sometimes carried by fellow workers through difficult terrain.

"He would teach the Bible, taught the tribal children how to read and write, talked about the importance of education, and told Bible stories," Ramsey notes. Dr. Leslie started the first organized educational system in these villages, Ramsey learned.

It took some digging for Ramsey to uncover Leslie's identity. "The tribal people only knew him by one name, and I didn't know if that was a first or last name. They knew he was a Baptist, and he was based in that one city and they knew the years."

When Ramsey returned home, he did some additional investigation and discovered Dr. Leslie was affiliated with the American Baptist Missionary Union. The American Baptist Missionary Union was founded in 1814 by Adoniram Judson, who led a pioneering work in Burma.

Born in Ontario, Canada, William H. Leslie followed his intended profession as a pharmacist until his conversion in 1888. He moved to the Chicago area, where God began to grip his heart with the desire to become a medical missionary.

Dr. Leslie initiated his Congo service in 1893 at Banza-Manteke. Two years later, he developed a serious illness. A young missionary named Clara Hill took care of him until he recovered. Their budding friendship ripened into love and a marriage proposal. They were wed in 1896.

In 1905, William and Clara pioneered a work in Cuilo, Angola, where they overcame a hurricane that struck the night before one of their children was born, and more mundane obstacles like charging buffaloes and armies of ants.

Seven years later, they cleared enough of the leopard-infested jungle along the Kwilu River at Vanga for a new mission station perched on a small plateau. Some of the villages surrounding Vanga were still practicing cannibalism at that time.

They spent seventeen years at Vanga, but their service ended on a rocky note. "Dr. Leslie had a relational falling out with some of the tribal leaders and was asked not to come back," Ramsey says. "They reconciled later; there were apologies and forgiveness, but it didn't end like he hoped."

"His goal was to spread Christianity. He felt like he was there for seventeen years and he never really made a big impact, but the legacy he left is huge."

CHAPTER 11

Fastest Growing Church Has No Walls

For the last few years, researchers have credited the underground church in Iran as the fastest growing Christian church in the world. It has unique characteristics that defy comparison with churches in America and Europe, and in the opinion of some who know it well, the church in the west could learn by studying it.

"The fastest growing church in the world has taken root in one of the most unexpected and radicalized nations on earth," according to *Sheep Among Wolves*, the outstanding two-hour documentary about the revival that has taken place inside Iran. "The Iranian awakening is a rapidly reproducing discipleship movement that owns no property or buildings, has no central leadership, and is predominantly led by women."

The documentary was produced by Frontier Alliance International (FAI), which supports disciple-making teams targeting the "unreached" and "unengaged" within the 10/40 Window.

There is a mass exodus leaving Islam for Christianity within Iran, according to FAI.

"What if I told you Islam is dead?" one unidentified Iranian church leader says on the film. "What if I told you the mosques are empty inside Iran? What if I told you no one follows Islam inside of Iran? Would you believe me? This is exactly what is happening inside of Iran. God is moving powerfully inside of Iran."

Many of the ruling class still follow Islam, "because that's where the high paying jobs are," according to the film, but the majority of the ordinary people love God and recognize that Islam is the problem.

"What if I told you the best evangelist for Jesus was the Ayatollah Khomeini?" an Iranian church leader asks. He maintains the ayatollahs brought the true face of Islam to light and people discovered it was a lie, a deception. "After 40 years under Islamic law—a utopia according to them—they've had the worst devastation in the 5,000-year history of Iran."

Efforts by the ayatollahs to destroy Christianity have backfired, but have served to refine and purify the church. "What persecution did was destroy the church that were not disciples, and destroy the church that were about converts," the Iranian church leader noted. "All these church planters found out that converts run away from persecution, but disciples would die for the Lord in persecution."

"So, our model inside Iran is that we don't convert to disciple, we disciple so we can convert."

Often a disciple making movement (DMM) begins the first moment someone comes into contact with an unbeliever. "Everything is foundational on prayer. We find people of peace through prayer. We even find locations through prayer," the Iranian church leader noted.

"When we do DMM, Jesus has gone faster than us. He has come in their dreams, or He's come miraculously in their lives. When we hear this, we know that Jesus has gone ahead of us."

Surprisingly, their emphasis is not planting churches; it is making disciples. "He is letting unbelievers lead other unbelievers to Himself and the kingdom of God. If you plant churches, you might make disciples. But if you make disciples, you will plant churches," the Iranian church leader said.

"One thing powerful with DMM is that it is obedience-based discipleship. It is based on the authority of Scripture, and every time you read the Scripture, you must obey it. This is how people become conformed to the image of Christ and sanctified. They are not just reading the Bible for information. They are reading the Bible to get transformed."

About 55% of the disciple makers are women, according to one Iranian leader.

"What's fascinating right now is that the most powerful leaders in Iran are women, but it's not in a bombastic, humanistic way ... in fact, they are the most gentle women. They are leading this movement, going out in the highways and byways sharing with prostitutes, drug addicts, with everybody they come into contact with, and that takes courage. They are courageous women."

The women leaders in Iran have not embraced a feminist theology, according to one of the U.S.-based leaders with FIA. "In a biblical way, they are submissive to proper structure and the order of the church, but when it comes to what Satan is doing, they are fierce. These are not like modern, angry, liberal women that are just upset. No, there is a gentleness and submissiveness that is beautiful and follows the biblical pattern."

One stereotype of Iran promulgated by the nightly news involves crowds of angry Muslims shaking their fists and chanting, "Death to America" and "Death to Israel."

But the film presents a different reality beneath the surface. "The most mind-blowing aspect of the church in Iran is that central to their redemptive theology, and their understanding of not only who Jesus is, what He came to do, and what He will return to do, is a covenantal theology that has Israel at the center."

"When you ask most people what the most existential threat is to Israel, they will say Iran—and that's true. But behind the curtain of what God is doing, God is raising up one of the fastest growing movements of former Muslims that are falling in love not only with the God of Israel, not only Israel's king, not only Israel's Messiah, they are actually falling in love with the Jewish people. As a result of this, you have a prayer movement in Iran that is crying out for the salvation of Israel."

The film cites one Iranian couple that had the opportunity to move to the U.S. After living in America for a matter of months, the wife decided she wanted to move back to Iran, telling her surprised husband: "There is a satanic lullaby here. All the Christians are sleepy, and I'm feeling sleepy."

One leader with FIA notes the alarming nature of her conclusion. "That story was disturbing because that woman was discerning a threat to her faith that was a greater threat than the kind of persecution that happens in Iran. She saw that spiritual sleepiness is a greater threat to her faith than persecution."

The film observes that the only church in the book of Revelation not critiqued by Jesus was under persecution and suffering. "If freedom is such a great thing for the kingdom, then why is Europe and America in the state they are in?" an Iranian believer asks.

"When we walk outside, we really don't care if we get arrested, we are not upset if we get arrested. What is fifty years in prison compared to eternity with Jesus?"

The filmmakers contend the church in Iran offers wisdom to impart. "I believe that what is happening in the church in Iran is going to become a measuring stick for the global body of Christ. It is not something we will be able to admire from afar. It is going to be something we are required to participate in. It is going to disrupt our lives," one U.S.-based leader with FIA says.

"I believe the Lord is going to take this issue of the testimony, the story, the witness of the church in Iran and thrust it into the heart of the global body of Christ, that we would follow in their footsteps and learn from them. I believe the Lord is putting this message on blast for us to prepare us for the days ahead."

Chapter 12

How Islam Progressively Takes Over Countries

In Dr. Peter Hammond's book, *Slavery, Terrorism and Islam*, he documents the way Muslims slowly develop a presence in various countries, and as their population numbers build, become more aggressive and assertive about exercising Sharia Law.

"Islam is not a religion, nor is it a cult. In its fullest form, it is a complete, total, 100% system of life," Dr. Hammond notes in his book. "Islam has religious, legal, political, economic, social, and military components. The religious component is a beard for all of the other components."

Their takeover of a country, what Dr. Hammond refers to as "Islamization," begins when the population of Muslims reaches a critical mass, and they being to agitate for various privileges.

Open, free, democratic societies are particularly vulnerable. "When politically correct, tolerant, and culturally diverse societies agree to Muslim demands for their religious privileges, some of the other components tend to creep in as well," he notes.

This is how it works, according to Dr. Hammond:

When the Muslim population remains under 2% in a country, they will be seen primarily as a peace-loving minority and not as a threat to other citizens. This is the current situation in*:

United States — Muslim 1.1%

China — Muslim 1.9%

As the Muslim population reaches 2% to 5%, they begin to recruit from ethnic minorities and disaffected groups, sometimes within prisons and street gangs. This is happening in:

Australia — Muslim 3.2%

Canada — Muslim 4.9%

Italy — Muslim 4.2%

Philippines — 4.8%

United Kingdom — Muslim 2.2%

Spain — Muslim 2.1%

Sweden — Muslim 3.7%

Switzerland — Muslim 3.2%

Thailand — Muslim 4.3%

"From 5% on, they exercise an inordinate influence in proportion to their percentage of the population," Dr. Hammond notes. "For example, they will push for the introduction of halal (clean by Islamic standards) food" and increase pressure on supermarket chains to feature such food on their shelves, along with threats for failure to comply. This is happening in:

Denmark — Muslim 5.4%

France — Muslim 5.7%

Germany — Muslim 8.7%

Norway — Muslim 5.6%

The Netherlands — Muslim 8.0%

Soon, they begin to apply pressure to allow Sharia Law within their own communities (sometimes ghettos). "When Muslims approach 10% of the population, they tend to increase lawlessness as a means of complaint about their conditions," Dr. Hammond notes. "In Paris, we are already seeing car-burnings. Any non-Muslim action offends Islam, and results in uprisings and threats, such as in Amsterdam, with opposition to Mohammed cartoons and films about Islam." These tensions are seen on a regular basis in:

India — Muslim 13.6%

Israel — Muslim 19.3%

Kenya — Muslim 9.8%

Russia — Muslim 10.6%

The violence increases when the Muslim population reaches 20%. "After reaching 20%, nations can expect hair-trigger rioting, jihad militia formations, sporadic killings, and the burnings of Christian churches and Jewish synagogues," such as in:

Ethiopia — Muslim 33.8%

"At 40%, nations experience widespread massacres, chronic terror attacks, and ongoing militia warfare," such as in:

Bosnia-Herzegovina — Muslim 51.2%

Chad — Muslim 57.6%

Malaysia — Muslim 55.7%

United Arab Emirates — Muslim 52.2%

From 60%, persecution of non-believing "infidels" rises significantly, including sporadic ethnic cleansing (genocide), use of Sharia Law as a weapon, and Jizya, and a tax placed on infidels. After 80%, expect daily intimidation and violent jihad, some State-run ethnic cleansing, and even some genocide, as these nations drive out "infidels," and move toward a 100% Muslim society, which has been experienced to some degree in:

Albania — Muslim 97.9%

Bangladesh — Muslim 90.5%

Egypt — Muslim 99.8%

Indonesia — Muslim 88.3%

Iraq — Muslim 97.7%

Jordan — Muslim 99.2%

Lebanon — Muslim 88.2%

Pakistan — Muslim 97.7%

Qatar — Muslim 87.5%

Saudi Arabia — Muslim 94.1%

Sudan — Muslim 97.6%

Syria — Muslim 95.3%

Tajikistan — Muslim 99.4%

Turkey — Muslim 99.2%

West Bank/Gaza — Muslim 91.2%

Achieving nearly a 100% Muslim society will theoretically usher in their version of peace—the peace of "Dar-es-Salaam"—the Islamic House of Peace. "Here there's supposed to be peace, because everybody is a Muslim, the Madrassas are the only schools, and the Koran is the only word."

Afghanistan — Muslim 100%

Iran — Muslim 99.5%

Morocco — Muslim 100%

Somalia — Muslim 99.9%

Yemen — Muslim 99.8%

Dr. Hammond observes this Islamic ideal is seldom realized. "Unfortunately, peace is never achieved, as in these 100% states the most radical Muslims intimidate and spew hatred, and satisfy their blood lust by killing less radical Muslims, for a variety of reasons."

"It is important to understand that in some countries, with well under 100% Muslim populations, such as France, the minority Muslim populations live in ghettos, within which they are 100% Muslim, and within which they live by Sharia Law," he states.

Dr. Hammond is also concerned by demographic trends. "Today's 1.5 billion Muslims make up 22% of the world's population," he observes. "But their birth rates dwarf the birth rates of Christians, Hindus, Buddhists, Jews, and all other believers. Muslims will exceed 50% of the world's population by the end of this century."

*These percentages are from the Joshua Project, 2022.

CHAPTER 13

Woman's Near-Death Vision of Heaven Confirms Other Accounts

She had been a Christian since she was nineteen, raised in a conservative church that came out of the Anabaptist movement. In her early sixties, she had such a powerful vision of heaven, she could barely speak of it, a vision closely matching other contemporary accounts popularized in recent years.

"In all humility, I felt like I was not worthy to speak about what I saw," says Carol Meyer. She and her husband, Vern, live on a "gentleman's horse farm" in Michigan, consisting of a few acres, their modest home, a horse barn, and one tree standing alone in their pasture.

Carol was vice-president of a small bank in Indiana before they retired to their farm in Michigan.

Fourteen years ago, while she slept in the middle of the night, Carol said she was transported to the "edge" of heaven. She had been suffering with a life-threatening gastrointestinal disease that led to a hospitalization immediately before her experience.

Fire, lightning, thunder, and water swirled around her as she landed on the floor of paradise with a "whoosh." "It was scary and exhilarating all at the same time," she recounts. "I instantly knew I was in heaven. As I was standing there, this incredible peace overtook me. There were no more earthly emotional holes in my spirit. I was completely whole. It was an incredible feeling. This state of being is no doubt part of the scripture that there will be no tears or sorrow in heaven. It was a very profound experience."

Carol looked to her right and saw a large angel soldier, dressed in a brownish gown, with no visible wings. His face was set like flint—similar to earthly soldiers guarding important landmarks.

Just beyond him were three-foot diameter metal tubes sloping down into a cavernous area. Then she delighted as she glimpsed one of her favorite creatures on earth—butterflies.

Oh God, you have all these butterflies up here. This is so awesome! she thought. These butterflies were large and blue, unlike any variety she had seen in North America.

When Carol looked up, she beheld magnificent colors in the sky unlike anything she had ever seen. "It was much more than a beautiful sunset. There were more colors than you've ever seen."

She saw flowers in abundance and heard the sound of either rushing water or a swirling wind. She looked down at her feet and was surprised.

"I was standing on a crystal floor, like gold at its purest point. It was moving in a slight wave." There were pathways leading in different directions. She was amazed by all the activity she witnessed.

To her left, she saw the beginning of a sparkling blue river flowing gently along. "I called it a rushing river, but the sound was coming from God."

Then she saw the Lord, who walked out from a ledge covered with grape vines. "He was so beautiful. He had on a soft white linen gown, with a shine to it." His eyes looked deeply into her soul, and she knew instantly He was and is the King of Kings and Lord of Lords.

Just as suddenly as Carol was transported to heaven—whether in the body or not, she doesn't know—she awakened in her bed. "I woke up in my bed, curled up in the fetal position," she recounts. "I couldn't believe what happened to me."

It took her several days to tell her husband and another six months before she could share her story with other relatives.

The following spring, she visited the Meijer Gardens in Grand Rapids, Michigan. Every spring, the gardens play host to a massive butterfly show, featuring thousands of varieties of exotic specimens. She almost fell over when she glimpsed the same blue butterflies she had seen on her heavenly visit, a tropical species native to South America.

Many years after her vision, she read *Heaven Is for Real*, the story of four-year-old Colton Burpo's trip to heaven after his own near-death experience. She was fascinated by his reference to a painting of Jesus by Akiane, the young art prodigy who also had a vision of Jesus.

A friend told her a copy of the painting was at their local Christian bookstore, so she raced there to see it for herself. She almost burst into tears when she viewed it. "The feeling was so powerful. I grabbed it and held it to me." The painting was so close to the One she saw in her vision, it was uncanny.

Years later, she almost begins to shake when she recalls what she experienced in heaven. "It got me so much, I almost couldn't handle remembering it. That was the effect it had on me. It was like it was so holy, it couldn't come out of my mouth."

CHAPTER 14

Airline Pilot Prompted by Holy Spirit to Speed Departure Before Disaster Struck

The Holy Spirit prompted a Christian airline pilot to speed the departure of his Batik Air flight from Palu, Indonesia carrying 140 passengers, narrowly averting a potential disaster with the loss of many lives.

The epicenter of a powerful 7.5 magnitude earthquake struck Friday, September 28, 2018, in a mountainous area of Central Sulawesi, forty-eight miles from the provincial capital of Palu. Only minutes later, underwater landslides apparently triggered a massive ten-to-20-foot tsunami that swept through Palu and other coastal areas.

The waves were intensified by Palu's location at the end of a narrow bay. At least 4300 people perished from the combined effects of the earthquake and tsunami. Smaller villages in the surrounding area were entirely swept away.

"All day Friday, I had been feeling unsettled, and I didn't know why," Captain Icoze Mafella recounted at a Jakarta church, Duta Injil BIP, two days after the disaster.

To displace his feelings of unease, Captain Mafella, a strong Christian, began to loudly sing worship songs on his flight from Ujung Pandang to Palu. "Usually I only hummed, but that day, I wanted to praise the Lord as best I could," he said. "I think you should make a CD of worship songs," his Muslim co-pilot told him, jokingly.

When they were about to land at the Palu Airport, the wind was unusually strong, and he "heard a voice in his heart" directing him to circle again before landing.

The Palu airport is squeezed between two mountain ranges, and some pilots refer to airports situated in this way as "valleys of death," so once again, the pilot felt prompted to be extra careful in landing and recited the twenty-third Psalm:

"I may walk through valleys as dark as death but I won't be afraid. You are with me and Your shepherd's rod makes me feel safe," he said.

After they landed, the Holy Spirit prompted him once more that he needed to be quick. He instructed his crew to take a shorter break before the plane was due to take off for Jakarta via Ujung Pandang.

"I didn't even leave the cockpit and requested permission from the control tower to depart three minutes ahead of schedule," he recounted.

He received approval for the expedited time for takeoff from Air Controller Anthonius Agung, and they prepared for departure.

He felt such an urgency that Captain Mafella broke with standard flight procedures and took over some of the co-pilot's responsibilities to speed up their exit.

The moment arrived for takeoff, and Captain Mafella barreled down the runway. "I don't know why but my hand kept pushing the lever causing the plane to speed up as it took off," he said.

As they sped down the airstrip, the massive earthquake began to strike Palu, and both pilots felt the plane sway noticeably to the left and right. The Muslim co-pilot glanced at Captain Mafella with a look of fear in his eyes.

"If I had taken off three minutes later, I would not have been able to save the 140 passengers, because the asphalt on the landing strip was moving up and down like a curtain blowing in the wind," he testified.

Several minutes after takeoff, he attempted to communicate with the control tower but there was no response.

Then he looked down and saw an unusual sight. "The seawater on the coast was forming a very large hole so that the foundation of the seabed could be seen," he reported. "I saw circles getting bigger and bigger. I thought it was very strange."

Prior to a tsunami, the shoreline often recedes dramatically, exposing areas that are normally submerged.

When the plane arrived in Ujung Pandang, he was told the shocking news that there had been an earthquake and tsunami in Palu.

The air controller, Anthonius Agung, twenty-one, made sure their plane (the last to leave the airport) had safely taken off before he jumped from the crumbling control tower at the height of the quake.

"They said people tried to call him to get away from the tower, but he said, 'No, the aircraft isn't airborne yet.' Then the roof started collapsing and he jumped."

Tragically, he broke his legs, arms, and ribs because of the fall and died from internal injuries on his way to the hospital.

"In this difficult time, during the split seconds of decisions, he waited for me until I was safe before he jumped. That's why I call him my guardian angel."

Many others are calling the air controller a hero—along with Captain Mafella.

"It is important that we hear the voice of God," he said.

"And whatever happens, we must be calm, not in a panic, so that we can clearly hear the voice of God coming to us by the Holy Spirit."

CHAPTER 15

Good Book Survived Nashville Tornado

The cluster of storm cells firing across western Missouri with baseball-sized hail caused the first tornado warnings to be issued at 11:02 p.m. on March 2, 2020, as many were dropping off to sleep.

An hour and a half later, when most were already in a deep sleep, a more direct warning was issued for Nashville, but it was too late for many to take cover. Within six minutes of the warning, the tornado hit with over 160 mile per hour winds, a ferocity that toppled trees and buildings, shredding many structures to small, unrecognizable fragments.

Twenty-five people were killed in the disaster, with more than 300 injured, and thousands left without power.

Then a great and powerful wind tore the mountains apart and shattered the rocks before the Lord, but the Lord was not in the wind. (1 Kings 19:11)

Yet one singular book of infinite value survived the tempest—the Holy Bible, without any damage, resting in the bough of several forked branches, as if set there by an angel.

"My friend's house was hit hard, and while cleaning, I noticed one thing!" Big Cee O'Neal reported in a short video clip reposted by CBN.

As he helped his friend with the cleanup effort, he happened to glance upward and see something amazing.

There was the Bible resting in the tree, completely unscathed and balanced perfectly between the trunk (vine) and one surprisingly sturdy branch.

It was an excellent place for God's Word to abide—between branch and vine.

CHAPTER 16

Top Female Porn Star Found Jesus

In 2010, Maxim magazine named her one of the top female porn stars in the world. Little did they know, she was already on a rocky road to sanctification as a new creature in Christ.

Brittni, who used the professional name Jenna Presley, started dancing to earn extra money as a freshman at Santa Barbara City College in 2005. Two men approached her after one of her performances and asked if she would like to make "romance movies."

"You mean porn?" she joked. They nodded affirmatively, but it was no joke.

"I didn't know what to expect," she admits now. "At eighteen, I was only a baby. I was looking for love in all the wrong places."

Brittni was insecure as a result of her upbringing in a home with a "verbally abusive" mother and passive father. For the first time in her life, she began to receive positive affirmation, and it felt good. She traveled to L.A. and shot her first pornographic scene.

"I felt so loved that day because they did my hair and makeup. I was told I was beautiful and that I was going to be a star. In the first few months, it felt good."

Producers worked her relentlessly in the early phase of her career because of her youthful, fresh appearance. "I already looked like I was twelve," Brittni recalls. They dressed her in "little girl" clothing and pigtails, which made her uncomfortable.

The inescapable conclusion is that filmmakers wanted to appeal to the depraved fantasies of men with pedophile tendencies. "It's disgusting how they can portray you as a little girl," she says today. "It's complete perversion."

During this period, she worked as much as sixty days without a day off, shooting two and sometimes three sex scenes a day. "I didn't know how to say no," she notes. "I didn't know how to stand up for myself. Before this, my mother made every decision for me."

The youthful spark that made her such an attractive commodity began to fade. "It left me feeling drained," she says. "I was so robotic; I was like a rubber Barbie doll. I had no emotions."

Initially, she made $900 for each sex scene she filmed, but the money quickly disappeared. As hopelessness and emptiness overwhelmed her, she turned to drugs to numb the pain. "I started with cocaine. Then it became a downhill spiral to heroin."

"I had many lonely nights when I cut on my wrists. I tried to kill myself. I spent all my paycheck on drugs."

After three years in the adult film industry, she was fed up. She placed a 911 call to her grandmother. "I need you grandma," she said. "I'm done with this. Come and get me."

During her stay with her grandparents, they took her to the Rock Church in San Diego, led by Pastor Miles McPherson. Brittni was "bawling" through most of the sermon. In response to his invitation, she raised her hand to receive Jesus as her personal Lord and Savior.

The church gave her a Bible, and after she got home, she devoured Genesis. "I always wondered how we became human. Finally, I had the answer, and I was so excited. I couldn't put it down."

She began to date a man she met at church, but the relationship had a tragic ending. As they sat together at Los Panchos restaurant in San Diego one evening, men from a rival motorcycle gang approached their table and began to beat her boyfriend with brass knuckles. "He got murdered, stabbed in front of me," she recalls. The attackers were in and out of the restaurant within minutes.

Traumatized by the incident, her burgeoning faith was derailed. "That began another spiral into more drugs and suicide attempts," she says.

She began to date someone close to her former boyfriend. He encouraged her to get off drugs and get baptized, and she began to get involved with church again. In another bizarre turn, this man turned out to be a wolf in sheep's clothing. "He ended up being a pimp and got me back into the adult film industry," she says.

Brittni began to straddle two worlds ruled by opposing powers. "I was on the Howard Stern show preaching the Word, and I was preaching on the set." She kept making adult films for two more years to make ends meet, as she battled contradictions that left her weary and dry. "It was a big mess," she admits.

"The devil wanted me back, but God kept tugging at me," Brittni says. "The devil had a plot, but God has a plan."

The ministry of XXX Church, which employs creative outreach strategies to the porn industry, caught Brittni's attention at a porn convention. Their booth at the Exotica convention blares to attendees, "Jesus loves porn stars." Remarkably, they distribute hundreds of Bibles at these venues.

One of the young women who ministers to the girls, Rachel Collins, made an impression on Brittni. "She brought coffee, Bibles, lip gloss to the girls in the industry," Brittni recalls. "She was so sweet and loving; there was a glow to her."

After Brittni saw Rachel's photo in one of their magazines, she contacted the ministry and eventually filmed an interview with Rachel about her experience with adult films.

In November 2012, Brittni filmed her last sex scene. "It was seven long years," she laments. "I hated what I was doing, but I wondered what I would do next." After Brittni left adult films, she found work with a limousine company and makes a decent income.

"I look forward to waking up every morning," she says. "There is life after porn; there is life after drugs and prostitution."

Brittni also reconciled with her parents and has a wonderful relationship with them today. Recently, her entire family sat together in church. "I love my mom so much," she exclaims. "My sister got baptized with me, and my brother prayed the prayer of salvation with me on the phone."

"God is alive and He is working!" she says. "He is in the business of miracles. I have finally encountered the unconditional love of God, and I will never go back."

Chapter 17

Winston Churchill Warned About the Dangers of Radical Islam

Winston Churchill was one of the greatest leaders of the 20th Century, who served as Prime Minister of the United Kingdom during World War II, and again, from 1951 to 1955.

He was also a historian, writer, and artist. He is the only British Prime Minister to have been awarded the Nobel Prize in Literature and was the first person to be made an honorary citizen of the U.S. following the Second World War.

As an officer of the British Army in 1897 and 1898, he fought against a Pashtun tribe in the northwest frontier of British India and also at the Battle of Omdurman in Sudan. In both of those conflicts, he had eye-opening encounters with Muslims. These incidents allowed his keen powers of observation and always-fluid pen to weigh in on the subject of Islamic society.

While these words were written when he was only twenty-five years old (in 1899), they serve as a prophetic warning to western civilization today.

"How dreadful are the curses which Mohammedanism (Islam) lays on its votaries! Besides the fanatical frenzy, which is as dangerous in a man as hydrophobia in a dog, there is this fearful fatalistic apathy."

Churchill apparently witnessed the same phenomenon in several places he visited. "The effects are apparent in many countries: improvident habits, slovenly systems of agriculture, sluggish methods of commerce and insecurity of property exist wherever the followers of the Prophet rule or live."

He saw the temporal and the eternal tainted by their belief system. "A degraded sensualism deprives this life of its grace and refinement, the next of its dignity and sanctity," he wrote.

The second-class status of women also grated at the young officer. "The fact that in Mohammedan law every woman must belong to some man as his absolute property, either as a child, a wife, or a concubine, must delay the final extinction of slavery until the faith of Islam has ceased to be a great power among men," he noted.

"Individual Moslems may show splendid qualities, but the influence of the religion paralyzes the social development of those who follow it. No stronger retrograde force exists in the world."

Well before the birth of modern Israel, its terror tactics and drive for world domination were felt. "Far from being moribund, Mohammedanism is a militant and proselytizing faith. It has already spread throughout Central Africa, raising fearless warriors at every step, and were it not that Christianity is sheltered in the strong arms of science, the science against which it (Islam) has vainly struggled, the civilization of modern Europe might fall, as fell the civilization of ancient Rome."

Churchill's quotations are from "The River War," Volume II, pages 248-250, published by Longmans, Green & Company, 1899.

Chapter 18

They Called Themselves Christians, But Refused to Forgive

Alec Rex was driving down a busy street in Adelaide, Australia on February 15, 2016, when he suffered a massive heart attack and his heart stopped.

He slumped forward on the steering wheel, traffic stopped around him, and a woman came rushing over to his car.

"She opened the door and tried to get me out, but I was in a seatbelt," Alec recalls.

As she struggled to free him, she forgot to turn off the ignition, and the car began moving forward. "The car took off and got up to about thirty miles per hour. She was still hanging on to the car."

When she saw they were going to hit another vehicle, she let go and fell headlong to the pavement. "It was a miracle she wasn't killed. She hit the ground and saw me hit the vehicle. She pulled herself together and ran one hundred yards."

The young woman was a corrections officer who just left her shift. When she started CPR, she was certain Alec was dead.

Providentially, an ambulance was among the vehicles caught in the traffic jam. "A couple doctors raced over and started working on me. In the police report, it says they resuscitated me five times. That means I died five times. They put me in the ambulance and took me to the hospital. I was dead."

Doctors could find little reason for hope, but then Alec surprised them. "They didn't know what to do with me. I came back to life. I was thrashing about, punching them. I came back to life. They were stunned."

"According to the MRI, my heart was badly damaged because one of the main arteries was blocked. They put a stent in there."

The hospital also discovered pneumonia in his lungs, so they placed Alec in an induced coma following his surgery.

"My heart was so badly damaged they said to my wife there was a possibility I would have a ten percent chance to live. If I survived, I would be a vegetable."

But God was about to demonstrate His power in a way that would surprise the doctors. And while Alec was hovering between life and death, he was transported to a nether region beyond this world.

"In front of me was like a veil, the gates of hell," Alec recounts. "I was at the gates of hell, but not in hell." Everything appeared two-dimensional to him, like he was watching a TV.

Then he heard a voice say, "Jesus I know but you I don't."

But to his right, another voice said: *I am the Lord God. I am going to heal you and make you new.*

Alec recognized that Jesus was speaking to him, and He could read Alec's thoughts.

Jesus' presence provided the light for Alec to see. "Others there couldn't see Him or hear Him."

Then the Lord impressed on his heart: *I will do what I want to bring your healing. I will show you the power of the Holy Spirit.*

Then an astonishing sight met Alec. "Around me was a sea full of people," he recounts. "I couldn't see their faces. They were joined together in chains."

Jesus impressed on his heart: *These people call themselves Christians, but they couldn't forgive their brothers and sisters.*

Jesus mentioned to Alec to pay attention to the Parable of the Unforgiving Servant and instructed him about its meaning. "I was taking this all in. He only allows you to remember what He wants you to remember. I can't add to what he told me."

During his near-death experience at the gates of hell, Alec says that Jesus also told him a worldwide revival is coming that will be greater than Azusa Street or the Welsh Revival. *There will not be anything like it,* Jesus told him.

"It is not just people getting saved," Alec adds. "It is the bride being made perfect, without spot or blemish."

The Lord communicated to him: *What the world deems insignificant is what I am going to use in this revival.*

Alec was in a coma for three weeks. During that time, doctors debated about whether or not to turn off his life support.

But then, God breathed new life into his body. "They were going to switch off the machine," he recounts. "God brought me back to life. It is a medical fact I was dead for twenty minutes in the hospital. My brain is now 100%."

"Praise God everything changed. I am one miracle after another."

After Alec came out of the coma, the head ICU nurse told his wife Beth, "Your husband's vital signs are 100%."

The next morning, Dr. Matthew Worthley, a cardiologist and professor at the Royal Adelaide Hospital, came into his room, looked at his file, and said, "You were dead but you're alive. You're a miracle!"

Other doctors were equally amazed. "At the surgery, there was a vascular heart surgeon, Dr. Raja. He shook his head and said, 'I was there when you came back to life. I was there when they took the MRI of your heart. It was so badly damaged. I can't understand it. There is no sign of a heart attack, no sign of any scarring. Your heart is 100%.'"

When Alec left the hospital, he got a standing ovation from the nurses. "They said, 'This is the guy who was dead and came back.' I thanked all the nurses and doctors. There were doctors there with tears."

While Alec is grateful to be alive, he is even more ecstatic about what God is doing. "I believe the bridegroom is coming soon—two years, five years, ten years—I don't know when, but it's exciting. Impossible things are happening. The bride is going to be beautiful—her appearance, her apparel, and her beauty."

CHAPTER 19

Encounter with Jesus on the Moon Left Astronaut Changed

In the rounded, gray Apennine mountains of the moon, Apollo 15 astronaut James Irwin had an encounter with God he would never forget. Irwin was the eighth man to walk on the moon and the first to ride in the Lunar Rover. Apollo 15 was a "J Mission," which meant he and fellow astronaut David Scott spent an extended period on the lunar surface—almost three days, where they collected 170 pounds of geologic material including the famous "Genesis Rock."

Scientists believe the rock dates back to the time the original lunar crust was formed, which they estimate at 4.5 billion years. "It was remarkable," Irwin commented later. "It was sitting on a pedestal rock almost free from dust. It seemed to be saying, 'Here I am, take me.'"

Irwin and Scott worked for an extended period with little rest prior to their liftoff. "Apparently, when Jim was suiting up, his water tube kinked so he wasn't able to get any water," recalls Mary Irwin, his wife.

Outside their spacesuits, the temperature on the lunar surface was 150 degrees. "He perspired like crazy," Mary says. "He was losing his electrolyte balance. An imbalance of sodium and potassium can trigger a heart attack," she notes.

While Irwin did not suffer a heart attack, flight surgeons on earth who monitored the men were alarmed when they saw both astronauts develop irregular heart rhythms.

Irwin's situation was more severe, with abnormal heartbeats every other beat. Neither man was told about their condition by Mission Control. Flight surgeons reasoned they were already getting 100% oxygen, they had continuous monitoring of their vital signs, and they were at zero gravity—conditions that partially replicated or even exceeded an ICU unit back on earth.

NASA also had concerns about wider dissemination of this sensitive health information. "If doctors said something and it was on the loop, who knows who would have leaked that to the press," Mary notes. "They didn't need that kind of situation terrifying people."

As Irwin moved about the lunar surface, apparently unaware of his precarious health situation, he was struck by the size of the earth—about the size of his thumbnail.

"I was just amazed to see the earth," he said. "It reminded me of a Christmas tree ornament, a very fragile one, hanging majestically in space. It was very touching to see earth from that perspective."

At one point, Irwin had trouble with a planned experiment. "He was erecting an experiment that wouldn't erect, due to a cotter pin or something of that nature," Mary recalls.

Frustrated in his attempts to get the experiment to work, Irwin decided he would pray.

While raised in a Christian home, and a believer and churchgoer since age ten, he was a nominal Christian at this stage of his life. "Maybe he walked away from his walk with the Lord a little," Mary suggests. "He described himself as a 'bump on a log Christian.'"

But he really needed wisdom due to this problem and he said, "God, I need your help right now."

Suddenly, Irwin experienced the presence of Jesus Christ in a remarkable way, unlike anything he ever felt on earth. "The Lord showed him the solution to the problem and the experiment erected before him like a little altar," Mary says.

"He was so overwhelmed at seeing and feeling God's presence so close," she says. "At one point, he turned around and looked over his shoulder as if He was standing there."

This unusual encounter with Jesus—some 238,000 miles from earth, changed Irwin's life forever.

After his return from the moon, Irwin rode in a ticker-tape parade through the streets of New York. "There were thousands of people lining the street, and he was trying to see all their faces," Mary recalls. "God dropped it in his heart that he had a responsibility to mankind to share Jesus with everyone after that."

Like other men in church history who have experienced dramatic encounters with God, the result was an increased power to witness for Jesus Christ, a confidence and boldness that fueled his passion to become an emissary for Jesus Christ to the nations.

Within a year of Irwin's return from space, he resigned from NASA and formed High Flight Foundation, which is on a quest to reach the world as "goodwill ambassadors for the Prince of Peace."

"God decided that He would send His Son Jesus Christ to the blue planet," Irwin said, "and it's through faith in Jesus Christ that we can relate to God. Jesus Himself said, 'I am the way and the truth and the life. No one comes unto the Father except through me.'"

"As I travel around, I tell people the answer is Jesus Christ, that Jesus walking on the earth is more important than man walking on the moon."

For two decades, Irwin traveled the world and presented small flags he carried from the moon to the leaders of various countries. "These flags were so powerful," says Bill Dodder, a close friend to Irwin. "He took flags to each country as a means to witness for Jesus Christ."

Dodder traveled with Irwin on several expeditions to Mt. Ararat in search of Noah's Ark. "We ran the Great Wall of China together," Dodder recalls.

Irwin continued to suffer heart problems after he left the space program. On the 20th anniversary of the Apollo 15 mission, he spoke in Aspen, Colorado. The next day, he took a long bicycle ride to the Maroon Bells near Aspen. After the ride, he collapsed due to a massive heart attack and went to live forever with the God he loved—the same one he encountered on the surface of the moon.

It is ironic, perhaps, that his heavenly homecoming was within hours of the 20th anniversary of his earthly homecoming from the moon.

Dodder was with Irwin on the day he passed away. "The day before he died he said, 'All I want to do is be faithful.'"

CHAPTER 20

How God Answered Francis Chan's Ridiculous Prayer for a Son-In-Law

Many Christian parents have prayed for their children to meet and marry another Christian—preferably a faith-filled, sold-out follower of Jesus.

But when noted author and preacher Francis Chan was impressed by a young man involved with his ministry, he lifted up a bold, audacious matchmaking prayer, and God answered in a way that confounded Francis himself.

"Earlier this year in February, I prayed, and I asked God for something that was just ridiculous," Francis Chan told a group at the Finishing the Task conference.

Francis had begun to notice a young man involved with his ministries named Justin Clark and became impressed by the insights gained in the younger man's devotional life. "I would come home and say, 'Honey, this guy, the way he talks about the Word and the way he talks about his prayer life, I've never met anyone like him.'"

"You have a little crush going here," his wife, Lisa, said, lightheartedly.

"I do, I love this guy," he replied.

A short time later during his quiet time with the Lord, Francis took his interest in Justin to another level. "Lord," he prayed, "you answer everything and you're so good to me, and I'm just going to ask, can you make him my son-in-law?"

"He doesn't even know my daughter, but make him fall in love with my daughter and make my daughter fall in love with him."

After he lifted up the prayer in February, weeks and months went by, nothing happened, and Francis began to forget about the prayer.

Five months later, Francis woke up and said to the Lord,

"God, I'm so used to you answering things, and I feel distant from you. I've never prayed this before but I'm sorry, I feel insecure this morning."

"I feel like a neglected housewife," he continued. "I know you love me and I know it's not about feelings but I'm just going to ask, can you show me some love this morning?"

An hour later, Justin approached him and said, "Can I ask your daughter out?"

"What??? Yes, yes ... do you have enough money? Please, please, please ... "

Justin and Rachel began dating in July, and several months later, he proposed to her on a bluff overlooking the ocean in San Francisco. "He took me on a small hike and told me that he loved me for the very first time," Rachel noted on the couple's wedding blog.

As they continued walking, she noticed rose petals on the forest floor, but she wasn't sure if they were for someone else. "We kept following the petals, and Justin led me to believe they were someone else's, but eventually I heard music and realized it was one of my favorite songs."

The trail opened up to a clearing on the bluff, with a spectacular view of the ocean as a backdrop. Justin got down on one knee and asked Rachel to marry him.

She said, "Duh ... yes!"

Then Francis and the rest of their family emerged from hiding places to surprise her.

Nearby, Justin had placed a few of Rachel's favorite things, including Chinese food and a live dwarf rabbit he rented. "Needless to say, he put a ring on it!" Rachel exclaimed.

Rachel and Justin's wedding took place December 3, 2016 in Redwood City, California.

"When I walked my daughter up the aisle, I was bawling," Francis recounted. "I haven't cried that much in years."

"When we got to the altar, I was ready to hand her off, and we hugged up there, just holding each other for probably a minute. It was so uncomfortable, and everybody was thinking, *Is he going to let go or is she going to let go?*"

As they held each other, Francis thought, *God, you're so great. I remember how she rebelled against you and now you brought her back. I remember her as a kid jumping in my lap. I remember all of this, and now I get to pick who she marries, and you answer like that?*

"The last few months have been a sweet season with God," Francis said. "Sometimes I don't get it. I feel overwhelmed. I feel like an only child and think, *There's no way You listen to everyone like this.*"

"I love you; I love you. I love you. I adore you; I adore you," Francis gushed, his heart overflowing with gratitude for the remarkable way God answered his 'ridiculous' prayer.

CHAPTER 21

Jesus Appeared to Muslim Family, Said He Was Sending a Man to Tell Them More

Tyler Connell with the Ekballo Project has been touring college campuses around the U.S., sharing stories and videos from his most recent trip to Middle East, where he documented a dramatic move of God among Muslims, particularly with refugees.

In the last few months, he and his team visited Harvard, MIT, Iowa State, Clemson, and the University of Georgia, among other campuses. "In every stop, we saw the presence of Jesus break into these college campuses and touch students, with bodies healed, people saved, and people giving their lives to serve in the mission field," Connell exclaims.

College students are amazed to learn what God is doing in Iraq and the surrounding region. "Jesus is moving in these Middle East nations," he says. "Many there are disillusioned and broken and just want to know the truth. Now more than ever, there is a harvest among Muslims that has not been seen in history."

His first film chronicles a young missionary named Daniel*, twenty-four, originally from Vermont. Two years ago, Daniel moved to the Middle East to work with Syrian refugees.

"They go house to house and visit these Muslim families and sit with them and talk with them and find out their names, their stories, and love them. As trust is built, they begin to open up about the Gospel."

One afternoon, Daniel walked into a white tent with a family of eight people inside. "Hi, I'm Daniel, and I'm here to tell you about Jesus," he announced.

He wasn't quite prepared for their reaction. "The family

freaked out, they looked at each other, almost turned white. The father was excited, yelling."

What's going on? Daniel wondered.

The interpreter explained that the night before Daniel's visit, the whole family was sitting in their tent having tea together, and a man in white opened the door to their tent and stood at the entrance. The man was glowing.

"Hello, my name is Jesus, and I am sending a man tomorrow named Daniel to tell you more about me." Then he disappeared.

So, when Daniel arrived at their doorway and told them his name, they were completely undone. "They asked him to tell them more about Jesus, and he gave them the Gospel and the whole family gave their lives to Jesus," Connell reports.

The father had been a part of the Free Syrian Army. "He had known bloodshed. He was a devout Muslim. This man and his family are now planting underground churches and are seeing a harvest among Muslims."

Recently, the father was dismayed by a large cell phone bill, and he asked his fifteen-year-old daughter about it. "It's because I'm telling all our relatives in Saudi Arabia about Jesus," she said.

In another Syrian refugee family, Connell felt God's presence breakthrough in a powerful way. "The joy that broke out among these people was incredible," he notes. "Jesus' presence was stronger than I have ever felt, in that little dirty room, with cat pee everywhere."

"There was about twenty-five people in there and Jesus' presence was stronger than any conference, any prayer room, any camp-high moment. Jesus was there in the middle of the desert, in the dirt, with Muslims. He is attracted to the brokenhearted, the contrite, the desperate. The King of heaven was right there with the poor in spirit."

Over the last three years, Connell and his team have responded to an assignment from God to capture what He is doing in the most unreached parts of the world, the 10-40 Window. "This Window has the three giants of Islam, Buddhism, and Hinduism. Currently, there are 2.9 billion unreached, who have yet to hear that Jesus is the way to the Father."

"We felt God told us to go to these places, the dark places, and capture what He is doing through the lives of missionaries that have given their lives, left everything they had here, to live overseas. We follow them with our camera and capture what God does and show it on college campuses to ignite students to live for something bigger than themselves."

In May 2015, his team spent eight days in the Middle East, going house to house among the refugees. "They were all Muslims but they all said they were disillusioned with Islam and they didn't know what they believed anymore," he observes.

"They asked, 'What is the truth?' There was a perfect cocktail of circumstances that caused them to be open to the preaching of the Gospel."

Going to the Middle East, his team had to confront their fears. "We realized that intimidation and fear was only a smokescreen. On the other side of that fear was our greatest breakthrough of joy and laying down our lives and seeing Jesus move like we never imagined."

The name has been changed for security reasons.

CHAPTER 22

D-Day Chaplain Carried No Weapons, Led Men off Landing Craft

He was the only man on his landing craft to come ashore at Omaha Beach with no "visible" weapons to protect himself. But that didn't stop this chaplain from being the first man out of his boat.

"I had the sword of the Spirit," said Lt. Col. George Russell Barber, USAF (Ret.), who started his career with the horse cavalry along the Mexican border before World War II. "We were all afraid," he explained, as the men came ashore June 6, 1944, amidst a hail of bullets and fiery explosions. "If a man says he's not afraid, he's lying—but we had our faith."

My last visit with Colonel Barber was six months before his passing on December 17, 2004, at age ninety. He wanted to attend the dedication of the World War II Memorial in Washington D.C. in 2004, but health concerns kept him away. Although the strength in his legs was failing, his mind was sharp and his grip still strong.

He served his country in four wars, and one of his most powerful memories was the D-Day invasion on Omaha Beach. "On the Sunday before D-Day, I held services on eleven different ships in Weymouth Harbor for thousands and thousands of soldiers," he said. "I gave away a lot of pocket Gideon's Bibles–there are no atheists in foxholes."

On the fateful morning of the invasion, he went over the side of his ship on a rope ladder into a flat-bottomed landing craft that held thirty soldiers.

"When we hit the shore, they let down the ramp, I stood in front and led my men off," Chaplain Barber recalled. "They were shooting at us all around."

To the right, Barber witnessed a horrible sight. "Just before we landed, I saw a landing ship hit a mine," he said. "It blew up and killed all thirty men. They were floating in the water and on the beach."

Without hesitation, Barber rushed to the sides of the wounded. "I talked to as many as I could and prayed with them. I said, 'Trust in God.'" As men died in his arms, he recited John 14:1-2: *"Do not let your hearts be troubled. Trust in God; trust also in me. In my Father's house are many mansions ... "*

"Men were being killed all around me," Barber said. "We were all trying to dodge the bullets. Thank God, I wasn't hit." Miraculously, none of the four chaplains landing on the Normandy beaches that day were killed, according to Barber.

If they survived the barrage of hostile fire, the next challenge for Barber and his men was to climb over steep cliffs just beyond the shore. "I couldn't get over the 100-foot cliff, so I had to dig my own foxhole that night on the beach," he recalled. "I prayed as if everything depended on the Lord, and I dug as if everything depended on me."

"The Lord and me got that foxhole pretty deep."

Unable to sleep, Barber crouched in his crude shelter amidst the storm of battle. Through the night, he stared up at a frightening display. "I watched the sky lit up by tracer bullets. Every fifth bullet is a tracer bullet, so you can see it go up and come down."

"The next morning, I got over that cliff, and I met Ernie Pyle, the famous war correspondent for *Stars and Stripes*," Barber recalled. "We split a can of Spam together." Later that day, the two men walked Omaha Beach, past the bodies of over 1500 who had fallen in battle. "We saw all the carnage and death and destruction."

Pyle wrote his own account of their walk that day. "The wreckage was vast and startling," he wrote. "In the water floated empty life rafts and soldiers' packs and ration boxes ... but there is another and more human litter. It extends in a thin little line, just like a high-water mark, for miles along the beach."

"Here are socks and shoe polish, sewing kits, diaries, Bibles, and hand grenades. Here are toothbrushes and razors, and snapshots of families back home staring up at you from the sand."

Then Correspondent Pyle did something on their walk the chaplain remembered vividly. He bent over and picked up a pocket-sized Gideon's Bible that was next to a fallen soldier. "I picked up a pocket Bible with a soldier's name in it and put it in my jacket," Pyle wrote. "I carried it for a mile or so and then put it back down on the beach. I don't know why I picked it up, or why I put it back down."

"I can't prove it," Chaplain Barber said, "but I probably gave that soldier that Bible only two days before that." Less than one year later, Pyle lost his own life near Okinawa when a Japanese sniper killed him as he covered the war in the Pacific.

Chaplain Barber also survived the Battle of the Bulge and was at the Remagen Bridge spanning the Rhine River immediately before it collapsed. Later, he and his men visited a concentration camp at Nordhausen, Germany. Before Allied troops arrived, Germans crowded 200 Jewish men into a building and set it afire. No one survived the flames. "War is ugly. War is hell," Barber said.

After the war, Chaplain Barber met two members of the Polish underground while he stayed at a hotel in Germany. One day, the three men decided they would climb one of the highest mountains in Germany. "It was a windy and snowy day," Barber noted. They pulled themselves up some of the steep faces using a steel cable someone had left behind.

As a bitterly cold wind stung their faces, they reached the summit, and Barber found something surprising. "There on top of one of the highest mountains in Germany, we found a large white cross," he says. The wind at that elevation made it hard for the three men to keep their balance. "We held on to the cross as we looked over the edge."

"What better thing to hold on to in the storms of life than the cross of Christ," he said.

Chapter 23

The Early Roots of the Jesus Movement

Lonnie Frisbee could barely read and write. Abandoned by his father, raped as a child, he tripped out on LSD as a teen and indulged in gay sex. Yet God chose him to be the key evangelist at the heart of the Jesus movement in the 1970s.

God used Lonnie to help ignite and propel the rapid growth of two major movements—Calvary Chapel and the Vineyard.

"When we got saved and started reading the Bible, we just believed everything we read," said Lonnie's wife, Connie. The two separated in 1973.

Both Lonnie and Connie had rocky pasts—making them more than qualified to be the sort of "cracked vessels" God delights in using to emit His glorious light.

Lonnie was sexually abused by a male babysitter at the age of eight years old, while his mother worked. He dreaded every day she left for work and faced abuse almost daily for at least a year, according to Connie.

Lonnie's father ran off with another woman, and that woman's jilted husband tracked down Lonnie's mother and the two wounded spouses found solace in one another and married. Lonnie's new stepdad was a "classic 50s tough guy and rode a motorcycle."

By contrast, Lonnie had a clubfoot, was unathletic, and grew to love cooking and artistic pursuits such as painting. By his late teens, he had become a self-described "nudist vegetarian hippie."

Connie was also drawn to the lifestyle of the flower children of the sixties. "I didn't become a hippie because I thought that's what I wanted to be when I grew up. I became a hippie because I was in juvenile hall, and I was in a home where my father was very violent, and my mother was an alcoholic and a drug addict."

"My mother beat me naked in front of my stepfather at thirteen. It was horrendous the kind of stuff I went through. So, I would run away from home because literally my mother was trying to kill me."

When the beatings or "torture" intensified, she ran. "From thirteen on, I was in some pretty harrowing situations. I was riding with motorcycle gangs, and then I would be in juvenile hall, and then I would be back at home with this woman who was completely out of her mind."

At the time she met Lonnie, Connie lived in a commune in Silverado Canyon, California, with a group called the Brotherhood of Eternal Love. What started as a commune with several homes in the area morphed into a major drug distribution channel for LSD and hashish.

"They dealt LSD for Timothy Leary," Connie recounts. "They were the main people bringing hashish into Southern California from Afghanistan."

While still in high school, Lonnie came to the commune where Connie lived to buy marijuana and LSD. "Everybody thought Lonnie was really a square ... goofy," she recalls.

One time, Lonnie joined her group on an excursion to Tahquitz Falls, near Palm Springs. "We would leave Silverado Canyon and drive out to Palm Springs at maybe one or two o'clock in the morning. We would hike to the first seventy-foot waterfall in the dark."

As they hiked, Lonnie lagged behind the others. "Finally, he caught up to me, and he had this Army duffel bag over his shoulder. He had a small frame, so the duffel bag was almost as big as him."

"What have you got in there?" someone asked.

"I have a couple bottles of wine and some French bread ... and a microscope," he said.

Finally, they arrived at the foot of the waterfall. "We would unroll our sleeping bags, drop our LSD, wait until we woke up, and then we would just be on for a new day."

In the morning, they climbed to the top of the seventy-foot waterfall and then used ropes to drop down to the other side, where "it was just one waterfall after another."

On one of these excursions, Lonnie packed a Bible, rather than one of the mystical books he often carried, and began reading from the book of John.

The power of the Word stirred his soul, and he cried out, "God if you're really real, reveal yourself to me!"

Years later, in 1980, Lonnie described what happened next: "The whole atmosphere of this canyon that I was in started to tingle and get light and started to change and I'm going, 'Uh oh ... I didn't want to be here.'"

Then the Lord spoke to his heart: *I am Jesus. I build nations and I tear them down. It is better for a nation never to have known me than to have known me and turn their back from me.*

Initially, Lonnie couldn't fully comprehend what that meant.

Then Jesus continued: I am the Way and the Truth and the Life. No man comes unto the Father but by me. I am the Door of the sheepfold. If any man enters in by another way, that man is a thief and a robber and the Gatekeeper will not open unto him.

Prior to this, Lonnie had subscribed to the popular notion that there are many pathways to God. "I always thought all roads led to Rome, but He explained to me that He was the only way to know God."

The power of the Word and the Spirit broke through his drug-fueled haze. He accepted Jesus as his Savior and Lord and was born again.

Then the Lord impressed on Lonnie's heart: *I'm going to send you to the people.*

"And I saw a vision of thousands of people and they were wandering around in a maze of gray darkness, bumping into one other, with no direction or purpose for their lives. Then the Lord showed me that there was a light on me that he was placing on my life and it was Jesus Christ and I was going to go bear the word of the Lord."

After Lonnie graduated from high school, he went north to attend the San Francisco Academy of Art. The timing of his educational sojourn to the Bay Area coincided with the Summer of Love, when as many as 100,000 young people converged on the city's Haight-Ashbury neighborhood.

As a new convert full of zeal, but not well-grounded in the Scripture, Lonnie began preaching on the streets of Haight-Ashbury, where he bumped into the leaders of a Christian commune known as The Living Room.

"They found Lonnie talking about Jesus in Haight-Ashbury, and he was mixing flying saucers into the Gospel and stuff like that," Connie recounts. "They ministered to Lonnie and he saw the ability to be in service all the time so he moved in with them."

Some believe the Jesus movement began in this communal house known as The Living Room, located in Novato, a suburb of San Francisco. Within the large house were four couples that had banded together apart from the organized church. They had committed themselves to live like the book of Acts.

"I find this story about these four couples as big as the story about Lonnie, because these people were in their thirties, and they had jobs. They had lives that were already moving in a direction," Connie notes.

They quit their jobs, sold and gave away their possessions, and kept only what they needed to function as a unit at enormous sacrifice.

The couples were Ted and Elizabeth Wise, Steve and Sandy Heefner, Jim and Judy Dopp, and Danny and Sandy Sands. They devoted themselves to prayer, the study of the Word, and bold outreach to the city.

The families also had seven children between them. The wives made a giant pot of soup every day. "It would be made for the men to take to the city the next day for their lunch. They would invite people to partake with them. They would take three cars into the city and would bring as many people back as they could." In the evenings, they poured over the Scripture, answering questions that arose.

"There was a basket and in this basket was all the bills these married couples had. And in the basket was all the money for the household." The men picked up tent-making jobs on the side to support their ministry activities.

Even though Lonnie and Connie had lost touch with each other, God brought them together on the streets of Haight-Ashbury. Connie had parted ways with the Brotherhood and moved in with a group involved in white witchcraft.

When Lonnie recognized her in the streets, he called out: "Connie, where are you going?"

"We're hitchhiking to Southern California, going up to Joshua Tree."

"Well, I'm going too," he replied.

It had taken Connie and her friends three weeks to hitchhike from Big Sur to San Francisco. "But as soon as Lonnie got in the car, we got one ride after another, and in no time, we were dropped off on his mother's front lawn in Costa Mesa," she recalls.

They rolled out sleeping bags, slept on the lawn, and Lonnie invited them in and made breakfast the next morning. Then they hitchhiked to Palm Springs and made their way to Tahquitz Falls.

As a new believer, Lonnie was still rough around the edges, straddling his nascent faith with his "roper doper," drug-filled past.

"We dropped acid out there, and Lonnie led me to the Lord. When I got saved, I was under the influence of LSD and I was naked," Connie admits. Lonnie and the other two men were also unclothed.

"I knew what LSD felt like and this was different. It had to be, or my life wouldn't have changed."

"When Lonnie led me to the Lord, my experience was so over the top. I was crying. I had a vision. He baptized me in water, and I came up out of the water and got baptized in the

Holy Spirit. I could not stop crying for the first twenty-four hours."

"Everything changed that day. The way I perceived the world changed. I didn't see one ugly person from that moment on. I perceived people differently. Everything was different."

"Had it not been for God saving me, I'm sure I would have died with a needle in my arm on the Sunset Strip being a prostitute," she says.

Neither one of Connie's fellow travelers got saved, but they hitchhiked on to Joshua Tree, and Lonnie left to go back up to The Living Room in Novato.

It seems a group Connie lived with at Mt. Shasta in a teepee had decided to winter in Joshua Tree. When Connie and her friends reached them, a woman greeted them at the door with a surprising question: "Every day we've been throwing the I Ching, and every day it comes up you have a message for us. Connie, what is the message?"

(I Ching is a form of ancient Chinese divination, consisting of sixty-four hexagrams and commentary based on the symbols. By randomly generating the six lines through various methods and then reading the commentary associated with the resulting hexagram, the participants supposedly receive an oracle.)

Surprised by the rather abrupt inquiry, Connie paused for a moment and said: "God is real, and He did have a Son, and you can be saved through Him and live eternally."

That shocked her friends! The next day, they began to pepper her with questions, far beyond her understanding as a new creature in Christ. When she was hit with a tough question, she looked down at her toes, closed her eyes, and asked God for the answers.

"When I opened my mouth to speak, the answer would be given. I would hear the answer for myself because I didn't know either. Out of that group, I got my first convert."

Her bold witness invited pushback from the evil one. "After some days, the animosity, hate, and real dislike manifested."

Connie left with the new convert and went to stay with a

woman who had a bottle farm—an acre and a half full of bottles. "After a while, the Lord told me this woman was poor, and we were making her much poorer by having to feed us, and so I told my convert we were going to have to leave."

She returned to her parents' house for the first time after a long absence and discovered a surprise. "There was a note that Lonnie 'miraculously' left word for me on the same day I arrived. I hadn't been there for a year and a half!"

Lonnie left his new family of believers in The Living Room with an unusual message—he told them he was going to find the girl he would marry. When he left, he wasn't even sure of Connie's exact location.

When they reconnected, "He came and picked me up right away and took me up to Novato."

Connie didn't know about Lonnie's romantic intentions. She saw him as more of a friend at this stage of their relationship.

"He was attracted to me spiritually, and I became attracted to Lonnie spiritually. I began to see him in a completely different light after I was able to see through my spiritual eyes," she notes.

When Connie arrived at the commune in Novato, everything she owned was in a small backpack, a backpack she found on a rock in Big Sur. The clothes had been discarded by kids from all over the U.S. When they arrived in the hippie "Never Never Land," they dropped their old clothes in a huge pile in Big Sur.

Connie and Lonnie slept in sleeping bags in the living room of the large house in Novato. The group also operated a storefront coffeehouse in the Haight-Ashbury neighborhood.

"There were some magazine articles being written about us at that time," Connie recalls. Because the men didn't shave their beards and cut their hair or dress conservatively, they had some friction with a Christian outreach in Haight-Ashbury operated by Dave Wilkerson.

"We were ... preaching the Gospel on the streets and preaching in Golden Gate Park. Sometimes we went down to Market Street and even hit the dirty bookstores at that end of town."

"We had runaways. People would send us pictures of their kids from all over the country. There were on a wall in the basement—all these kids' pictures.

"Once in a while, God would send us one of these kids, and we would recognize them, and we would ask them to call their parents. We would usually be able to get them to do that. Most of them went back home ... these were kids that were under eighteen from Nebraska or New York and ended up in the Haight. This was 1967 and 68, at the very peak of the hippie movement."

Connie remembers how hard the women worked in the commune. "Although I was single at the time, I quit going into the city almost completely to stay home and watch the children, to help cook and clean, to lighten the burden."

"We had bulgur wheat for breakfast. Most of the time, God provided very well for us. We had a huge, long table that would feed almost twenty people in the big house. Every night, there was a meal laid out of homemade breads and chicken enchiladas and vegetables we grew."

"We brought as many people to the house as we could and witnessed to them. We had all kinds of characters come through there. We would sit around and play conga drums, beat on books or maracas, and worship the Lord that way. There wasn't a set pattern. It wasn't like every Sunday we do this. It was really moving in the Sprit. We saw so many miracles ... we just knew God was doing stuff in our lives all the time. All of us have continued to live our lives that way."

After several months on the floor in sleeping bags, Connie and Lonnie's romantic feelings for one another grew and they decided to marry. "I was nineteen and he was eighteen when we got married. Neither of us really realized how much our past would play into our relationship," she said.

"We never had a honeymoon. We had a honeymoon in a tent in his parents' backyard."

Connie knew there was abuse and homosexual activity in Lonnie's past. "Lonnie never looked at himself as being a homosexual. He did answer all my questions because I had questions. He thought he was saved out of that. In speaking to me about it, he said that because homosexuals can't procreate, they have to recruit other people to be homosexuals. That's what he told me, that he was recruited."

"His whole perception of when he got saved ... he fell so in love with God. So did I. That's why Lonnie came back to marry me."

CHAPTER 24

The Communal Hippie House That Became Ground Zero for Jesus Movement

They called it the Big House, a large ranch house in Novato, California, situated on a former egg farm, where four hippie couples set their careers aside to live together with their children at the height of the sixties.

Evangelist Lonnie Frisbee crashed on their living room floor during the formative months of his early Christian life and grew under their influence, before he joined Pastor Chuck Smith and rode the wave of the Spirit in Southern California.

Steve and Sandi Heefner were influential in getting the four couples together. Steve, a disc jockey, landed in the Bay Area with his wife in 1965. "We moved a lot, every year, because of radio, to get to a bigger market," he notes.

They settled in Sausalito and began reaching out to make friends. Sandi went to a Newcomer's Club put on by the city and met Liz Wise, who appeared "exotic."

Sandi, a nominal Roman Catholic, planned a dinner party with Liz and her husband, Ted, a former agnostic who had recently become a Christian. Sandy also invited Jim and Judy Doop, grade school friends from the East Bay. The three couples hit it off in a spectacular fashion.

Once they got to know each other, Ted and Liz invited friends from Berkeley, Danny and Sandy Sands, into their group.

"This was not an accumulation of Christians wanting something to happen, we were just friends trying to get to know each other," Sandy notes.

Ted Wise had recently been tripping on LSD, trying to figure out what to do with his life, when he met Jesus Christ and was born again. Some credit Ted as being the first convert of the Jesus People Movement.

"Ted began to talk about putting something together that would further Jesus Christ into ordinary lives," Sandi recalls. "We started discussing this thing and decided we would have potlucks together." Then the idea progressed to finding a house where they could live together—including the seven young children between them.

Sandi was initially wary about communal living, but Ted and the others were swept up in the enthusiasm of "what was happening at the time."

"I was not for it," Sandi admits. But then she had an unusual experience that changed her thinking and renewed her faith.

"Steve and I were having a lot of marital problems and were not getting along," she recalls. "Our arguments and differences were becoming public."

One weekend, Steve and Sandi decided they would go camping together along the coast. They couldn't seem to find the right campsite and stopped at a hamburger stand, where the couple began arguing in public.

"That night, I was so pissed, I didn't even put my sleeping bag near him. I was crying to the Lord. I knew my marriage was dissolving."

As Sandi looked up at the night sky, she saw an unusual formation of stars she had never seen before. "I saw a huge figure eight made out of stars."

She recognized it as a sign from God, that "He is contacting me and I'm supposed to be the eighth member of this community. I knew that was His signal to me personally and I understood I was called. But I was way out of my element as a Roman Catholic," she says.

As far as they knew, they were the first Christian hippie community in northern California. "We were the first one I had heard of, of real families with small children and careers, dropping everything to become an evangelical arm."

"They gave up everything, sold everything, and moved in together," Connie Frisbee recalls. "Many people think this is where the explosion happened. I find this story about these four couples as big as the story about Lonnie, because these people were in their twenties and had jobs. They had lives that were already moving in a direction."

"It would be like coming to me after I worked at UPS for ten years and had kids and saying quit your job, take your kids, and move in with these other four couples, sell everything you have and just keep what you need to function as one unit. That was an enormous sacrifice."

"They decided to live like the book of Acts," she adds. Some referred to their commune as the House of Acts.

People in the neighborhood noticed. "The word got out in Novato that there was a hippie community, so we attracted all the teenagers from Novato," Sandi says. "So, every day after school, there would be a bunch of kids sitting in our living room wanting to know what was happening. There was magic in the air. We witnessed to them about Jesus. On Friday nights, the house was jammed with teens, the Lord brought the crowd. Many souls were harvested."

As the four couples and their children settled into the Big House in 1967, an unusual social phenomenon was taking place that summer in San Francisco. Thousands of young people in hippie attire were converging on the city's Haight-Ashbury district.

"We started taking donuts on a Friday night into San Francisco because so many kids were coming into town," Steve recounts. It turned into street conversations, with the couples witnessing for Christ.

The need was so great, they decided to set up a mission in the city that became known as The Living Room. "The Living Room was a little storefront," Connie Frisbee recalls. "It was one block down off Haight on Page in what is called the Panhandle." Several churches in the area provided support to help them get started.

The four women in the Big House made a huge batch of soup using a baby bottle sterilizer, and the men carried it into the city in the morning and it was given away for free. "People would come in and chat and have soup. One day, Charles Manson came through and that was rattling. He was just a weird kid that came to lunch."

"You never knew when you woke up that morning where God was going to send you to minister that day," Sandi says. Sometimes they would go to Market Street or Golden Gate Park to spread the Gospel. They would go out wherever God was leading them for the day, in twos or threes.

When the men returned to the house from their daily outreach in the city, they always had extra guests with them. The guests could stay for several days. "Every night, there was a meal laid out of homemade breads and chicken enchiladas and vegetables. We brought as many people to the house as we could and witnessed to them," Connie Frisbee recounts. Much of the food was donated by local stores.

"We would sit around in the evening and read the Bible, play conga drums, beat on books or maracas, and worship the Lord that way. We would talk about our day with the Holy Spirit. Had God given anybody any insights? Did they read something in the Bible they didn't understand? We would discuss and come to a better understanding of it."

"There wasn't a set pattern. It wasn't like every Sunday we do this. It wasn't like that. It was really moving in the Spirit. We saw so many miracles and so many coincidences. We just knew God was doing stuff in our lives all the time."

The kids they invited to stay were rough around the edges. "Some had not bathed but covered it with patchouli oil. I can't stand the smell of it. Every sleeping bag and towel reeked of that oil," Sandi recounts.

With four couples, seven children, plus additional guests, there were usually twenty mouths to feed every night. "We had these extra kids coming and had no income at the time. We were living on the graciousness of our Father."

"Some of the men would get painting jobs," Connie Frisbee recalls. "One was a cigarette salesman. Ted Wise was a sail maker. Steve Heefner was a disc jockey but lost his job because he told people he accepted Jesus as his Lord and Savior."

Steve and another one of the men made $20 a week sweeping a church. "We could count on $20 a week for food,"

Sandi notes. "We had a communal moneybox on the wall in the kitchen. If you got any money, you put it in, and if you needed any, you took it out. All four families lived on that little box. For a year and a half, we never knew how we were going to be fed that day, and God never missed a meal."

The couples had surprisingly little conflict. "We were so busy evangelizing, there was no time for minor skirmishes," Sandi says.

The largest bedroom in the House of Acts was given to the children. "All seven children were in one bedroom. My son was out of his gourd; he was so excited. The room was trashed almost every day. We asked, 'Who did this?' They would all point to someone else, so you would have six different versions of who did it. The kids loved it. But we were working all the time."

Steve met Lonnie Frisbee in Haight-Ashbury walking down the street. At the time, Lonnie was attending the San Francisco School of Art. "Lonnie was a spectacular character. He was an out front, open witness at that time, known on the street," Steve says.

Lonnie was also a new believer that needed some help sorting out his theology. "They saw him telling people about Jesus on the streets, but he had flying saucers mixed in with the presentation of Jesus," Connie Frisbee recalls. "They ministered to Lonnie, and he saw the ability to be in service all the time, so he moved in with them."

Lonnie began sleeping in a sleeping bag on the living room floor of the Big House. "Lonnie was very L.A. and a showbiz kid," Sandi says. "He was out there even for us. He did spectacular things—miracles."

"Lonnie would be driving down the road and tell somebody, 'Turn at this corner, stop at the next stop.' There would be somebody standing on the corner that he knew when he was a child. Lonnie would jump out, and the person would get saved right there on the corner."

"It happened over and over and over again. He had long hair like Jesus and wore robes. When it came to spiritual matters, Lonnie could produce. He was an extension of our community."

Lonnie brought Connie into the Big House, and she eventually became his wife. When Connie noticed all the work the women were doing, she immediately started helping with the children, the laundry, and the cooking. "She was fabulous," Sandi recalls. "I've never seen hunger for the Word like Connie."

Steve and Sandi went away one summer for an intensive Bible study on a farm in Ohio under the direction of Victor Paul Wierwille, the originator of The Way International.

When they returned from Ohio and Connie learned about their study of the Word, she began to follow Sandi around. "Every morning before I got out of bed, she was dressed and sitting at the door of my bedroom with a paper and pencil ready for me to teach her. She followed me all day long, day after day. This went on day after day. She was waiting for me to get up and teach her. I never saw anybody with that kind of hunger for the Word."

"As Connie and Lonnie hung around, they ended up courting and marrying," Steve adds.

When the living room of the House of Acts filled up with young people, shoulder-to-shoulder, they asked a Lutheran church nearby if they could use one of their large meeting rooms. "They allowed us access to their church every Friday night. So, we had hundreds of kids come in and many got saved there," Sandi says.

After Steve and Sandi returned from their summer away, they thought their community was slipping into legalism. One of the women living with them had a heavy cigarette problem. "The community decided that since she had a problem, nobody could come in who had any cigarettes on them. We knew it was wrong, not based on the Word."

After living in the Big House for eighteen months, Steve and Sandi began to seek God about leaving. They were the first couple to depart. "I know some people think we broke it up by being the first to leave, but in reality, it was legalism that broke it up," she says.

Looking back, they recognize they were at the forefront of the Jesus movement—the first to catch the wave. "We had to be among the first. I didn't realize, as a Catholic, there was such a thing as revivals. I wasn't looking for it. I didn't recognize it when we were in it and living it. But years later, I looked back and realized we were at the cusp of a revolution and revival."

The other couples stayed in the house for a while, then went back to their own lives again. "We continued to minister and cooperate with each other," Sandi says.

"We never stopped ministering and continued Bible Studies in our home. I think the country is ready for another revival. I'm hoping I get to see it. I would love to see it come back to the United States."

"We had no idea what we were doing. All we know is that we loved the Lord. Every time we got up in the morning, we had no idea what He had in store for us that day."

Chapter 25

The Untold Story of Pastor Ray Ortlund's Homegoing

Ray Ortlund, the beloved pastor, author, and radio broadcaster—who touched the lives of many through small-group discipleship—bravely endured the complications of pulmonary fibrosis, an insidious lung disease that also claimed the life of Campus Crusade Founder, Bill Bright.

Ray and his cherished wife, Anne, founded Renewal Ministries after he led two of the most prominent churches in Southern California. Together, they authored more than twenty-five books and traveled extensively throughout the world, speaking on behalf of renewal and revival among God's people. For nineteen years, Ray was the speaker for the Haven of Rest radio broadcast.

Ray went to be with Jesus on July 22, 2007. Five years after his homegoing, his wife and daughter recount the untold story of the months and final days of his glorious life.

In the progression of pulmonary fibrosis, normal lung tissue is replaced by scar tissue, which causes the sufferer to slowly suffocate to death. "When these growths cover your lungs, the air is all around you, but you can't take it in," notes Anne Ortlund. "It's like drowning, a very hard way to go."

Ray fought this insidious disease at the same time Bill Bright suffered with the same malady. "They talked about it over the phone," Anne recalls. Bill encouraged Ray to seek the same therapy he was receiving in Florida; however, Ray's disease had advanced far beyond what the therapy could offer. In the often-difficult days before their passings, the two families shared encouragement and prayer.

In the last six months of his life, Ray periodically had ten-to-fifteen-minute emergencies when he fought desperately to get air. "When those periods were over, more than once he said, 'This is God's gift to me.'"

In January 2007, Ray was invited to preach his final sermon at a church on the verge of a split. "The pastor had gone into heresy, and he invited people to follow him after he was kicked out," Anne recalls.

Ray, concerned about his breathing and physical stamina, told Anne, "Pray I won't cough when I'm preaching."

In the service, Ray climbed the stairs as soon as his introduction began, so he could regain his breath before he began to speak.

"It was a powerful sermon about love in the body," Anne recalls. "The Lord was so kind. He never coughed once, and nobody left the church."

"The Holy Spirit used that sermon to convict then that they needed to stay together."

A month later, Ray suffered a stroke and a heart attack almost simultaneously. Because Anne was ill, daughters Sherry Harrah and Margie McClure had to make the decision to put a breathing tube down Ray's throat.

"Due to the stroke, he couldn't write. He couldn't speak because of the tube," Sherry recalls. "It was a very hard family time." Ray—one of the great communicators of all time—was reduced to conversing with a nod.

After nine days, the breathing apparatus was removed. His vocal cords were damaged, and he could only speak with great labor for about two months. One night, he woke up and told Anne, "Glory to God!" By God's grace, his vocal cords healed, and he was able to speak well until the day he went home with Christ.

One week before his passing, Ray and Anne had dinner with Sherry and her husband, Walt. While Anne and Sherry were in the kitchen, Ray voiced an inner concern to Walt. "I'm dying," he told Walt. "Mom doesn't get it, and she doesn't want to get it. I need your help to make her believe that."

"We had a heavy conversation at dinner about his death—he brought it up," Sherry recalls. It was clear that Anne was struggling with the concept of life without her husband and best friend of more than sixty years.

After Anne voiced her concerns, Ray offered his calm assurance. "Anne," Ray said wisely, "God will provide for you without me. This is a new reality."

A few days later, Anne woke up abruptly to find Ray sitting on the edge of the bed, fighting for breath. "He was in such agony," she recalls. She immediately called 911. A normal oxygen level in the blood is 95-100% as measured by a pulse oximeter. When paramedics arrived, Ray's count was 37%.

He arrived at Hoag Hospital in Newport Beach, California on Thursday, and for the next two days, family members began to gather. "They didn't know this was actually the end because he had been in and out of the hospital so many times," Anne notes.

"I was alone with him, and Ray started singing, 'Shall We Gather at the River.' We sang it together—it was a precious moment."

"Shall we gather at the river,
where bright angel feet have trod,
with its crystal tide forever
flowing by the throne of God?
Yes, we'll gather at the river,
the beautiful, the beautiful river;
gather with the saints at the river
that flows by the throne of God."

When Anne left the room, Ray shared some inner fears with his nurse, Patrick.

He conveyed that he had another friend, besides Bill Bright, who had pulmonary fibrosis and that his death was agonizingly painful. He told Patrick that he did not want to go that way. "I want my family to be around me, and I want to be in my right mind."

Ray made it clear he wanted no drastic measures to prolong his life. He emphatically refused the insertion of another breathing tube.

"With the Lord being my helper, I promise I'll keep you comfortable," Patrick said.

In the early hours of Sunday morning, the Lord impressed on Ray's heart that it was time. He awakened abruptly at 4:00 a.m. and called for Patrick. "I'm going," he said with certainty. "Phone my Anne and tell her to come and tell the children to come."

"There were eight of us around the bed, and we had three hours of the most precious time," Anne says. Ray sat up and Patrick removed the oxygen mask from his face so he could talk.

"We would give verses of Scripture and we sang hymns," Anne says. "We remembered things that happened in the family and would thank each other."

Ray stayed true to his calling to the very end. "Ray was leading it all like a pastor leading a service," Anne recalls. "He was really in charge."

"We sang everything we knew—'Great Is Thy Faithfulness' and even 'Jesus Loves Me.'"

"Like Jacob, Ray went around the room from one person to the next and gave an admonition and a benediction." With tears flowing freely, each member of the family kissed him or held his hand.

He came to Anne last, who sat next to him. He looked at her as she held his hand, "Obey your children," he said.

In the final moments of Ray's life on earth, the family recited in unison the Aaronic benediction, found in Numbers 6:24-26, NKJV:

"The Lord bless you and keep you;
The Lord make His face shine upon you,
And be gracious to you;
The Lord lift up His countenance upon you,
And give you peace."

Then Ray said by himself, "Amen and amen."

At that moment, he looked up and raised his hand, as if greeting the Lord. His head fell gently forward on his chest and he slept, not to wake again on this earth.

"When he said 'Amen,' his head dropped forward and he

was with the Lord," Anne says. "His death was as glorious as his life."

"It felt like such a gift from the Lord and a gift from daddy to bless us in the way he did," Sherry says. "He died as he lived his life. He was always thinking of the Lord and of others and trying to connect the two."

"He was being who he always was, loving the Lord and loving on us."

CHAPTER 26

Anne Ortlund's Valentine Remembrance

They met in a prayer group at the University of Red-lands. As they listened to each other talk to God, the beginnings of a passionate love affair began to stir.

"You can learn a lot about a person's heart just by listening to them talk to God," says Anne Ortlund, the popular Christian author and speaker. "The first few weeks, we talked to the Lord more than we talked to each other," she says, referring to the young Navy man, Ray Ortlund, who joined the prayer group with twenty-two other sailors waiting for their deployment in World War II.

Two weeks after joining the group, Ray asked Anne out on their first date—a moonlit horseback ride in San Bernardino, California. With their horses sauntering along the trail on a balmy night, and moonbeams lighting up the rocks and bending boughs of shadowy trees, Ray began to sing an old hymn:

"Far away in the depths of my spirit tonight,
rolls a melody sweeter than psalm;
in celestial strains it unceasingly falls
o'er my soul like an infinite calm.
Peace, peace, wonderful peace,
coming down from the Father above!
Sweep over my spirit forever, I pray
in fathomless billows of love!"

Anne joined Ray in song, and the resulting harmony surprised them both. "I didn't know he could sing, and he didn't know I could sing," she notes. "While we were singing that song together, we fell in love. We both knew we were made for each other."

Ray went home that night and wrote to his parents, telling them he found the girl he would marry.

They dated every weekend for the next few months. Then shortly before Christmas 1944, as war raged in far-flung corners of the world, Ray proposed. He dropped to his knee, pulled a pocket New Testament and Psalms from the breast pocket of his Navy uniform, and recited Psalm 34:3, KJV: *"O magnify the Lord with me, and let us exalt his name together."*

After Anne gushed her acceptance, Ray faced the somewhat intimidating prospect of approaching her father, U.S. Army Brigadier General Joseph B. Sweet. "Ray had never seen a general before, much less ask for his daughter's hand in marriage," Anne recalls.

While General Sweet was home from the war for a few days, Ray took a walk with him around the block near their home. After Ray summoned the courage to state his intentions, he found that God had already prepared the heart of a praying general.

"Yes, I'm sure this is God's will," General Sweet told Ray. "Just one thing—make my Anne happy."

With Ray's meager Navy salary, he couldn't afford an expensive ring for Anne. So, he went to a jewelry store and offered a $5 down payment on a humbly adorned band.

As he plunked the bill down on the counter, the jeweler stared at it for a moment and said, "That's not much."

"It may not be much for you but it's a lot for me," Ray replied. Feeling compassion for the young sailor, he let Ray walk out with the ring.

Anne received the ring for Christmas, but then Ray left for service overseas. He would be gone for the next eighteen months. The separation was difficult for the engaged couple, but today Anne has a more mature outlook.

"That was God's blessing, because we were so in love, it would have been dangerous if we'd been together," she says.

After the war ended and Ray was honorably discharged, they married at the Fourth Presbyterian Church in Washington D.C., then left for their honeymoon in the Shenandoah Valley. It was late April, and the dogwood trees and azaleas were in full bloom—a magnificent sight for the pair.

"Praise God, we are not separated anymore!" they exclaimed to each other again and again.

During their honeymoon, Ray let down his guard and shared some of his deepest insecurities with Anne. He told her about growing up with dyslexia, in an era when it was seldom diagnosed properly. "He always had bad grades in school and thought he was stupid."

Within his own family, he felt like an outsider. The youngest of five, he was a "surprise" baby, and there was no room for him to sleep in the family home. "When evening came, he went next door to his aunt's house," Anne says.

While he adored his two older brothers and attempted to follow them around, they often rejected his companionship. "They would say, 'Get away from us, dumb little Ray.'"

As Ray opened up his heart, Anne poured grace on his insecurities and anxieties. Surprised that she loved him anyway, he later referred to their honeymoon as one of the great turning points of his life. "He went from thinking he was a nobody to thinking God could use a nobody."

Their romance extended from the very beginning to Ray's last breath. "Do you know what elevators are for?" she asks.

"They are for kissing—if nobody else is in the elevator." It was one of the reasons they chose a high-rise condo for their final years. "Sometimes, we would get on and kiss and kiss and then realize nobody had punched the button."

They usually emerged from empty elevators with large grins on their faces.

In public, if one of them left to use the restroom, Ray would always say to Anne, "I'll miss you," as she walked away. In their fifties, the Ortlunds were eating in a restaurant when Ray suddenly put his fork down, stared at Anne for a few seconds, then began to cry.

"Ray, what's the matter," Anne asked.

"You're just so beautiful," he told her.

Often when Ray preached, he would lean over from the pulpit and say to Anne, "Do you have any idea how much I love you?"

Anne says their best years were the twenty-three years at the end of Ray's life. After Ray retired from active church ministry, and the Ortlunds started Renewal Ministries together, they found more time for each other. "In ministry, the church is a rival to the wife," Anne notes.

"From age fifty-eight on, we were never separated," she says. "We always spoke side-by-side. He always wanted me beside him."

Ray constantly advised other married couples, "The closer you get to Christ, the closer you get to each other and the less there will be between you."

From 1970 until Ray's passing, the Ortlunds read through the entire Bible once a year, following a daily schedule. "We were on the same page every day and could talk about what we read," she notes, which helped to build greater unity and purpose in their marriage.

Before they went to sleep each night, they prayed together. In Anne's eyes, Ray grew "happier and happier, wiser and wiser, sexier and sexier."

Five years have passed since Ray's graduation to heaven, but Anne still feels very close to him. "I'm still his soulmate," she says. "I talk out loud to him because I miss him."

She acknowledges they won't be married in heaven but prays they will be dearest friends. "The exciting marriage is between Christ and the church," she observes. "That wedding will be off the charts."

Before Ray's passing, he wrote several love notes to Anne and hid them around their house for her to find later. One note she found within the last few months that said, "How can I thank you for all you mean to me?"

Another note said, "I was born to love you."

"That's a good Presbyterian for you," she laughs.

"He always had me on his mind," Anne says. "He was so happy because he lived in the presence of God, but he was conscious of me too."

CHAPTER 27

Jesus Movement Prodigal Slid into Sin

He was swept up in the euphoric early days of the Jesus Movement in the 1970s, but some abuses in his past left him with gaping vulnerabilities and a rocky road to sanctification.

"I was repeatedly molested by a number of men in my neighborhood as a very young boy," says author and speaker Joe Dallas. "That awakened a sexual precociousness a kid should not have."

The premature awakening of these desires led to successive sexual experimentation, while stolen pornography from the local liquor store fueled his erotic fantasies. The power of lust became a growing part of his experience as an adolescent.

By the eighth grade, Dallas was sexually active, then he became promiscuous with both sexes in high school. Extensive drug use was another accelerant on his wayward path.

But at a critical moment, a high school girlfriend invited him to church—a "little place" called Calvary Chapel, in 1971. He decided to check it out.

"You had to arrive two hours early to find a place on the floor," Dallas recalls. "I had never seen so many on-fire Christians together under one roof."

He was intrigued because he had never heard such a clear presentation of the Gospel, a message that penetrated to the depths of his heart.

He wrestled under the conviction of the Holy Spirit for two months after his first visit to the church. Dallas describes being "hounded, dogged, aggressively pursued" by God's Spirit.

One day, he couldn't take the pressure any longer. He went to a park across the street from his high school in Long Beach, California and began to pray:

"Lord, I do believe You are there and that You hear me. I believe You died on the cross, and I'm tired of fighting. I'll have You if You'll take me."

At that moment, he was born again. "It was incredible and unforgettable," he says. "No matter what has happened since then, that will always be the reference point." After his conversion, Dallas was baptized by Lonnie Frisbee, the charismatic hippie evangelist at the center of the Jesus Movement.

For the next few years, Dallas was on fire for Jesus. With his long hair and a car covered with Christian bumper stickers, he resembled many in the burgeoning movement. "I toted a Bible to school the size of a phone book and witnessed to anything that breathed," he recalls. He and other friends shared the Gospel with sailors and prostitutes in downtown Long Beach.

"I was very zealous and that was part of the spirit of the time," Dallas notes. "There was a strong emphasis on evangelism, and it was assumed that if you were a born-again believer, you would be witnessing."

In 1972, Dallas joined an outreach of Calvary Chapel in Long Beach that became known as Shekinah Fellowship, led by Brant Baker. When Dallas was ordained by the church the following year, he was eighteen years old. As an associate pastor, his primary focus was in music ministry. He also did pastoral counseling and conducted weddings and funerals.

Dallas describes Brant Baker as "a very charismatic minister" who wanted to follow in the footsteps of Kathryn Kuhlman, the well-known faith healer and evangelist who had a weekly television program in the 1960s and 1970s called "I Believe in Miracles." More and more, Baker's services became healing services modeled after Kuhlman's, and he began to draw large crowds. Greg Laurie was part of the church at that time but left shortly after Dallas's arrival to start his own ministry in Riverside, California.

The same year Dallas was ordained, he married a committed, young Christian woman after a very brief courtship. "In those days, there was no dating or much courtship to be done because we thought the Lord was coming back Tuesday before lunch," he says.

He and his wife worked alongside each other at Shekinah Fellowship, but now he sees the folly of marrying so young. "We weren't mature enough to handle the stresses of marriage and ministry," he says.

The church began to develop some serious internal problems, according to Dallas. "The leader was in his mid-twenties, and you had very young men and women with more responsibility and power than they were ready to handle," he says. "There were power struggles and ego clashes," he says sadly. "We lost some of the simplicity and integrity that we had when we began."

Dallas and his wife left the church to find work in the secular job arena. At first, it appeared to be a good decision. But after a year away from his ministry involvement, Dallas' mind began to drift in the wrong direction.

His curiosity was aroused by an adult bookstore that recently opened in the area. "Up to that point, my life was very consecrated, and I wouldn't dream of using pornography or acting out in any form of sexual sin," he says. "But I started to compromise first in my thought life."

He gave himself permission to walk into the adult bookstore, and that began a breathtakingly rapid decline. "I began using pornography and hired a prostitute," he says.

"Then I got involved in an affair with a friend's wife, which culminated in a pregnancy and abortion."

Dallas separated from his wife and started going to gay bars after that. "There was a mystique about gay bars that was attractive to me," he says. "My attraction to men was inflamed by the pornography."

"I was drinking heavily and acting out, and I didn't even want to think about God," he recalls. He ignored his spiritual life for a year, the same length of time he had his first extended relationship with another man.

At that point, he reached a dilemma. "I realized I was a

Christian, and I couldn't pretend I wasn't. But I also wasn't willing to give up my homosexual behavior."

An answer to his inner conflict arose in the form of the Metropolitan Community Church (MCC), a liberal church started in 1969 that promoted a "gay theology" through its reinterpretation of key biblical passages. "I heard about a church where you can practice homosexuality," he says.

Dallas attended the church for five years, while he promoted the idea that the Bible does not condemn homosexuality. Whatever his inner qualms, he pushed those aside for several years.

During these years, Dallas learned that two key leaders of the Jesus Movement, Lonnie Frisbee and Brant Baker, both had separate struggles with same-sex attraction. Both men ultimately died of HIV-AIDS. "When I joined MCC, I met people who said, 'We all know Brant Baker. We see him at gay bars.'"

"I didn't believe it," Dallas says. "I said that can't be true."

"I was so naïve," he continues. In the early days of the Jesus Movement, "there was such simplicity and such innocence. I wouldn't have known a sexual sin if it mugged me." Yet, a search of the pages of Scripture reveals that almost every leader God used in powerful ways had deep flaws.

As Paul's letter to the Corinthians says, *"But we have this treasure in jars of clay to show that this all-surpassing power is from God and not from us."* (2 Corinthians 4:7)

By some measures, Dallas' quality of life was high during this period. He held a good job, led an active social life, and lived in a comfortable apartment.

"The circumstances of my life seemed pretty good to me," he notes, "but an inner turmoil kept growing. I couldn't pretend I was doing the right thing." Sometimes he woke up in the middle of the night, sat bolt upright, and wondered, 'What am I doing?'"

Dallas decided it was time to open the scriptures once again, and he revisited all the Bible passages he could find that dealt with human sexuality and sanctification. "It became clearer and clearer I had been kidding myself," he admits. "I repented that night, and that became another reference point in my life."

He shared his story with his gay friends, which was difficult, but a huge relief. "They reacted very reasonably and very kindly. It was very classy of them," he notes.

Dallas left the Metropolitan Church behind and, like the prodigal returning to his father's house, made his way back to Calvary Chapel in Costa Mesa. He moved from his apartment, found a new job, and started seeing a Christian counselor he found in the yellow pages. "It was important for me to change everything," he says.

Between his renewed fellowship in a Bible-based church, his time spent in the scriptures, and his Christian counselor, Dallas was able to learn some important lessons.

"I was an older and wiser prodigal at twenty-nine," he notes. 'I thought if I was really a spiritual man, I wouldn't have these kinds of temptations, and, if I had them, it would be too dangerous to admit them."

"Now I realized that if I wasn't able to admit them, I would be setting myself up for another downfall." He came to realize that struggles and temptations are an ongoing reality. "No one is immune from that slippery slope—whatever their weakness is, if they entertain it like I did. The key issue is what we do about temptation when it comes."

Dallas does not believe anyone is born homosexual. He theorizes that some are born with certain personality structures that make them more susceptible to same-sex attraction. This, along with family dynamics and other variables, may work in combination to increase these vulnerabilities.

After several years of counseling, Dallas studied to receive his own degree in counseling. His intent initially was to focus on chemical dependency and alcoholism, but he couldn't find an internship in that specialty. After he attended a conference in 1987 that dealt with homosexuality from a Christian perspective, he began to see the need for counseling designed to help Christians with struggles like his own.

"At first I thought my story was rare, but I was wrong," he notes. "I began to dream about starting my own ministry for Christians caught in sexual sin."

Today, Dallas directs a biblical counseling ministry for those dealing with sexual and relational problems, and with their families as well. He has authored six books on human sexuality from a Christian perspective, including *Desires in Conflict* (Harvest House), *The Game Plan* (Thomas Nelson), *When Homosexuality Hits Home* (Harvest House), *Five Steps to Breaking Free from Porn* (Harvest House), and *Speaking of Homosexuality* (Baker).

CHAPTER 28

A Mechanic's Cry for Help

Bruce Van Natta, forty-two, traveled around Wisconsin doing on-site repairs on diesel engines. On a mild fall day, he had fixed the coolant leak on a mammoth logging truck, put his tools away, and was ready to leave, when the truck's driver asked him to look at one more thing.

"There's an oil seep in the front of the engine somewhere," the man said. Bruce got on the creeper on the floor and slid under the huge chrome bumper, feet first. The truck was still running.

"Why don't you jump inside and shut it off," Bruce called out. With the front wheel removed and the truck jacked up, there was barely enough room for Bruce to slip under the axle that ran from wheel to wheel.

Bruce noticed the driver hadn't positioned any safety equipment to support the jack—no blocking or jack stands. But Bruce had done the same thing many times himself to save time, so he wasn't concerned.

But as the other man hopped up in the truck's cab to shut off the engine, he watched the huge truck shift and rock slightly. "Out of the peripheral vision in my left eye, I saw movement," Bruce says. "I turned my head just in time to see the jack wiggle around and shoot out like a rocket."

The leading edge under the massive engine, the truck's axle, came down on Jack's body like a blunt guillotine, with a crushing blow across his stomach nearly cutting him in half. It created the loudest noise Bruce had ever heard.

"Lord help me!" Bruce cried out twice. The force of the trauma on his stomach caused blood to shoot into his throat suddenly; he coughed and spit out a large blob. He bled internally from major arteries severed in five places.

Bruce looked at the left side of his body and saw he was only one inch thick. "I was thinner than the thickness of my spine," he recalls. Because the axle went up at a slight angle, the axle crushed him to about two inches on the right side.

"Call 911!" Bruce screamed. The driver went into shock when he saw Bruce's condition. After he placed the emergency call, he grabbed the jack to hoist the truck off Bruce's body, but the only place he could find to attach it was one of the springs near the wheel—a precarious and unstable position.

As the engine lifted above his crushed stomach, Bruce thought it would be impossible to look this way and still be alive. It was somewhat surreal; he thought his flattened body resembled a cartoon character.

I'm probably going to die, he thought. *This will probably kill me.*

"Get me out from under the truck," Bruce yelled, fearful the truck might fall again. But the other man refused to touch him. With two shattered vertebrae, it was not a good idea to move his body.

Bruce reached back and grabbed the chrome bumper himself, then used all the strength he could muster. "I pulled as hard as I could and got my head out," he recalls, but the rest of his body was still under the truck.

Immediately after that exertion, Bruce passed out. He believes he died at that moment or had a near-death experience. "I can say I died because when the medical people got there, I didn't have a pulse."

Then something very strange happened. "My spirit left my body and went up in the roof of the garage. My spirit was up there looking down, at perfect peace."

The other man knelt over Bruce's body, crying and running his fingers through Bruce's hair. "I'm sorry, I'm sorry," he said repeatedly.

Then looking down from above, Bruce witnessed something even more startling. "I realized there was a huge angel on either side of my body," he says. He estimates the angels were about eight feet tall, very muscular, dressed in white robes.

"There was a light shining off both of them," he recalls.

"They were identical in appearance, like matching bookends." Their long hair flowed to the middle of their backs.

The angels' robes were woven in such a way as to create a course, patterned material. "The robes were tight enough that I could see muscles bulging out of their shoulders, backs, and arms," he notes. Their arms were positioned under the bumper, angled toward Bruce's body.

Bruce estimates he was watching from above for about thirty to forty minutes. Because he was in a rural area, the closest town was Adams Friendship, Wisconsin— the emergency responders were a volunteer fire department.

Immediately, they grasped the severity of his injuries and called for a helicopter that would transport him to UW Madison Trauma Center. The chopper came relatively quickly, but then turned around because there was no ambulance on the scene—no way to get his body into the helicopter.

Even though Bruce was 'dead' or 'unconscious,' he could later identify the ten people who arrived, even the fact that two of them entered the building by the wrong door, something he could not have known unless his spirit observed from above.

One of the volunteers, Shannon Cila, kneeled down next to him and began lightly slapping his face.

"Bruce Van Natta, open your eyes. Bruce Van Natta, open your eyes," she said. She continued, as her voice rose.

From the ceiling, Bruce felt his spirit inch closer as she called out to him.

"All of a sudden, I shot back into my body, and I'm looking at this woman eye-to-eye."

In his body, he suddenly felt excruciating pain. "In the ceiling I was at perfect peace, but back in my body I realized, 'Oh crap, I'm the guy who was under the truck.'"

He glanced to the right and the left but couldn't see the angels anymore. Somehow, he sensed they were still there.

"I realized I was on the edge of life and death, and I got scared." Every time Bruce shut his eyes, his spirit left his body and began to "rocket" down a tunnel. Then Shannon lightly slapped his face and called his name and his spirit returned.

"Do you want to live?" she asked him. "Do you have a wife and kids?"

His wife, Lori, and their four children jumped into his mind. *I can't die*, he suddenly thought. *I've got to be here for my family.*

"No matter how bad it hurt, I decided I had to keep my eyes open," he says.

It was more than two hours before Bruce received medical attention at UW Madison Trauma Center. The emergency room doctors on duty who examined Bruce's initial CT scan, Dr. Scott Pinchot, Dr. Fumito Ito, and Dr. Daniel McKenna, got into a vigorous disagreement because the CT scan indicated that Bruce should be dead.

With his superior mesenteric artery severed in two places, and other arteries and veins cut, he should have bled to death within minutes. What stunned the doctors is that he still registered a weak blood pressure, and his heart was still beating.

Dr. McKenna, the chief resident in the trauma department, told Bruce later: "We were looking at the CT scans of a dead person. You were dead, but your eyes were open, and your heart was pounding like a twenty-year-old man running a marathon."

"We couldn't make sense of it," he said. "Was something in the CT scan lying to us? You had bled out; we had no flow. We didn't know what to make of it."

Bruce believes the two angels followed him during the emergency and intervened to keep him alive. In addition to the severed arteries and veins, his pancreas and spleen were crushed, two vertebrae were broken, and most of his small intestine obliterated.

Doctors were so certain he would die within hours, they opened Bruce up and repaired the major arteries, attempting nothing more. They decided to wait four hours, believing he would die within that timeframe. They ultimately waited another twelve hours before any further intervention, they were so certain he would die. But his heart kept beating.

Next, they placed Bruce into an induced coma. Eventually, he endured five surgeries over the next twelve months. After that, he had a year and a half of rehab.

Bruce credits his wife's prayers in his miraculous survival. "When she first got the news, she got down on her knees and said, 'Lord, I can't deal with this. I need your help. If Bruce can't be the man he wants to be, then take him. But if he can be who he wants to be, then please save him.'"

"She only took her Bible into the hospital and never left my side for three weeks except to go to the bathroom," he says. "It was touch and go for a long time. There was miracle after miracle. God healed my spleen and my pancreas."

When Bruce came out of the coma, he got some bad news. "They only expected me to live one year because I didn't have enough small intestines," he says. While the average small intestine is twenty feet in length, Bruce only had three feet remaining, and that small portion was not functioning properly.

"They told me they could only feed me intravenously for a year and then I would die," he notes. His weight dropped from 185 to 124, and he began to have the look of a concentration camp victim.

But a man named Bruce Carlson heard about Bruce Van Natta's medical case from a prayer chain, then God woke Carlson up two mornings in a row with a special assignment: buy a plane ticket and fly from New York to Wisconsin to pray for Bruce's healing.

Carlson argued with God about the $900 plane ticket. "I wasn't looking for this," Carlson notes.

"He showed up at the hospital and prayed for me," Bruce recalls. Carlson placed his right hand on Bruce's forehead, and then he prayed a bold prayer:

"Lord, I add my prayers to all the other prayers for Bruce. In the name of Jesus, I command you small intestine to grow back right now."

Instantly, Bruce felt an "electric shock" and heard a snap. "An electricity, the power of God, came right out of his hand and went into my intestines. I could feel them rolling around," he says.

"It felt like a snake came uncoiled inside my stomach," he continues. "I felt something cylindrical rolling around and moving inside my stomach." Doctors confirmed the miracle later through x-rays and CT scans: his small intestine grew an additional seven feet in response to this prayer in Jesus' name.

Not only did the intestine grow back, but it also worked perfectly. "When they tested it, the small intestine worked exactly as if I had all my intestines. I was losing weight and then, all of a sudden, my weight leveled off."

Sometime following the accident, Bruce left his business and entered full-time Christian work. Bruce authored a book about his miracle, *Saved by Angels* (Destiny Image), and is working on a new book.

He formed Sweet Bread Ministries, a non-denominational, evangelistic ministry dedicated to bringing people of all backgrounds into a closer, more intimate relationship with Jesus Christ.

"I'm in great health now," Bruce says. "God is real, and He is still doing miracles today."

CHAPTER 29

Researcher Finds True Location of Jewish Temple

*It is the glory of God to conceal a matter;
to search out a matter is the glory of kings.*
(Proverbs 25:2)

The Temple Mount on Mt. Moriah is considered the most sensitive piece of real estate on the face of the earth. Abraham, in obedience to God, traveled there to offer his son, Isaac, as a sacrifice, then God provided a substitute.

A thousand years later, God directed King David to buy a threshing floor from Araunah (Ornan) and the surrounding land on Mt. Moriah as the spot for the first Jewish Temple, ultimately built by his son, Solomon.

The thirty-seven acres that comprise the Temple Mount is considered deeply sacred to Christians, Jews, and Muslims, with several Islamic holy sites there, including the Dome of the Rock and the Al-Aqsa Mosque.

Many Christians believe a third temple will be built on the site of Solomon's temple in line with Bible prophecies (Daniel 9:27), but the Mount is currently controlled by the Islamic Waqf of Jordan. Some maintain the Dome of the Rock is situated on the spot of the former Jewish temple, which creates a massive problem for plans to rebuild.

Any efforts by the Jewish people to construct their Temple on or near the Dome of the Rock could potentially trigger all-out war.

Christian Widener, a PhD in mechanical engineering and formerly a professor at the South Dakota School of Mines, did a deep dive to discover the exact whereabouts of the former Temple in his book, The Temple Revealed.

He didn't begin with any preconceived ideas about the location. "I wasn't trying to develop my unique view of where the Temple was located," he said.

"I wanted to know precisely where it was and could it be known reliably or not?" he explained. "For many Christians, the rebuilding of the temple signifies the final steps before the physical return of Jesus Christ to the earth."

There are four primary views as to where the Temple was originally located. The view with the greatest popular opinion places it in the middle of the Temple Mount platform—in the same place as the Dome of the Rock. The other views place it north of the Dome of the Rock, south of the Rock, or in the Ophel area south of the Mount, in the city of David near the Gihon Spring.

After exhaustingly sifting through the competing theories about the true location, Widener's conclusion is a modification of the view held by Dr. Asher Kaufman, a professor at Notre Dame, which located the Temple in the northern portion of the Temple Mount, with the Holy of Holies situated on the Dome of the Spirits (Tablets), which Widener convincingly demonstrates as the original threshing floor of Araunah.

"When God chooses a place for his foundation, they will not be lost and cannot be moved," Widener notes. The stone in question on the Temple Mount is roughly ten feet in diameter, a flat piece of bedrock, its surface pockmarked by time, the elements, and the possible movement of an ox pulling a sledge in a circular fashion around it, separating the wheat from the chaff.

Behold, I am laying in Zion a stone, a tested stone, a costly cornerstone for the foundation, firmly placed. (Isaiah 28:16, NASB)

Like a datum point used by a heavenly builder, the surrounding Temple Mount platform was set to the level of this stone.

Widener goes a step beyond Dr. Kaufman in presenting the Temple's alignment with the Golden Gate, the gate that faces east, seen prominently when standing on the Mount of Olives. "The famed Golden Gate is the true eastern gate of the First and Second Temples and marks the east-west line of where the temple should be rebuilt."

"To make sure it would never be opened again, the Ottoman sultan Suleiman the Magnificent had it walled up in stone in 1541. It is reported that he sought to prevent the Messiah of the Jews and Christians from ever entering through the gate," he notes. (The gate had already been nailed shut for centuries when Suleiman walled it up.)

The 3,000-year-old gate has been shut for most of the last 2,000 years, in line with a prophecy in Ezekiel 44:1-2: *Then the man brought me back to the outer gate of the sanctuary, the one facing east, and it was shut. The LORD said to me, "This gate is to remain shut ... because the LORD, the God of Israel, has entered through it."*

Jesus, the Messiah of the Jews, rode through that gate on a donkey, in his triumphal entry into Jerusalem on April 6, A.D. 32, presenting himself as King, fulfilling one of the most amazing prophecies in the Bible, contained in Daniel 9. (Date cited by Don Stewart and Chuck Missler in their book *The Coming Temple*.)

After Israel gained control of East Jerusalem in the Six Day War (1967), Moshe Dayan inexplicably surrendered control of the Temple Mount to the Muslims. However, this too fulfilled a prophecy from Ezekiel 44:8: *You have not kept charge of My holy things yourselves, but you have set foreigners to keep charge of My sanctuary.*

Widener believes the Temple could be rebuilt without disrupting the Muslim holy sites. "It's not a case of either the Dome of the Rock or the Jewish temple. Clearly the Jewish temple could be rebuilt now without a significant impact to existing Islamic religious sites. This large open courtyard is essentially a blank slate where building could begin almost immediately and in earnest (political obstacles notwithstanding)," he writes.

"Political obstacles" may be Widener's greatest understatement in the book. But many Christians in the 1800s could not envision a rebirth of the state of Israel. More recently, it seemed politically problematical to move the U.S. Embassy to Jerusalem or for the Abraham Accords to be achieved. So, if God has ordained it, it will happen in ways we might think improbable.

Widener lays out a few scenarios in which a joint use plan for the Temple Mount could be implemented. "If Jordan ever became destabilized then they may no longer be in a position to properly manage the Waqf, in which case Israel would likely assume control for security reasons," he posits.

"As a compromise, I believe it would be possible to use the northern approximate one-third of the temple complex to house an Israeli-controlled area ... The southern portion would then be mostly a separate Muslim zone including the Dome of the Rock and Al-Aqsa Mosque that would remain under status quo conditions," Widener explains.

He imagines a comprehensive peace plan put together by Israel, moderate Islamic nations, and the U.S., which includes Jews being allowed to pray on the Temple Mount and rebuild their holy temple.

"God says I chose this place for my throne and for the soles of my feet. When Christ comes to rule and reign, He has chosen that spot. I believe Him. I take His Word as truth."

Chapter 30

Born with a Hole in Her Heart

No one guessed little Giselle had a heart problem until a routine doctor's check-up at seven months old.

"I don't know why Giselle was born this way," says Tamrah Janulis, Giselle's mother. "That's one of the questions I will ask God."

At seven months, doctors discovered a congenital heart defect known as tetralogy of Fallot, the most common cause of blue baby syndrome. Tamrah and husband, Joe, were completely surprised when doctors informed them that Giselle lacked a pulmonary valve and arteries.

"I thought there was nothing wrong," Tamrah recalls. "I wasn't prepared. I was at the hospital, and my world completely stopped. I was in shock, speechless."

Some medical experts said Giselle, the youngest of four children, could live to be thirty, others said she should not be alive at all.

Two months later, doctors performed heart surgery and discovered the connections between Giselle's heart and lungs looked like "a bowl of spaghetti" or "a bird's nest," with small thread-like veins that had sprung up, attempting to compensate for the missing arteries.

After this surgery, experts recommended a variety of additional surgical options, some rare procedures considered risky.

Tamrah and Joe decided against further surgeries, but followed doctors' prescriptions for a litany of medicines. "I gave her meds every other hour and shots twice a day," Tamrah says. "I carried her everywhere and never let her out of my sight."

A bright child, Giselle learned the alphabet at ten-months-old. "Nothing stopped Giselle," Tamrah says. "She loved going to the zoo. She rode horses with me. She did everything."

"We're a very musical family, and Giselle was always singing," she adds.

As the months went by, Giselle's hands, feet, and lips began to exhibit a slight bluish hue, telltale signs her heart was not working properly.

After her second birthday, she had her first vision of Jesus. It happened in their family room, only a few weeks before her condition took a turn for the worse.

"Hey Jesus. Hi. Hi Jesus," she said, to her mom's surprise.

"What do you see, babe?" Tamrah asked.

"Hi Jesus. Hi," little Giselle continued, her eyes wide with delight.

"Where is He?"

"Right there," she pointed.

Giselle had at least two more visions of Jesus in the succeeding weeks. One happened in the car while they were driving and another in a store.

One day in the car, Giselle began to spontaneously sing, "Rejoice! Rejoice! (E)mmanuel ... " She had not learned to pronounce 'E's,' so it came out as 'Manuel.'

"How does Giselle know that Christmas song?" sister Jolie Mae wanted to know.

According to Tamrah, Giselle had never heard the hymn before. Also, in the ensuing weeks, she would suddenly begin singing "Hallelujah" as she walked around the house.

Cindy Peterson, Giselle's grandmother, believes the veil between heaven and earth was pulled back slightly, in preparation for eternity. "She had a foot on earth and a foot in heaven," Cindy believes. "She was joining with the worship in heaven."

A short time later, Giselle was lying in bed, not feeling well. As Tamrah studied her daughter's face, Giselle pointed up at a corner of the ceiling. "Hey horsey. Hi!" she said.

"Where's the horsey?" her mom asked.

"There ... " she pointed.

She also pointed to a "kitty cat" but Tamrah is convinced

she saw a lion, a glimpse of the wondrous menagerie of creatures inhabiting heaven.

A few days later, Tamrah and husband Joe still didn't know how long she might live. But in the fullness of time, Giselle's condition deteriorated.

"She was getting weaker and weaker," Tamrah says. "Her hands and feet started tingling, and the tissue started dying. Her feet, hands, and lips were increasingly blue."

Little Giselle left this world in her mother's arms, at home. Joe was embracing both mother and daughter on their king-sized bed.

In the minutes before her homegoing, Giselle let out a soft wail. Joe thought she was crying because she was going to miss her family.

"My miracle is that she lived as happy as she did," Tamrah says. "Every day with her was like a miracle to me."

"It gives me hope that she saw the Lord, and she is in heaven with Him. I know she is up there, and she is waiting for me."

CHAPTER 31

Businessman's Near-Death Experience of Hell

He was attending a business convention with his brother and another family member when random shots sprayed a crowd outside an Atlanta restaurant.

Three intoxicated, young men were denied entrance to the eatery and retaliated with a burst of nine-millimeter bullets from an Uzi submachine gun. One of the shots entered the back of Matthew Botsford's head, lodging itself in the frontal lobe of his brain.

"They were angry, so they took a shot straight up the sidewalk," says Matthew. "If you took a hypodermic needle, heated it up, and stuck it in your head, that's what I felt," he says. "It was a searing hot pain, then things went black."

His body slammed to the pavement, and the last thing he remembers is the cold, hard cement amid "inky" darkness.

He was at the edge of death, if not clinically dead, three times after his heart stopped: once on the sidewalk, once in the ambulance, and once in the emergency room of Piedmont Hospital. But weak vital signs returned, and doctors induced a coma that lasted twenty-seven days to reduce brain swelling.

Matthew's wife, Nancy, described the horrifying ordeal in her book, *A Day in Hell; Death to Life to Hope* (Tate Publishing).

Prior to this incident, Matthew had a minimal belief in God. "I knew there was a God, and that Jesus is His son," he recalls. "But never had I made a commitment to say Jesus is the Way or made any effort to get to know Him."

"It was all about me. I had my own plans. At twenty-eight years old, I felt young, vibrant, and strong."

When the lights went out, Matthew entered a different

conscious reality. "Immediately, I shifted from the temporal realm I lived in, to the eternal realm of hell," he recalls.

In the book, Matthew describes a horrifying scene in what he believes was hell, with his body suspended in midair, arms outstretched, shackled with ancient black chains clasped around his wrists and ankles, suspended over a deep glowing red abyss.

He saw four-legged creatures roaming about in apparent agony, as they attempted to stay clear of flowing lava. Smoke billowing up from the magma seemed to carry the souls of the lost. He heard awful screams emanating from the depths of hell. None of the screams were intelligible—just cries of pain, loss, and anguish.

"It was obvious by the countless screams I heard, I was not down there alone, yet isolated. I was in my own torment."

The lava flow got closer to Matthew, and globules of magma splashed on his shins and feet, which burned his flesh to the bone. "I smelled my own flesh searing and burning away. I saw and felt my flesh reform only to be burned off again and again."

Demons with dark oval eyes looked at him, judging and mocking him. "I could see some of the faces of these demons, and bodies ... short and stout covered with scales and horns of varying numbers, sizes, and lengths upon their heads, denoting their levels of authority in Satan's realm."

"Demons with sharp teeth peeled the skin off my backside, which resulted in tremendous pain. I heard the sound of my skin being ripped off in ribbon-like fashion. I smelled their stench like rotten carcasses or rotten flesh. Over and over and over, this repeated itself. There was to be no end to the torment. I understood this was to be an eternal existence for me."

On the night of the shooting, Nancy was at their home in Michigan waiting for a phone call from Matthew. When he didn't call, she went to bed at 11:00 p.m. thinking something wasn't right.

She woke up at 2:00 a.m. with a sick feeling in the pit

of her stomach. Matthew's father called moments later, and Nancy's first words were, "Is he alive?"

When she flew to Atlanta that morning with Matthew's parents, she didn't know the severity of his condition.

Like Matthew, Nancy had only a nominal faith in God and did not even think about praying on the journey to the hospital.

A nurse informed her for the first time Matthew was shot in the head and tried to prepare her for her first visit to his bedside. In ICU, she saw Matthew's head wrapped up, with numerous wires and tubes protruding from his body. Believing his passing to be imminent, five organ harvesters stood nearby with red and white containers and began to pressure her to sign agreements for his vital organs.

Later in the afternoon, she met with the doctor, who provided little reason for hope. "I took out a grapefruit-sized portion of brain matter, skin, skull, and bullet fragments," he began. "But I had to leave the bullet in place in the frontal lobe because it was so impacted."

"He has a 30% chance of making it through the night," the doctor said. "Even if he lives, he may have paralysis or, due to the brain injury, need to be institutionalized."

The bleak assessment was too much for Nancy to bear, and she stood up abruptly and left the room, apparently in shock. "I was losing it," she recalls. "I couldn't comprehend his words. This was more than I could handle."

She started to walk down the hallway, but then something unusual happened. She felt a hand grab her right shoulder. She whirled around, thinking it might be her mother, but no one was there.

"Instantly, I knew it was Jesus!" she says. "It was a touch from Jesus. Every cell of my body knew it was Him."

She ran back to ICU, knelt down by Matthew's bed, and began to pray fervently. "Lord, bring back my husband. Bring back his personality, his heart. Even if he's in a wheelchair, I promise to stay with him."

It is impossible to know the time that elapsed between Nancy's prayer and Matthew's rescue from hell. But in response to her prayer, help appeared in the most dramatic way, as Matthew recounts:

"In my realm in hell, I saw a massive finger begin to protrude in from the outside which led into the entirety of a man's hand." He says the hand was cracked and creviced like any man's hand, yet of "great age" and massive size.

"This hand of God methodically descended towards me and grasped me about my waist, instantaneously causing the shackles to drop off, demons to flee, blackness, fear, and hopelessness to be vanquished."

Matthew recalls hearing heavenly music and saw a brilliant white light. Then he heard a voice that sounded like thunder, a bolt of lightning, and mighty rushing waters say, "IT'S NOT YOUR TIME!"

When Matthew awakened from his coma, he was paralyzed on his left side, weighed ninety-five pounds, and had the functional capabilities of an infant. For the next two years, he endured intensive rehab to relearn "everything."

After his rehab, he asked one of his neighbors about finding a church. The neighbor invited him to The Rock Church in Gainesville. At first, Matthew and Nancy cried throughout the worship. There was a "gradual unveiling" for them as they both grew in faith.

"The moment I believed, there wasn't a question," Matthew says. "Yes, Lord! I get it now. I finally understand."

Matthew still has some paralysis on his left side and wears a brace on his right leg. But he would not trade the gunshot and the day in hell for anything. "I still have deficits," he says. "But I was spiritually dead, and that bullet brought me to such a great life. I would never have known Jesus. I can say I was in the right place when I was shot."

Matthew and Nancy started Seeds of Love Ministries and frequently share their testimonies with churches and other groups.

They want everyone to understand what is at stake between heaven and hell. "I don't want anyone else to experience what I experienced," Matthew says. "People need to have an answer to a huge question: 'Where will you spend eternity?'"

CHAPTER 32

Vincent Van Gogh's Unappreciated Journey with Christ

A record 1.2 million visitors came to the giant retrospective of Van Gogh's work in Amsterdam in 1990, which coincided with the 100th anniversary of the Dutch Post-Impressionist's death. What visitors did not see at that major exhibition were Van Gogh's Christian-themed paintings, which were left in the basement of the museum.

"None of the religious imagery was in the show. It was deliberately kept in the basement," says William Havlicek, Ph.D., author of *Van Gogh's Untold Journey* (Creative Storytellers). "In Western art, there has been a move toward secularization through existential thinking," he notes, which followed the disillusionment of many artists after two world wars.

Havlicek spent fifteen years researching and studying more than 900 of Van Gogh's letters. His revealing book dispels many of the myths that surround the painter's tumultuous life. "Vincent's letters portray a very different story than the popular tale of the mad artist who cuts off his ear," Havlicek notes. "What emerges instead is a story of selfless loyalty, the epitome of the Gospel's sacred counsel—'love one another.'"

"Many of his religious letters were held back and only released in the last five or six years," Havlicek adds.

Vincent's father and grandfather were pastors, and it seems many in the Van Gogh family gravitated toward religion or art. His father, Theodorus, a Dutch Reformed minister, was not known as a compelling preacher, but a "welfare pastor" who distributed food and clothing to the poor, Havlicek explains.

As Vincent's zeal for Christ grew in his early twenties, he wanted to study theology, but failed his entrance exam for seminary. Instead, he went off to serve as a missionary to coal miners in the Borinage district of Belgium.

He found miners who were sick and starving, living a bleak existence, without adequate food, water, or warm clothing. A mining explosion had left many in a horrible condition. Fighting for survival, they apparently had little interest in his evangelistic appeals.

In response to their plight, Vincent gave away everything he owned, including most of his clothing. To tend to their medical needs, he ripped up his own bedsheets for bandages and slept on straw on the ground. "By such actions, he won the admiration and respect of the workers and was able to convert some of them," Havlicek notes.

"Vincent was a very generous man. He understood that unconditional love of God extended to unconditional love for others. He would never recognize love that was not an action." Van Gogh was also inspired by the writings of Charles Dickens which revealed his compassionate response to human suffering.

Sadly, a church committee overseeing Vincent thought he suffered from excessive zeal and fired him because he did not dress well or preach eloquently. "It did not seem to matter to them that he literally poured out his life in sacrifice and service on behalf of the diseased and destitute," Havlicek laments.

Vincent went home to his parents, but the physical and emotional ordeal of caring for the miners and the rejection by the church hierarchy had taken its toll. He appeared to suffer a nervous breakdown, which caused his father to make his first quiet inquiries about committing Vincent to an asylum.

At the same time, the drawings Vincent had made of miners and others captured his brother Theo's interest. He persuaded Vincent to begin formal art studies at the Académie Royale des Beaux-Arts in Brussels. Van Gogh wanted to continue to serve God with his art, stating: "To try to understand the real significance of what the great artists, the serious masters, tell us in their masterpieces, that leads to God. One man wrote or told it in a book, another in a picture."

In 1881, he fell in love and proposed marriage to a woman

who was seven years older. She turned him down, but his advances persisted in a clumsy manner. Exasperated, the woman and her parents forcibly rejected Vincent, partly due to the struggling artist's inability to support himself.

During the time Vincent lived with his family, Vincent and his father got into more and more heated arguments. After one particularly violent exchange on Christmas day, when Vincent refused to go to church, Vincent left to live on his own in The Hague.

The following year, Vincent attempted to rescue a prostitute, Sien Hoornik. He wrote of his unusual relationship with Hoornik in his letters: "I met a pregnant woman, deserted by the man whose child she carried. A pregnant woman who had to walk the streets in winter, had to earn her bread, you understand how, I took this woman for a model and have worked with her all winter. I could not pay her the full wages of a model, but that did not prevent my paying her rent, and, thank God, so far I have been able to protect her and her child from hunger and cold by sharing my own bread with her."

As one might imagine, his family was shocked he had taken in a prostitute and pressured him to alter his living arrangement. His parents continued to explore the idea of committing Vincent to an asylum due to his errant behavior.

Vincent's father died of a stroke in 1885, and Vincent's sisters blamed him for "murdering" his father, due to the emotional fallout from their intense discussions and unresolved conflict.

After his father's death, Vincent went into a tailspin. "Vincent embarked on a three-year drinking binge in Paris," Havlicek notes. "This was the most destructive period of his life. Even so, he continued to produce some remarkable work inspired by the Impressionists who exhibited in the great city."

He experimented with absinthe, which was a highly popular drink in some circles made from unstable wormwood alcohol. The unpredictable side effects for many users included nerve damage, blindness, and insanity. Absinthe may have triggered the epileptic seizures that began to plague Vincent during this period.

"After drinking a large quantity of absinthe, Vincent slashed off a portion of his ear," Havlicek recounts. "It's possible he had a grand mal seizure when he slashed the upper part of his ear," he says.

Most art critics and historians believe Vincent lost his faith sometime between 1882 and 1885. Yet, Havlicek found abundant evidence in Vincent's letters and his art that an abiding faith remained, even as his health and behavior deteriorated. Surprisingly, most of the Christian-themed paintings appeared in the last three years of his life.

For the sake of self-preservation, Vincent moved to Arles in southern France, where he had an unusual meeting one day in a café he frequented. A local peasant walked in who bore a striking resemblance to his deceased father. "This chance meeting led to some of the most emotionally wrought portraits in the history of art—a father's posthumous portrait painted vicariously using the face of another," Havlicek notes.

Vincent painted the man's hands clasped as if in prayer, holding a shepherd's staff. "He surrounded his father in a gold light, which is always a symbol of the divine," Havlicek notes. "It's a sacred work; Vincent loved sacred references."

Havlicek made the significant discovery that a saintly bishop's ruminations on the cosmos in Victor Hugo's *Les Miserables* inspired one of Vincent's most famous works, The Starry Night:

Victor Hugo wrote, "He was there alone with himself, collected, tranquil, adoring, comparing the serenity of his own heart with the serenity of the skies, moved in the darkness by the visible splendours of the constellations, and the invisible splendour of God, opening his soul to the thoughts that fall from the Unknown. In such moments offering up his heart at the hour when the flowers of night inhale their perfume, lighted like a lamp in the centre of *The Starry Night* ... "

Vincent used the same title for his painting, and Havlicek notes the striking similarities. "The theme of *Les Miserables* is redemption," Havlicek observes. In Van Gogh's painting, "the stars are painted like flowers. There is an interaction between the earth and heaven. It is as if heaven is reaching down."

"Starlight implies in Vincent's view that the darkness of sin, guilt, and death are overcome by divinely mediated grace."

"Van Gogh's interest in the Gospel is very profound," Havlicek says. His paintings, *The Good Samaritan*, *The Raising of Lazarus*, *The Sower*, and *The Sheaf-Binder* (or harvester), all display Christ-centered themes.

Havlicek even sees the work of Christ in Van Gogh's famous painting of sunflowers. "In 1886, Van Gogh found sunflowers thrown in a street gutter in Paris. He went home and painted these beautiful cast-off flowers. The way the flowers were transformed through love shows redemption."

Van Gogh died under unusual circumstances in what most label a suicide, but Havlicek has some doubts. "No gun was ever found," he says, and there were no powder burns near the fatal wound to his abdomen.

Two boys admitted they were target shooting near Van Gogh and had an encounter with him that appears suspicious. "One wrote a confessional letter years later saying they were harassing Van Gogh. He didn't admit he shot him, but he said there were things he did to him he wish he'd never done."

Vincent lingered for two days after the fatal shot. When he was interviewed by police, Vincent said, "I'm hurt but don't blame anybody else."

Havlicek believes that if he was shot accidentally by the boys, it was consistent with Vincent's character to withhold that information. "He had a very sacrificial aspect to his personality. There were several times in his life when he took the blame for someone else," he says.

"He loved Christ enormously at the end of his life," Havlicek maintains. "He said Christ alone among all the magi and wise men offered men eternal life. In spite of a broken life, something glorious emerged."

CHAPTER 33

For the Burpo Family, Heaven Is for Real

When doctors inexplicably missed four-year-old Colton Burpo's burst appendix, and the resulting infection nearly took his life, his father railed at God as Colton's life seemed to slip away.

Pastor Todd Burpo found a small room in the hospital after Colton was taken into surgery, and he unloaded some raw emotions toward heaven. "Where are you God? Is this how you treat your pastors? Is it worth it to even serve you?" he shouted, as recounted in the *New York Times* bestseller *Heaven Is for Real*.

After Colton's surgery and a time in ICU, the fair-haired boy made a remarkable recovery. It wasn't until four months later, on a family car ride to South Dakota, that Colton's parents realized something very unusual happened to Colton as doctors fought to save his life.

Colton shared with his astonished parents that he left his body in the hospital and visited heaven, where he sat on Jesus' lap and met departed family members, along with other remarkable details.

He watched his father praying for his life in the small room, a fact that even Todd's wife, Sonya, didn't know. Todd had confessed and repented of his "raw" attitude toward God in the hospital, but the realization that his son sat on Jesus' lap in the midst of his anger melted his heart.

"I screamed at God when he was holding my kid and it was wrong," he admits. "When I knew God had forgiven me for that, I knew it was okay to share it with other people."

Colton told his parents one of his favorite places in heaven was the throne room of God, with God seated on a huge throne, Jesus enthroned on His right, and the angel Gabriel on the Father's left. "People ask Colton, 'What does God's face look like?'"

"Colton says, 'His face is so big, I could hardly see it.'" Todd notes that his son "has nothing to measure God by—he was just a little kid." Colton estimated that God is so large, he could hold the world in His hands.

Everyone Colton saw in heaven had wings, except for Jesus. Colton described Michael the Archangel as the biggest of the angels—twice as tall as Todd.

Heaven Is for Real was on the *New York Times* bestseller list for months, with over ten million copies sold. An illustrated children's edition of the book came out later. "There are more details and memories in the children's book," Todd notes. "It's all first-person Colton and starts with him leaving the hospital."

In heaven, Colton was taken under wing by his departed great-grandfather, a man he never met, who passed away when his father was only a boy. He also met a sister he never knew, who was miscarried by his mother.

"When people say Colton met his little sister, he's quick to correct them. He says, 'She was not my little sister; she was my big sister.'"

"She was never born, but she aged to where she was Colton's big sister," Todd adds. This unnamed sister waits in heaven for the rest of her family to arrive, when they will delight in finally giving her a name.

It appeared to Colton that babies gradually age to their late twenties or thirties in heaven, while older people regain youthful bodies. "There is no death or dying in heaven," Todd notes. "Colton's memory is that you age to your prime and then you stop aging." Colton's great-grandfather appeared to be a man in his thirties, having reverted in age.

There are "gobs" of babies in heaven, according to Colton, but it remains unclear whether this is due to abortion or natural deaths. "The women in heaven, especially Mary, are involved with raising the kids," he says. According to Colton, Mary, the mother of Jesus, has dark hair, brown eyes, and is a little taller than his mother. Mary had a dark sky-blue sash and a light above her head. She seemed to be in her late twenties, like the other adults in heaven.

"Colton will tell you that King David and Samson were two of his favorite Bible characters he met in heaven. He always talks about how nice they were. David would show him around heaven and help him. He went to David a lot for help."

Even though Colton never read the book of Revelation, his description of a coming battle accurately reflects the events depicted in Scripture. "Colton says there's going to be a war," Todd notes. "He says 'Jesus, the angels, and the good people are going to fight the monsters and the bad guys.'" He saw Jesus throw Satan into hell.

One day, Colton asked his father, "Dad, why do I remember a dragon with seven heads and ten crowns?"

Todd looked at his son in amazement and said, "Colton, whatever you saw and whatever John saw is the same thing."

"Colton says, 'Satan looks like an angel, but his light was extinguished a long time ago. They showed me where he used to have a throne in heaven.'"

One of Colton's favorite activities in paradise was to attend a class taught by Jesus. "Jesus was his teacher and he had homework. We knew it had to be heaven because he hates homework down here," Todd says with a laugh.

Some wonder how Colton could have seen so much in a short period. By Colton's reckoning, he was only gone for three minutes from his earthly body. "Peter said that with God a day is like a thousand years and a thousand years is like a day. If you do the math, three minutes equals two years," Todd notes.

"God operates outside of time, and time doesn't limit God," he explains.

Todd showed his son countless artistic representations of Jesus before Colton decided on one that matched his memory of the Lord. The image that came closest was painted by a young prodigy named Akiane Kramarik, who had a powerful vision about Jesus as a child that led to her painting.

It may seem surprising to some that Colton and Akiane recall Jesus with blue-green eyes. "Colton says, 'Dad, Jesus' eyes are just so pretty.'"

"Many attack Colton and say 'Jesus was a Jew. He couldn't have had blue eyes.' However, the Bible doesn't say Jesus was a Jew. His mother was Jewish, but he was born of God—the Son of God."

Colton recalls that he could always hear people singing in heaven and one always feels God's love everywhere. "Heaven is not a place where you stand in the choir and sing the whole time," Todd notes. "It's a place where we get to be completely fulfilled."

Todd sympathizes with the skeptics who question his son's remarkable story. "When my son first started sharing this, I wondered how it could be true," he admits. "I tried to come up with explanations for what he was giving me. I tried to dismiss or explain away what he was saying, and I couldn't."

Colton's detailed information about his great-grandfather, along with the specific location of Todd and his wife while Colton was in surgery, erased his doubts.

Despite the book's enormous success, Todd would not choose to go through this experience again. "We didn't ask for this," he says. "Watching your child almost die—I don't ever want to go through that again. I can't tell you how awful that is. It was gut-wrenching."

"This was done to us, not because we're super-spiritual. Most of the things that happened were completely out of our control. It's because of God that this happened."

"If you look at the peace and hope people are finding because of the story, we can look back and say maybe God had a plan bigger than any of us could figure out at the time."

Chapter 34

Lost Forty-Seven Days at Sea

Louis Zamperini's record in the mile earned as a USC track star stood for twenty years. After he ran for his country in the Berlin Olympics of 1936, he had the dubious honor of meeting Adolph Hitler. But when his B-24 Liberator crashed in the Pacific during WWII, many thought a promising life was cut short.

The harrowing account of his ordeal at sea told in Laura Hillenbrand's outstanding book Unbroken reveals that God had another plan for his life.

"Talk about a miracle," Zamperini says today at age ninety-four. Stationed in Hawaii during WWII, Zamperini volunteered to search for a plane and its crew that disappeared one day in late May 1943.

When he agreed to undertake the mission, he knew the only plane available for the search was considered a "musher," because its tail flew below its nose due to undetermined mechanical problems.

His concern about the plane was confirmed when one of its engines sputtered and died during the search mission, which sent all aboard into a steep dive and a violent crash into the sea. Trapped inside the fuselage by wires from the electrical system, his ears popped and pressure inside his head intensified until he blacked out.

The plane sank deeper and deeper with Louis trapped inside. Like Jonah ensnared in the belly of the whale with seaweed wrapped around him, Louis couldn't free himself from the wiry tentacles.

Then mysteriously, he awoke and was freed from the wires! He was able to get through a window, then carbon dioxide canisters inflated the chambers in his Mae West jacket, which floated him to the surface.

"Why had he woken again? How had he been loosed from the wires while unconscious?" he wondered later. This first miracle suggested angelic hands sent by a God of deliverance and rescue—a God who still sets captives free.

Only Louis and two other crewmen survived. They spent weeks bobbing in the South Pacific in a struggle of faith and endurance. Their main concern was water, because they only had a few pints between them. Their food supply consisted of a few ration bars.

"On the raft, we had some chocolate bars," Louis recalls. Each Hershey Ration D bar was divided into segments, and they decided if they ate two squares a day, combined with a few sips of water, they might last for a few days until they were rescued.

But this sensible plan was quickly thwarted. "During the night, the tail gunner panicked and ate all the chocolate in one night," Louis says.

When Louis found out that Mac had eaten all the chocolate, he resisted the urge to beat the tar out of him. After four more days, they consumed all their water and none of them had a morsel of food.

"The next day, Mac started screaming, 'We're all gonna die; we're gonna die.'"

"I couldn't calm him down, no matter what," Louis recalls. "I had to crack him across the face and knock him on his butt to settle him down. I thought he would die because he ate enough chocolate for six people for a week."

Sharks continually circled the men as the relentless tropical sun beat down on them. After three days without water, a cloud the size of a man's hand appeared on the horizon. Storm clouds gathered and finally gushed over the men, as they craned their mouths upward to catch as much as possible. With a few improvised canvas rain catchers, they were able to fill a few containers with more water.

They caught a seabird but decided they couldn't eat it. Instead, they used it for bait and were able to catch a slender ten-inch pilot fish. It was the first raw fish the men had eaten in their lives and their first food in more than a week.

As Hillenbrand notes in her book, the previous record for raft survival by Navy crash victims in the Pacific was thirty-four days.

Louis had only prayed once in his life during childhood when he feared his mother might die. Now he prayed to God fervently for help. After they passed the two-week mark, Louis began to pray aloud. Without any church background, he recited bits and pieces of prayers he recalled from movies. Their third crewman, Phil, provided the amen chorus. Mac remained quiet.

After the water ran out again and they had been six days without a drop in their mouths, Louis prayed once more. He told God that if He would quench his thirst, he would dedicate his life to Him.

On the 27th day, they were strafed by a Japanese bomber. All three men jumped overboard and hid underwater as the plane's machine guns opened up on the raft. Unharmed, they were so weak, they could barely climb back on the raft.

The plane came back for a second pass. This time, Phil and Mac stayed on the raft and took their chances. Louis again dove underwater. This time, a shark made a charge toward Louis. He shoved his palm into the shark's nose, and it swam off.

When Louis climbed back aboard, he thought for sure the other men were hit. "Impossibly, there were bullet holes all the way around the men, even in the tiny spaces between them, not one bullet had hit either man."

"That was a miracle," Louis exclaims. "There were forty-eight bullet holes between their crotches and armpits. We were missed by an eighth of an inch," he notes. "You've got to believe in angels."

By the 32nd day, Mac had faded to a mere shadow of himself. With his own water tin dry, he pleaded for a sip of water. Phil refused him, but Louis obliged. Like the rich man and Lazarus, the man who made himself "rich" in stolen chocolate, longed for a drop to cool his burning tongue.

"Do you think I'm going to die?" Mac asked.

Louis couldn't lie to him. "Mac, I think you're gonna die tonight." Sure enough, Mac passed during the night.

"We buried him at sea," Louis says. "He sank like a rock. He had no flesh. We were all skin and bones."

On the 40th day, a number that always seems to carry biblical significance, Louis had a vision of angels singing. As recounted in Hillenbrand's book, "It sounded like a choir. Above him floating in a bright cloud, he saw human figures, silhouetted against the sky. He counted twenty-one of them. They were singing the sweetest song he had ever heard."

When Louis and Phil were picked up by the Japanese on the 47th day, they each had lost half their bodyweight from starvation. "We couldn't stand up or walk so they had to carry us over their shoulders."

"We were an attraction to the Japanese," Louis notes. "They spent hours at the raft, counting all the bullet holes," he recalls. "The Japanese couldn't believe it. They kept looking our bodies over to see where the bullets hit."

In the end, the Japanese shook their heads and came to the same conclusion reached by Louis and Phil. It must have been a miracle.

Zamperini spent the remainder of the war in a P.O.W. camp, where he endured horrible abuse at the hands of a prison guard nicknamed "The Bird."

After the war, he met and married the girl of his dreams, but post-traumatic stress disorder threatened to destroy his marriage. All the while, he dreamed of a return to Japan to hunt down and kill the former guard who tormented him.

"I had nightmares every night," he recalls. The nightmares followed Zamperini home like a crazed hound from hell. "No one knew about it, because I looked perfectly normal. I covered it up by drinking."

His wife, Cynthia, suspected something was terribly wrong, because Zamperini often woke up in a cold sweat, shouting. One night, he dreamed he was strangling The Bird. In fact, he was on top of his pregnant wife with his hands around her neck, choking the life out of her. "I woke up and couldn't believe it," he says.

His life spiraled downward as he began to chase other women at local bars, where he and his Olympic buddies often got free drinks. "I began to fall apart," Zamperini recalls. "My wife decided she wanted a divorce."

About that time, a new couple in their apartment building talked about a young evangelist preaching in a large tent in downtown Los Angeles. "In those days, 'evangelist' was a dirty word because there were so many crooked ones," Zamperini notes.

The young evangelist was Billy Graham, the object of William Randolph Hearst's famous order to his news editors—"Puff Graham"—that led to 10,000 people jamming the tent each night. Cynthia went with the couple to hear Graham, but Louis refused to go. When Cynthia returned home after the event, Louis immediately noticed something was different.

"She started speaking of a peace and joy in her heart," he recalls. Still, Louis stubbornly resisted her invitation to hear Graham. "She knew that to save our marriage, I would have to be converted."

Despite her appeals, Louis continued to dig in his heels. "I wanted no part of it."

But then Cynthia said something that got his attention. "Because of my conversion, I'm not going to get a divorce," she announced.

The next day, Cynthia was all over Louis again, and this time, he relented. "Ok, ok, I'll go," he said. "But when that fella says, 'Every head bowed and every eye closed,' we're getting out of there."

That night, Graham spoke from the eighth chapter of John about the woman caught in adultery. "He began to preach and quote Scripture that reminded me of my life," Louis notes. Still, his heart was hardened. At the end of the message, when Graham asked people to bow their heads, Louis grabbed his wife's arm and bolted from the tent.

As they got in their car, he said, "Don't ever get me back in a place like that again."

Louis suffered a fitful night's sleep that night, with more nightmares about The Bird. The next morning, Cynthia was just as firm in her resolve that a change in Louis's heart was the only possible way to save their marriage. She went after Louis again and convinced him to go back a second time to hear Graham. Louis warned his wife, "If he says, 'every head bowed and every eye closed,' we're out of there."

This time, Graham spoke about why Christians suffer and why God seemed to allow communism to flourish. At the end of the message, when Graham asked people to bow their heads, Louis got up to leave. As he moved to the end of their row and stood in the aisle, he hesitated and stopped.

Something Graham said about people "at the end of their rope" who turned to God triggered a flood of memories. He thought about his ordeal in the Japanese P.O.W. camp, when he and the other men prayed daily. He promised God then, "If you get me home alive, I'll seek You and serve You."

Likewise, his mind returned to his suffering on the raft. "On the raft, we were at the mercy of the elements on the ocean. I came back alive. God kept His promise," he realized, but he had not kept his part.

"What a heel I've been," he muttered to himself.

Instead of heading for the exit door, Louis turned and walked toward the prayer room. There, he fell to his knees and gave his life to Christ. "The Holy Spirit came into my heart, and I became a member of the true church, the Body of Christ."

Something unusual happened as he knelt humbly before God. "When I was still on my knees, I forgave all my guards, and I knew I was through smoking, drinking, and chasing women."

That night, his nightmares stopped abruptly. "The miracle that happened," he says, "it was the first time in years I never had a nightmare. I haven't had one since."

Zamperini rummaged through their apartment the next

day. He tossed out all the liquor, cigarettes, and girlie magazines hidden in various places. He dug out his WWII Bible, walked to a local park, and began to read. "I got to the crucifixion, and I started crying like a baby."

He left the park and hurried back to see Cynthia. "A miracle has happened in my life," he said excitedly.

"The same miracle happened to me," she said. "That's the miracle of conversion—it happens the moment you believe!"

The following day, Louis found Billy Graham and Cliff Barrows and told them about the marvelous change that happened. "I was bubbling over with joy," he recalls. Louis insisted, however, they would never get him up on a platform talking about his faith.

But God had other plans. "The next day, Cliff Barrows gave me a train ticket to Modesto." Zamperini boarded the train and headed for his first participatory Graham event, where he shared about his newfound faith. "I only knew two or three scriptures," he admits. "Since then, I've been on platforms all over the world."

Zamperini notes that one of the reviewers of *Unbroken* faulted the book in one respect: "He couldn't understand how someone with post-traumatic stress disorder could get over it in a moment."

"The reviewer didn't know the scripture, *'Therefore, if anyone be in Christ, he is a new creation; old things have passed away; behold, all things have become new.'*" (2 Corinthians 5:17, NKJV)

CHAPTER 35

Mysterious 'Jesus Photo' Stirs Faith, Brings Comfort and Peace to Many

It was a blustery Saturday, along the coast of Maine, with whitecaps forming to the horizon's edge. Jane Dobson received some jolting news that morning, October 2, 2010. A close friend in Wisconsin had passed away the night before.

"She was a beloved sister in Christ, a very dear friend of mine," Jane notes. "Her husband got up and thought she was asleep, but suddenly he realized she wasn't breathing." Her friend, Kathleen, died from a massive, unexpected heart attack at age sixty-seven.

Jane began to grieve for her friend. The Dobson house was full of weekend guests, their kids and old family friends, which made it more difficult for Jane to find time alone with God. Before she received the bad news about her friend, she had been praying that Jesus would reveal Himself in new ways to her houseguests.

"The wind was blowing so hard, I couldn't open my windows even an inch," Jane recalls. But then suddenly, about 2:00 p.m., the wind stopped. "It went from big whitecaps to flat calm—like a mill pond," she notes. "That usually doesn't happen in October in Maine."

Due to the favorable weather change, Jane's husband, Bill, suggested they go for a ride on their boat. Everyone quickly agreed, and the group of ten piled into the Dobson's thirty-six-foot Hinckley picnic boat, "Lady Jane," and set out along the coast of Maine.

Jane continued to grieve on the boat. "Everybody left me alone because I was so sad," she notes. Jane, a retired nurse with an active prayer ministry, offered praise for Kathleen's life and asked Jesus to send comfort.

After an hour on the vessel, Jane felt a noticeable change in the atmosphere. As their boat rounded a bend close to

Owls Head State Park's majestic lighthouse, something unusual happened.

"I felt God's presence so powerfully, it was astounding to me," she says. "It was like someone flipped a switch, and I went from horrific grief to inexpressible joy." She was so overcome by the peace and presence of God that her grief vanished.

Jane's daughter, Kirsten, recalls the same moment. "We were both praying for peace and comfort for Kathleen's daughter," she says. "All of a sudden, the most amazing sense of peace came over us."

About five minutes later, they heard their friend, Michael, say excitedly, "Who is this guy in white in the picture?" Michael had a new Sony digital camera and felt inspired to attempt some artistic shots on their outing.

"I was trying to be creative with the photos I took that day," Michael recalls. "My wife, Elizabeth, and I were sitting there, and I was looking at her glasses. I thought that would be a cool picture to take a shot of the reflection in her glasses."

Immediately, he pulled up the images on his digital camera, and there appeared to be an unknown figure captured in the tenth photo. "Who is this in Elizabeth's glasses?" he asked, as those who sat nearby began to look curiously.

In the photo, a mysterious hooded figure dressed in white stood on the inside edge of the boat, leaning slightly forward, with his head bent down, as if praying.

"Nobody could identify this person," Michael says. "We went through every scenario, and after a while, we determined there was nobody who looked like that on the boat, and nobody was standing on that side of the boat."

Kirsten left her mother and went over to see the photograph. "Oh my gosh; who is that?" she exclaimed. As her mind quickly processed the possibilities, she reached a dramatic conclusion: "I think that's Jesus."

"Mom, you've got to come over here!" Kirsten cried. Then Jane came over and scanned the digital image carefully.

"I'll tell you who it is," she volunteered. "It's either Jesus or one of His angels!" Without her glasses, she couldn't make a definitive judgment until they returned to the house.

When the passengers began to recognize the implications of this, powerful feelings emerged. "Michael was overcome," Jane says. "He knew that person wasn't on the boat, and he knew it wasn't a flesh and blood person." Their souls were rocked with holy fear, perhaps the way Moses felt when he heard God speak through a burning bush.

"We were all in a daze for the rest of the boat trip," Kirsten recalls. Some were scared by it. "Michael's father-in-law kept saying, 'It can't be that. There's no way that could be Jesus.'"

Michael sat there, incredulous. "I'm going to rethink my entire life after taking that picture," he said.

In the month that followed this unusual incident, Jane prayed for clarity about the identity of the person in the photograph. "I didn't want to say it was Jesus if it was an angel," she says. After a month, God gave her a striking vision that confirmed in her mind that the unknown figure is Jesus.

"I knew it was Him. He's bent forward as if He's praying, leaning against the inside of the boat."

Michael, who works in the financial services industry in New York, says he is not tech savvy. "There was no messing around with this photo," he says. "There was no editing to it." It could not have been a double exposure. He has not formed a conclusion about the identity of the figure.

Jane's husband, Bill, is an architect, a pilot, and works in the nursing home business. "I'm a skeptical person, the opposite of my wife," he says. "This blew my mind. There was no chance to alter the photo because we looked at it right after he took them."

"I fly airplanes. I don't see UFOs," he added. He is convinced the photo is Jesus.

Jane took dozens of copies of the photo to the funeral of her friend Kathleen. When she spoke, she recounted the way Jesus calmed the waters by His tangible presence that day.

God used the photo to bring special comfort to Kathleen's daughter, Trish, who now keeps a copy framed on her mantle. "What a beautiful gift of God it has been," Trish says. "That picture helps remind me He is right here in our midst." During several moments of great sadness, she feels the Holy Spirit has directed her to look at the image, and her anguish has been replaced with peace.

As Jane looks back, she realizes that God brought a most unusual answer to everything she prayed, when Jesus calmed the waters on a blustery day.

To listen to a podcast of the interview with Jane Dobson, go here:

CHAPTER 36

Satanist Plotted to Kill Prominent Pastor

During a satanic ritual, a death angel gave him an assignment: kill Pastor Craig Groeschel, senior pastor of LifeChurch.tv, one of the largest churches in the United States. But in the midst of his evil mission, he had an unexpected encounter with God's grace.

"I hated Christians," says Michael Leehan, who followed Satan for twenty years, and is also the author of *Ascent from Darkness* (Thomas Nelson), the gripping account of his enslavement to the powers of darkness.

As a young person growing up in Culver City, California, he faced "any kind of abuse you can think of" from family members. Some of the abuse was sexual, but mostly it was emotional and physical, including "savage beatings" by a grandmother who stuffed red pepper up his nose. Sometimes, he was hit with a two-by-four in the head. (Note: the details of the abuse are not contained in his book.)

"You never get over that," he admits. "It takes a lifetime to get over that."

Even though the family attended a mainstream denominational church, the dichotomy between their outer façade and what happened inside his home left deep scars. "The thing that kept me from Christ was Christians," he says. "They seemed double-minded and lukewarm."

The family relocated to Oklahoma City when Leehan was nineteen, and he began to sow wild oats. "I was sleeping around with everybody and drinking and getting high." The out-of-control behavior led to a serious drug overdose, and he almost died.

In the ambulance, he heard a man's voice say, "Not yet son, I have too much for you to do." In a daze, he mistook the voice for his father's, not thinking it might be a message from heaven.

Leehan married a young woman named Amber a year later, a nine-year union that produced three children. She filed for divorce, and he admits that his "mood problems" were more than she could handle.

Alone, depressed, and angry after the divorce, he made a tragic turn to the dark side. "God, in my mind, had abandoned me early in life," he notes in his book. "I decided that God was responsible for evil, controlled it, and was in fact both good and evil."

Through a misinterpretation of Isaiah 45:7, he concluded that God created evil.

"If He was responsible for all the suffering in my life, how could He possibly care about me? Since God didn't care about me, I might as well serve His enemy."

In the same way some give their hearts and lives to Christ, he gave his life to Satan. One Saturday afternoon, as he sat alone on his red corduroy couch, he went over the edge. "Satan, come into my life. You are now my god. Use me, have me, control me for your purposes."

At that moment, he felt an invasive power surge through his body, along with loathsome and perverted thoughts. Immediately, he went to a bookstore and purchased two books to guide his new path: *The Satanic Bible* and the *Book of Shadows*.

That night, he felt the urge to cut himself to show his allegiance to Satan. He used a sharp paring knife to cut the skin on his left forearm. It was the first of many such bloodlettings. "Not all cutters are Satanists," he observes, "but all Satanists are cutters."

As he got more deeply involved, he drew strength from his ritual time (RT, as he called it). "Typically, I would light candles, pray to Satan, and wait for things to happen. There was nearly always blood spilled. It was usually mine, but at times, it was a neighborhood animal, usually a cat."

One detail not found in the book is that Leehan considered Jim Morrison of the legendary rock group, The Doors, to be his spirit guide. Morrison died in Paris at age twenty-seven, allegedly from a drug overdose. "Morrison was dead, but I contacted him, and we would always meet up in the desert," Leehan recounts.

"I loved the guy; I literally saw his face. He would speak to me and tell me stuff to do. It was probably a demon in disguise." During the moment of his ritual blood sacrifices, Leehan often played the haunted and brooding Doors song, "The End," along with "Crystal Ship."

Leehan spent ten months in the Oklahoma County Jail due to his failure to pay child support. Given a New Testament, he sought to memorize as much as he could, so he could twist and manipulate Scripture when he confronted jailhouse preachers. He also tore out the pages to roll cigarettes he sold fellow inmates.

One night, when Leehan was home alone, he heard strange sounds emanate from his master bedroom, including scratching on the walls, guttural groans, and then chanting. "The demonic sounds from the unholy choir directed me to the living room," where he was engulfed by an evil presence that overpowered his will.

He felt an indwelling which seemed to be an angel of death. "This spirit gave me a mission: 'Kill Craig Groeschel.'" The satanic spirit explained that another man had been given the task but had backed down. Leehan was the chosen one to complete the assignment.

Groeschel founded Life Covenant Church in 1996 in a suburb of Oklahoma City, and it had grown to become the largest church in that area and one of the largest in the U.S.

For a year, Leehan stalked Groeschel with a 9-millimeter Glock and two clips, which he hid under his shirt as he sat in the foyer of the large church and studied the church's security arrangements. Leehan never ventured inside the sanctuary, because of his hatred of worship and the people of God.

On the day he decided to kill Groeschel, something unexpected happened. As Leehan sat and listened to the reading of God's Word, the praises of His people, and the message of the Gospel, it pierced his heart. The stone wall Satan had erected around his heart began to be dismantled, and the light of heaven began to work.

When an usher came over to him, Leehan confessed what he had been planning to do. The man stood there speechless, his eyes wide with shock and horror.

Leehan quickly left the church with his girlfriend, but the next week, his photo was plastered in the staff rooms of every Life.Church around Oklahoma City. A caption beneath his photo read, "If you see this man, call security or the police."

When he went back to the church the following Sunday, he forgot his weapon. As he sat in the foyer once more, an armed deputy sheriff confronted him, and Leehan was taken into the main offices. When Leehan was searched, they found no weapon on him.

"Why are you here?" one asked. "Is it to harm a certain staff member?"

"I'm done with that," Leehan replied. "I think I am seeking freedom from the life I've been living for so long. I think I'm seeking your God. I'm just not sure what to do next. I just need some time ... and a little space."

Somewhat perplexed by this strange turn of events, the staff decided to let Leehan go, they informed him they would talk among themselves, seek God's will, and decide what to do next.

"I was amazed I was allowed to leave the property ... and they didn't have me detained and arrested," Leehan recounts.

The next day, Chris Spradlin called him from LifeChurch. "I want you to know you are welcome at LifeChurch at any time. On one condition: you need to text John Ziegler (head of security) on Sunday morning and let him know which service you're going to be attending. John will be watching you ... you will need to sit in the same place every Sunday and conduct yourself in a way that would be pleasing to God. That's all we're asking."

"If you need anything from me, don't hesitate to ask. God bless you, Mike," Spradlin added.

Leehan couldn't believe it. They were welcoming him back without any pressure or forced meetings. The conditions seemed completely reasonable, considering he planned to kill their pastor only days before.

The grace shown to him began to melt his heart. "I had never seen that kind of love before," Leehan says. "I kept on going back because they let me go."

Over the next three months, Leehan attended the church, but Satan would not give up his possession without a fight. Leehan found himself engulfed in an intense spiritual battle for his allegiance.

Leehan grew increasingly miserable as his heart swung back and forth. On January 13, 2008, he decided he would kill himself. "That weekend, some people forced me to go to a men's retreat," he recounts. He went but told other men to leave him alone and cussed at several. "I don't know why I'm here," he told one man.

When Leehan tried to leave the retreat prematurely, his truck wouldn't start. He climbed up a hill by himself to write a suicide note. While he was up there, he poured out his heart to God for three hours.

"God, if you are real, help me now," he wrote. "I've lied and I have killed. I have lied and I have cheated. I have hurt everyone in my life, including You," he confessed.

"Satan took me in, why didn't You? Help me. Where are You? I need You and not tomorrow."

In the sky above, he saw dark, shadowy figures fighting with large, white images. "A battle seemed to ensue between the white figures and the dark figures, and the air swirled with turbulence," Leehan noted in his book.

Suddenly, a peace that surpasses understanding swept over Leehan. "I felt warm, safe, and protected. In an instant, I felt whole again. I felt as if the Word of God was being absorbed in the cells of my body."

When Leehan climbed down the hill and told the men at the retreat what had happened, they were overjoyed. That night, he went through an intense deliverance session for five hours with several other men at the retreat. "I gave my life to the Lord on the hill, but I couldn't say 'Jesus is Lord,'" he recalls.

At the end of the session, he could proudly announce his new allegiance to Jesus Christ. The other men baptized Leehan in a bathtub the same night.

Leehan maintains firm boundaries regarding the music and video he watches today. He recently walked out of the film, *The Wolf of Wall Street*. He will not be alone with a woman unless it's his wife. He has an occasional glass of wine at home but will not drink in public.

"Daily we are all being sanctified," he notes. "I'm not bulletproof. I can still fail."

One thing is certain, Leehan is determined not to be a lukewarm Christian. "I'm an all-in type guy. I love talking about the Lord and seeing Him work."

Whenever Leehan attends LifeChurch today, he sits in the front row, immediately in front of the pastor he intended to kill. But now, during the worship, his hands are raised in the air, praising God, joyful and free.

"Jesus Christ specializes in fixing broken messes just like me. He is, and always will be, the great Redeemer, and He is ready to transform your life whenever you call out to Him."

CHAPTER 37

Noted Physicist Says String Theory Suggests We're All Living in God's Matrix

Theoretical physicist, futurist, and bestselling author, Michio Kaku, has developed a theory that points to the existence of God using string theory.

String theory assumes that seemingly specific material particles are actually "vibrational states."

His view about intelligent design has riled the scientific community because Dr. Kaku is considered one of its most respected and prominent voices. He is the co-creator of string field theory, a branch of string theory.

"I have concluded that we are in a world made by rules created by an intelligence," he stated, according to the Geophilosophical Association of Anthropological and Cultural Studies.

Dr. Kaku has continued Einstein's search for a "Theory of Everything," seeking to unify the four fundamental forces of the universe—the strong force, the weak force, gravity, and electromagnetism.

The very purpose of physics, says Kaku, is "to find an equation ... which will allow us to unify all the forces of nature and allow us to read the mind of God."

Because string theory may provide a unified description of gravity and particle physics, it is considered a candidate for a Theory of Everything.

To reach his conclusions about intelligence behind the universe, Dr. Kaku made use of what he calls "primitive semi-radius tachyons."

A tachyon is a particle that always moves faster than light. Many physicists believe such particles cannot exist because they are not consistent with the known laws of physics.

As noted by Einstein and others, special relativity implies that faster-than-light particles, if they existed, could be used to communicate backwards in time.

Dr. Kaku used a technology created in 2005 that allowed him to analyze the behavior of matter at the subatomic scale, relying on a primitive tachyon semi-radius.

When he observed the behavior of these tachyons in several experiments, he concluded that humans live in a "matrix," a world governed by laws and principles conceived by an intelligent architect.

"I have concluded that we are in a world made by rules created by an intelligence, not unlike a favorite computer game, but of course, more complex and unthinkable," he said.

"By analyzing the behavior of matter at the subatomic scale affected by the semi tachyon pitch radius, what we call chance no longer makes sense, because we are in a universe governed by established rules and not determined by universal chances plane.

"This means that, in all probability, there is an unknown force that governs everything," he noted.

However, the unknown force, the first cause that set everything into being and holds everything together, is actually a person, Jesus Christ, Christians believe by faith.

In Dr. Kaku's understanding, the Universe is possibly a symphony of vibrating strings emanating from the mind of God, with His cosmic music resonating through an 11-dimensional hyperspace.

The Japanese-American physicist states, "Physicists are the only scientists who can say the word 'God' and not blush."

"To me it is clear that we exist in a plan which is governed by rules that were created, shaped by a universal intelligence and not by chance."

CHAPTER 38

Hostile Tribe's Chief Found Resurrection

The interior of Malaita in the Solomon Island chain had a long history of opposition to missionaries and other outsiders—sometimes violent resistance by the Kwaio tribal group.

In 1927, thirteen government officials from the UK were massacred by the Kwaio as they attempted to survey the area for taxation purposes. The British government responded by sending a warship to shell that part of the island, which resulted in the deaths of 200 Kwaio.

Later, several Roman Catholic priests were killed by the group. In 1965, a Protestant missionary from New Zealand was martyred as he attempted to evangelize the Kwaio. Ten years later, a medical missionary and his son were also killed.

But in the fullness of time, God had a plan to reach the Kwaio using missionaries from Fiji in 1990, as told in the compelling book, *Look What God is Doing*, by Dick Eastman, president of Every Home for Christ (EHC).

It seems several Fijian evangelists affiliated with EHC who had been part of a campaign to reach Fiji's 106 islands turned their attention to the 100 islands of the Solomon chain, 1,000 miles away.

They reached the island of Malaita and spent time evangelizing the coastal areas. One night, as their team sat around a campfire, a team member pointed to the rugged interior of the island and asked, "Are there people there who have yet to hear about Jesus?"

"Yes," one replied. "It's one of the most difficult areas in all of the islands to evangelize because of the rugged terrain and the hostile people."

An argument ensued within the team as they heard more about the history of the people group. Some were intimidated and urged caution. Cannibalism had been practiced until the end of the last century; who could be sure it had not ceased?

The team finally agreed they would pray and fast for seven days before attempting to send a team to reach the Kwaios.

With the help of two witch doctors who had become believers, a list of eighty-seven different evil spirits were identified that were said to hold sway in the region. They pointedly confronted each demonic entity with focused warfare prayer over the seven-day period, according to Eastman's book.

On the eighth day, Jack and Japta joined ten other Christian workers on a day-long journey into the rugged interior of the island.

About five o'clock in the afternoon, Jack and Japta reached one village where there was a large assembly of people, indicating something unusual might be going on. The two men were quickly surrounded by several large warriors, wanting to know where they were from and why they had come.

"Jack explained as quickly as he could in the Kwaio language that they were bringing the Kwaio people Good News," Eastman noted. "But the burly guardians led them away to be questioned by five village priests or elders. These were elders who had gathered in anticipation of the impending death of their chief."

"The strangers had arrived at a sacred moment and might be infringing on the customs of the Kwaio—a taboo of taboos that could meet with dire consequences."

As the Christians were questioned, they could not help but notice some of the large warriors standing near them had twenty-four-inch machetes and some carried bows with poison-tipped arrows.

"Why are you here?" one of the elders demanded.

"We have come to share Good News," they repeated once more, as they went on to describe the one true God who created everything in the heavens and on earth—including the

Kwaio. "Our eternal God sent His only Son to be like us, a man, and to sacrifice His own life willingly on our behalf."

The elders said they had never heard a message like this. They understood the concept of a blood sacrifice, however. After a few moments of heated discussion, one said, "We cannot believe anything you say unless our chief believes."

Jack and Japta requested permission to see the chief, knowing it was customary in many villages to seek approval from the chief. Once granted, that would open up opportunities for their message to be heard.

The elders refused because their chief, Haribo, was dying. Seeing him was out of the question.

Then one of the Christians had an idea. "When Jesus Christ came as the Son of God, He came not only to deliver men from their sins, but to heal sick people, too. God is quite capable of healing your chief." In response, the elders began to argue among themselves.

Jack and Japta spent the night locked in a hut, but at seven the next morning, the elders returned with surprising news. They were granted permission to pray for Chief Haribo!

When they entered the chief's hut, they could see he was very old and weak, struggling for breath, near death.

"Jack shared with him quickly God's plan of salvation, explaining that Jesus was the only way to eternal life," Eastman recounted.

The chief had a most amazing response. "I have waited my entire lifetime to hear this story," he told them. "I have always felt there was some sacred message like this. But no one ever came to bring us such words. How can I receive this Jesus into my life?"

Jack and Japta led Chief Haribo in the sinner's prayer. A few moments later, a profound peace transformed the countenance of the chief.

But two hours later, the chief died. For the rest of the day, his body was prepared for a traditional Kwaio burial. Meanwhile, Jack and Japta left the village and headed back to the coast.

But as dusk descended on the village, something shocking happened. Chief Haribo sat up and began to speak!

"Let the elders gather," he said to his startled hearers, "and let someone go and find the boys who came earlier to tell me about Jesus."

When they gathered, the chief related an amazing story about seeing heaven. "A being dressed in glorious white had taken him a great distance to the most beautiful place he had ever seen," Eastman recounted.

"A person called Jesus Christ, the Son of God the young men had told him about, was being worshiped by a huge crowd of people. The glorious being explained to him that this beautiful place was where people who believed in Jesus would go for all eternity to worship Him. So, everything the boys said was true."

"Peace had come to his life, Haribo said, and he had no more pain, nor had he seen any suffering among the people who worshiped Jesus."

Chief Haribo also gave the names of several Old Testament prophets he met in heaven.

"Then the being in white showed him another place—a place of great torment where people go who reject the message of Jesus."

The being in white told the chief he had to go back for a short time to tell the elders of the village that the message about Jesus was true. "This Jesus is the only way to experience eternal life," he said.

When the chief learned that Jack and Japta had left, he ordered runners to go after them and bring them back so they could preach to the rest of the village.

When Jack and Japta returned, they were astounded by what had happened. They presented the message of salvation again, this time to the entire village.

"Every person, including Chief Haribo's immediate family of twenty-one members, received Christ as their Savior. And soon, more than 300 villagers throughout the area (in ten nearby villages) had surrendered their lives to Christ."

"Haribo remained alive all that night and into the next morning. Then he laid back down quietly in his earth bed and went to be forever with Jesus."

By 2012, more than 8,000 Kwaios became followers of Jesus, including 1,000 in the most remote areas.

CHAPTER 39

Atheist Pilot Mocked God, until He Ran Out of Fuel in a Snowstorm

Raised in the secular seventies, completely un-churched, he had no room for God until he ran out of fuel in an Alaskan storm, miles from his destination.

"I was a God mocker," says Mark Rose, founder of Genesis Alive, and the author of *Last of the Long Hunters*, a story of the pilots who fly the Alaskan Arctic.

Rose learned to fly at sixteen, and by age twenty-two had become a bush pilot who helped take care of a fleet of helicopters that worked on the Alaska pipeline. "My ego meter was on 101," he admits.

One day, he flew some hunters to the upper part of a large river on the Arctic. But on his return flight, carrying one passenger, several things went wrong. First, herds of caribou had moved in, covering his first and second choices for a landing spot. Then he began to run low on fuel, so he called ahead for a weather check at the small airport near Kotzebue, on the Baldwin Peninsula.

"Come on in, the weather's fine," the FAA flight service operator told him.

He decided to take the chance his fuel would hold out, but then weather conditions changed dramatically. "I ran into a snowstorm at night, and I couldn't see the terrain, so I had to follow the gray ribbon of river below." In the days before satellite weather imaging, the man had given him bad advice.

"All my options were evaporating as fast as I could fly."

Rose had several friends, fellow pilots, who perished in similar flying conditions. *There must be a way out*, he thought. *I don't want to die at twenty-two. I won't get to experience marriage ...*

He had been flying on empty for thirty minutes. Then the engine started missing. "I was just waiting for silence and to have to crash at night."

His mind turned to his very last option—God. Rose had never prayed before, but in desperation, he lifted up a silent prayer. *If there is a God, I need Your help now.*

Then a voice spoke to him that was crystal clear. *Son, you said the right thing.* After he heard the voice, Rose also experienced the sensation of "a light bulb" that came on in his mind.

Immediately after his prayer, the plane popped out of the snowstorm! "Before me were the beautiful lights of Kotzebue—it might as well have been the lights of heaven," he recalls.

There was only one problem—he still had to fly another twenty miles over the Kotzebue Sound, a broad expanse of saltwater north of the Bering Sea.

"That was a breath-holder," he says. When he landed safely at Kotzebue Airport, his humanist worldview collapsed. There was no earthly reason his plane should have traveled such a distance with no fuel.

Rose believes God added an hour of fuel to his tanks to save his life. "When I landed, I was a different boy. I was not a Christian, but I was a believer in God."

He thought about his grandmother, the only Christian in his family. *So, gramma was right; there is something out there,* he thought.

Rose started to date a Christian woman who challenged him to read the Bible for the first time. As he read the pages of Scripture, something surprising happened. "I fell in love with the God of the Bible—his reasonableness, his forgiveness, his justice," he recounts.

But his stubborn heart was still not ready to make Jesus his Savior and Lord.

Then he had another brush with death in a helicopter that crashed, which completely flattened the seat he rode in.

About the same time, he missed a flight with some of the lead contractors for the Alaskan pipeline due to a schedule conflict. Shortly after the plane took off, it crashed, killing everyone aboard.

Later, on a flight to Fairbanks on a bush aircraft, he began to reflect on his life. *I'm not happy. This whole thing is not working*, he admitted to himself. *Everything I read in the Bible is either a lie or it's true. It's all or nothing. From reading the Bible, I understand God is my creator. If Jesus can raise someone from the dead and forgive my sins, that's exactly what God has for me.*

At that moment, Rose surrendered his life to Jesus Christ as his Savior and Lord. "When I landed in Fairbanks, I was a different boy, once again."

Chapter 40

Emma's Guardian Angels

She was bathed in prayer from the time she was in the womb. Her parents and both sets of grandparents are strong Christians. Still, when she began to point at angels and talk about them to her parents, they weren't quite sure what to think.

It started about a year ago, when she first began to talk. "Every morning when I would get her up, she would point up at the ceiling and say, 'Look momma, there's angels up there,'" says Caitlyn Sukut, her mother. "I thought, 'How cute, how sweet.'" Emma seemed to be seeing things she could not see.

"Is she imaging something?" Caitlyn wondered. "It's hard to know what a two-and-a-half-year-old is talking about," she admits. "I don't know how much is in her imagination and how much she's really seeing."

After naps, Emma would talk about the angels. "What does the angel look like?" Caitlyn asked. "She looks like auntie," Emma replied, referring to Caitlyn's sixteen-year-old sister, Hannah.

Several months ago, they had their first airline flight with Emma. "Look at the angels, momma," Emma said. "They are coming with us to help get us there and to protect us."

"When Emma first started talking about this, I had not taught her about angels," Caitlyn notes. "I never told her angels protect us."

Several weeks ago, Caitlyn went into Emma's room when she first awakened. "How did you sleep, Emma?"

"I slept great," she said. "The angels and the man came," Emma replied.

"Oh, what did they say?" Mom asked.

"The man protects us and loves us," Emma said. "The man's coming, Momma. The man's coming soon."

"Does the man look like Jesus?" Caitlyn asked.

"No," Emma replied.

Emma has seen paintings of Jesus at church, but Caitlyn isn't sure if Emma would confuse the person she saw in her room with the various artistic representations of Jesus. "We don't refer to people as 'the man' in our house," Caitlyn noted, so her choice of words seemed curious.

Once when mom and daughter walked into church, Emma cried out, "Look at all the angels singing to Jesus!"

"Where?" Caitlyn asked. Emma pointed up at the choir, dressed in long, flowing robes.

For a while, Emma seemed to be obsessed with angels and wanted to talk about them all the time. But as she gets closer to three years old, she is mentioning them less.

Caitlyn's grandmother, Lisa Hartman, has spent lots of time with Emma. "I asked her if there was an angel by me," Lisa says. Without hesitation, Emma got very serious and looked around her grandma. Then Emma walked behind her. She pointed and said, "Yes. Don't you see it?"

Lisa, who sometimes gets nervous on airplanes, was consoled by Emma before one of her flights. "There's angels on the airplane," she told her grandmother.

"It was so comforting to me," Lisa notes. "It was a fact to Emma. No one asked her if there were angels on the plane. She just offered it."

Lisa also noted that Emma sees angels around places that might be dangerous to small children, such as stairways, escalators, and even playgrounds.

"It's not surprising that little ones without the theology or teaching are able to see things," says Ron Sukut, Emma's grandfather. Sukut is the lead pastor at Cornerstone Community Church in San Clemente, California. "When God really starts to move in, angels start to show up," he notes. "The only way to get our attention may be for God to reveal Himself to a child who can't fabricate these things."

When Pastor Ron considers Emma's special sensitivity to the spiritual realm, he thinks about Matthew 18:10, KJV, "That in heaven, their angels do always behold the face of my Father which is in heaven."

CHAPTER 41

Muslim Struggled with Life-Threatening Shingles

He had the worst case of shingles in the history of Toronto General Hospital, and doctors prepared him for the worst. Raised a devout Muslim, he was stunned by an encounter in his hospital room with an unexpected visitor.

"My skin was burning as if someone had doused it with gasoline and then threw a match on it," says Dr. Nasir Saddiki. "I felt like I was on fire from my inside."

In a sterile room, on the eighth floor of the hospital, his doctor informed him, "The blisters are multiplying so fast I can literally watch them grow. Your body has stopped fighting back."

The next day, he contracted chicken pox and doctors placed him in strict isolation. His temperature soared to 107.6 degrees—a life-threatening level high enough to leave his brain permanently damaged.

For days, he continued to deteriorate. "My nerve endings became so inflamed that even a single hair drifting across my skin sent shock waves of fire rippling through my body," he says.

At thirty-four, Dr. Saddiki had already earned his first million dollars, but he wasn't prepared to handle his own mortality. "In facing death, I felt nothing but weakness and outright terror. I didn't have the slightest idea what might await me on the other side. I had been raised as a devout Moslem, and I had been taught that Allah was a god who did not heal sickness. I thought that my only hope was in medicine."

As Dr. Saddiki slipped close to death, he became listless and unresponsive, yet he could hear his doctors' conversations. "His immune system has simply shut down," one of them said.

"He's dying," he heard another doctor say. "His immune system must be compromised by AIDS."

I don't have AIDS, Dr. Saddiki wanted to say, but was unable to speak. The full weight of their remarks hit him like a sledgehammer.

If they have given up hope, where does that leave me? he thought.

Doctors delivered the bad news to his business partner. "In a few hours, he'll be dead," they informed him. "If by some miracle he lives, he'll be blind in his right eye, deaf in his right ear, paralyzed on his right side, and severely brain damaged." Then they walked out of the room, leaving him alone.

"I suddenly felt like a drowning man going down for the third time," Dr. Saddiki says. "Gathering what little strength I still had, I was barely able to whisper, 'God, if you are real, do not let me die.'"

Then in the middle of the night, something remarkable happened. He awoke suddenly to find a man standing at the foot of his bed. "I was shocked because rays of light emanated from him, which allowed me to see his body in my pitch-black room."

But one part of the man's body he could not view. "Amazingly, I was unable to see His face. It was too bright to look at it without hurting my eyes."

Even as a Muslim, he had an "inner knowing" that the one who stood there was Jesus Christ.

Dr. Saddiki felt no fear, only profound serenity in the presence of the one called the Prince of Peace. Although he couldn't speak, he wondered why Jesus would come to a Muslim when everyone else had left him to die.

He didn't hear an audible voice from Jesus, but these words came into his mind: *I am the God of the Christians. I am the God of Abraham, Isaac, and Jacob.*

"That is all He told me. As suddenly as He had appeared and woke me up, He disappeared."

The next morning, Dr. Saddiki's doctors returned to examine him. "The blisters have stopped growing," one physician almost shouted with amazement. Since he seemed more alert, they said, "We don't know why but your shingles have gone into remission."

The following day, still in severe pain and covered with blisters, Dr. Saddiki was discharged from the hospital with a suitcase full of drugs. "Don't leave your home," they cautioned. "It will be months before your blisters disappear, and when they do, you will be left with white patches of skin and severe scarring all over your body. The pain that you are experiencing can last for years."

"I looked like a cross between a leper and the Elephant Man," Dr. Saddiki recalls. "When people saw me, they literally fled to the other side of the street because I scared them so much. However, I wasn't concerned about my appearance because I couldn't stop thinking about Jesus' appearance. I was certain that His presence in my hospital room had stopped the shingles virus."

As a result of his unusual encounter with Jesus, questions swirled through his mind. "I knew very little about Jesus. I still had a consuming question in my mind. *Is Jesus the Son of God as Christians claim or is He just a prophet as Muslims are taught?*"

His first night home, he continued to suffer. "In spite of my medication, the pain and itching was so horrible, I almost had to tie my hands to a chair to keep from scratching myself to death." Mercifully, he drifted into a deep sleep.

The next morning, he woke up early and turned on the television. "While flipping through the channels, I froze when I saw the following words on the screen: 'Is Jesus the Son of God?' I watched captivated as two men spent the entire program discussing this topic, and in the process, answering all of my questions."

Before the program ended, one of the men led the television audience in a prayer. "My body was aflame with pain, but I knelt on my living floor anyway." As tears streamed down his face, he repeated the prayer and invited Jesus into his heart.

Immediately, the Holy Spirit brought a voracious spiritual hunger that caused him to want to know more about Jesus.

Despite his doctor's orders to stay inside, he went out and bought a Bible.

He devoured the books of Matthew, Mark, Luke, and John. "I still felt spiritually ravenous, so I then started in Genesis and read through the entire Bible during my sleepless nights."

His business partner, who happened to be a Christian, brought Dr. Saddiki books and teaching tapes, which further explained the Gospel to him.

As his faith began to grow, his prayers got bolder. "I dug out a picture of how I looked before I was attacked with shingles. I prayed and asked God to make me look that way again."

A few days later, something amazing happened. Dr. Saddiki awakened to find his pillow covered with blisters that had fallen off his face. "I crawled out of bed and stepped into the shower. What started on my pillow was finished in the shower."

"Every blister fell off my body!" he exclaims. "Instead of being covered with patches of white and scar tissue, my skin turned red. It then slowly healed, returning to its pre-shingles condition. When that occurred, I not only looked human, I actually looked like I did before I became ill, except for the scars that I still have on my chest."

Amazingly, none of the doctor's dire predictions came true. "My eyesight is now 20/20. My hearing is normal. My speech is unimpaired, and I suffered absolutely no brain damage at all."

"My healing was totally miraculous, swift, and complete. I never suffered from lingering pain or, in fact, any other complication. I had the most miraculous recovery the Toronto General Hospital has ever experienced."

Jesus showed up in a hospital room of a dying Muslim and brought healing. "But that wasn't the greatest miracle that He performed," Dr. Saddiki notes. "The transformation that occurred in my heart was even more dramatic than the one that occurred in my body."

From that day forward, Dr. Saddiki's passion has been to know and serve the Lord Jesus Christ.

CHAPTER 42

Raised by Gay Parents, He Shocked Them by Coming Out as a Christian

When he was two years old, his university-professor parents divorced, and his father and mother entered the gay lifestyle. His lesbian mom and her partner took him to gay pride parades, LGBT clubs, parties, and campouts, while his father remained "closeted" for several years.

"Mom was a political activist," says Caleb Kaltenbach, author of *Messy Grace* (Waterbrook Press). At gay pride parades, Caleb witnessed Christian demonstrators spray homosexual marchers with water and urine.

When he asked his mom why they were doing this, she said: "Because Christians hate gay people."

As a result, Caleb wanted nothing to do with Christianity or God.

In high school, a friend invited him to a Bible study, and he accepted with ulterior motives. "I thought I would pretend to be a Christian, learn about Christianity, and dismantle their arguments," he recalls.

He had attended a mainline denominational church with his father sporadically but was bored by it and didn't understand the liturgy. "They never discussed God, only social issues," he notes.

So, when he grabbed a Bible off his dad's shelf and went to the Bible study, he didn't realize there was a difference between the Old and New Testaments. Confused when they asked him to read a verse from 1st Corinthians, he began reading from 1st Chronicles.

"I was so embarrassed, but I wouldn't let these Christians get me down," Caleb says. He had lumped this group of believers in with the angry demonstrators he saw in the street.

But something amazing happened when he began to read the Bible for himself. "I really fell in love with Jesus," he recalls. "I learned that Jesus is really not like the Christians I saw on the street corners."

Later, he met a Christian friend at a restaurant and asked, "What do you have to do to be saved?"

As his friend, Gregg, waxed on about the realities of Jesus and His divinity, something stirred within Caleb.

"As Gregg was talking, it happened," he writes in his book. "I can't explain it. Something just shifted inside me. I truly believed what he was saying. There was no way around it—in that moment I became a follower of Jesus."

Baptized "covertly" almost immediately after he was born again, his dad grounded him after absorbing the shocking news. His lesbian mom and her partner were horrified when they learned and accused him of the ultimate betrayal—siding with bigots.

The next week, Caleb attended a Christ in Youth conference in southern Missouri. While there, he felt God's call to become a pastor and confessed before everyone he wanted to be a preacher.

Soon, he was attending Ozark Christian College and later, Talbot Seminary in La Mirada, California. In Southern California, he served on the staff at Shepherd of the Hills Church for eleven years.

After graduation, he accepted a call as senior pastor of a church in Dallas. Then something remarkable happened, both his parents independently made decisions to move to Dallas and began attending his church.

"What was even more incredible was that, as time went on, some church members were nicer to my parents than I was," he notes. As the church loved his gay parents without judgment, their hearts began to soften.

After three years of serving in Dallas, he felt called to move back to Southern California to lead Discovery Church in Simi Valley. "Two weeks before we left Dallas, both of my parents gave their lives to the Lord!"

"I was floored ... how did this happen? To this day, I'm still not sure. I do believe my parents are saved."

In Caleb and his family's remarkable journey of transformation, he has developed some unique perspectives because of his upbringing.

"I believe any expression of sexuality outside of heterosexual marriage is sinful," he says, "but I don't believe God called me to make gay people straight."

While Caleb holds to traditional doctrinal views, his ministry style is very open and accepting. "I completely concur that God designed sexuality to be between a man and a woman, but that's not the first thing I talk about with somebody that's gay," he continues. "I want to get to know them as a person, to build a friendship."

"I want to help them see Christ as their main identity. When they see Christ as their main identity, there is margin for discussion of holy living."

At his church in Simi Valley, he says, "We want to be a place where you can belong before you believe."

Chapter 43

Explosion and Fire Burned 95% of His Body

Billy Jack McDaniel knew the risks of work on drilling rigs. Injuries and death in the oil field are common, mostly due to human error. But when a pressure seal on his rig failed, which allowed natural gas to escape, he came face-to-face with eternity in a horrific explosion and fire.

"It didn't take much to ignite," recalls McDaniel, who found himself 150 feet high on a maintenance platform when the rig exploded. "I watched the fire. It came and got me. There was nowhere to go, nowhere to run."

His body ignited like a marshmallow too close to an open flame. But this was no Boy Scout campfire. McDaniel found himself seared by 2,000-degree temperatures. Usually, people's eyes melt at 1,200 degrees.

"The pain was intense, but there was no escaping it," he says. "It was constant, like hell."

As he watched his clothes quickly burn away, his skin bubble, and a sensitive body part catch fire "like a candle," he panicked. "I wanted to fall and die when the fire went out. I welcomed death."

From McDaniel's training as a volunteer firefighter, he knew what awaited such a severe burn. He knew he would stop breathing at any moment. He realized he was at death's doorstep. McDaniel contemplated throwing himself off the platform in a suicide dive.

As soon as the fire went out, driller Billy Humble clambered up a metal ladder to the platform, shooting past multiple rungs at a time to reach his friend and co-worker.

When McDaniel saw him, he was able to moan, "Promise me you'll take care of my wife and child."

Billy Humble nodded and said, "Yes, I will."

McDaniel was surprised when Humble suggested they pray, because Humble was not a church-going man.

A basket was raised up to the platform, and McDaniel was able to crawl into it by himself. "Nobody could touch me," he notes. "If they tried to touch me, skin and meat would have pulled off."

Most of his skin was burned off. Bone was exposed on his fingers, arms, chin, and jaw.

When the basket reached the ground, onlookers were stunned when McDaniel raised himself up and walked out. "My body was pouring fluid, so I was thirsty. I started to go to the drilling house to get a drink of water."

"Stop! Lay down!" someone shouted. He sat down in the dirt, and then he was placed on a gurney made from chicken wire.

When the ambulance arrived, people were again shocked when McDaniel stood up, stepped over to the vehicle, and laid himself down inside.

"I need you to call a few people," he told the nurse. He finally passed out when the ambulance hit a speed bump at the entry to the hospital.

After the explosion, rig manager Bob Quick went to the McDaniel home to inform Aleta, Billy Jack's wife. "You think about that knock on the door or call in the middle of the night," Aleta says. "But God had been preparing me for that exact moment for two years."

Aleta says God gave her a series of dreams that featured the dreaded knock. "Bob would be standing at my door in the middle of the night and say something happened to Jack," she says.

Due to her dreams, she felt more prepared to handle the shock. When Aleta arrived at LSU Health Sciences Center in Shreveport, she was informed by Dr. Kevin Sittig, director of the regional burn center, that there was a low probability of survival for her husband.

"Do you believe in God?" she asked Dr. Sittig.

"Yes, I do," Dr. Sittig replied.

"Do you believe He still performs miracles?"

"I do," he said.

"God and I had a conversation on the way here," Aleta told the doctor. "He told me He will deliver my husband alive. I'm not going to take anything less than one hundred percent," she said with assurance.

"I'll be praying right along with you. I'm not trying to be the bearer of bad news here. I'm just trying to give you a realistic picture of the challenges ahead. There is a greater medical probability he will not survive," Dr. Sittig said.

"However, if God wants him to live, he will live. If God wants him to die, he will die," he added.

Dr. Sittig was raised Catholic and spent twelve years in parochial school. He remains actively involved in his church. "When I get burns of this magnitude, the first place I go is right around the corner from the burn unit—the chapel," he notes. "I spend a great deal of time in that chapel."

"I'm not able to make a decision on who will live and who will die," Dr. Sittig says. "That's why I put it in the Lord's hands. I'm one of the Lord's tools."

There were no available beds in the ICU burn unit, so McDaniel was left in the hall near the nurse's station for seventy-two hours. "They thought he would die," Aleta maintains. "They thought it was a waste of time."

Dr. Sittig has a slightly different recollection of the initial prognosis. "I don't recall saying there is no way Billy Jack will survive," he says. "I will venture to say, that probably, the vast majority of burn units would calculate his mortality rate and would give him comfort care only."

"Parts of his body were so badly burned, that to a lay person, anybody would say there is no way in hell this man will survive."

When McDaniel confounded expectations and continued to live, he had the first of 115 surgeries and 80 blood transfusions.

McDaniel woke up in ICU two weeks after the accident, when he came out of an induced coma. He panicked because the room was dimly lit, and his eyes had been sewn shut. "When you wake up and you can't open your eyes, it scares you to death," he says.

He takes comfort knowing the Apostle Paul was once blinded, and when Paul and others in the Bible emerged from darkness, they were refined.

Before the accident, McDaniel was a "run-of-the-mill" Christian who attended church but lacked passion for God. Now, as he awakened from the coma after two weeks, he had a heart-to-heart with God.

"I can't do this," he told God. "I'm ready to die."

You don't have to ... If you let Me, I will carry you, God impressed on his heart.

When McDaniel first saw himself in the mirror, it was startling. "I saw a monster," he recalls. "There was nothing to identify myself. There was nothing of me there."

His six-year-old came to visit a week later. "Daddy, you still look real good," she said. "You can't quit, Daddy."

Initially, McDaniel's family was told he could be in the hospital as long as three years. But he walked out after four months and seventeen days, carrying eighty pounds on his six-foot, one-inch frame. Before the accident, he weighed 240.

"There may be one person a year burned over seventy-five percent of their body and lives," McDaniel notes. "There may be one person in a lifetime burned over ninety-five percent of their body and lives. But there is only one in the history of the world burned ninety-five percent who still has functionality. I am the one."

Today, McDaniel is often invited to conferences featuring burn specialists. "I'm a spectacle for the burn doctors. They can't explain why I lived," he adds.

His eyes should have melted at 1,200 degrees, but they're perfect, as clear as crystal. The inside of his nose, mouth, and lungs were not burned. His heart, liver, and kidneys never gave out. Even though his scalp was removed and re-grafted thirteen times, his hair is thicker now than it was before the accident. His ears fell off in the hospital, but they are growing back.

"Today I was on my tractor. I can hunt and fish and make love to my wife," he says. "I live my life just like everybody."

When McDaniel considers that aluminum melted on the drilling rig in an area above his position on the platform, he has only one answer. "There is no medical or scientific explanation. It was a miracle. That's the only thing it can be."

After he first got home from the hospital, McDaniel had a rough bout with suicidal despair. "My hell didn't start until I got home, because there is no help," he recalls. "I could do nothing. There was nothing to wake up for. I was junk."

One day, three months after his homecoming, he passed through a deep, dark valley. "I was waiting for my wife to leave so I could kill myself," he recounts. Even though he was slowly improving, he couldn't see the progress himself. Despondent, he picked up his Bible, and it fell open to Luke, chapter twenty-three, which tells about the crucifixion of Jesus.

"When Jesus was on the cross, He felt everyone's pain, sorrow, and sin at one time. He did it as a man. He didn't do it as God."

McDaniel had a startling realization. *Just my pain would have killed Him*, he thought. *If Jesus could take it as a man, then I need to shut up, get up, and get going.*

"Living with scars is hard," he says. "If I go into Wal-Mart, I get stares. If I go out to eat, little kids get scared."

But when Jesus first appeared to the disciples after his resurrection, they, too, were frightened. He showed them the scars on His hands and feet to prove He was alive.

"I use my scars to prove what Jesus has done for me."

CHAPTER 44

Muslim Husband Locked Christian Wife Out of the House

After a West African woman began to follow Jesus, her Muslim husband often beat her because of her newfound faith. Steadfastly, she maintained her quiet witness as she served him, all the while praying to God for his salvation.

It seems the woman wanted to attend a week-long church meeting away from home, according to her testimony, given to the mission organization, SIM. She meekly asked her husband if she could attend. Predictably, the man exploded in anger. "Her husband was livid. A whole week? Who would cook his food? Clean his house?" she recounted.

He told her she should focus on Islam and forget the Christian church. He beat her harshly once again.

In spite of her husband's violent response, she felt God's leading to attend this meeting, which would nurture her growth and provide needed fellowship with other women.

The man was so upset after she left, he locked up the house and declared to the neighbors that his wife would never enter his home again. To add a dramatic emphasis to his point, he threw her house key (hidden near the front door) into the river as he headed to his girlfriend's house for the week.

The woman stopped by the local market on her way home from the conference. "She planned to have a hearty meal ready for her husband when he came home from Friday prayers. She had no idea that her husband had already locked her out of her home for good," according to SIM.

After she got home, she thought it was strange that the house was locked up tightly. She wanted to start preparing the meal for her husband, so she borrowed a pot from her neighbor and began to clean the fish she had just bought.

"When she cut open the fish, a key fell out of its belly. Puzzled, she examined it and remarked to her neighbor that the key looked similar to her own house key. Her neighbor urged her to try it in the lock, and it worked! She opened the house, cleaned it, and got her husband's supper ready to wait for him," according to SIM.

As her husband walked home from the mosque, he was shocked when he recognized his house had been opened and a fire was burning in the outdoor kitchen.

Now he was really angry, thinking perhaps a neighbor had helped his wife bust open the door or break the lock. But when he examined the door and the lock, nothing seemed amiss.

"When he demanded to know how she got back into their house, she told him the strange story of the key in the fish's belly. Stunned, he didn't say another word."

The following night, he told his wife he wanted to attend church with her the next morning.

After the Sunday morning church service, the man asked if he could speak with the pastor privately. He told him the remarkable story about the house key and said, "I want to serve the God of the Christians. He is the One who knows and has power to do what no one else can."

The man surrendered his life to Jesus Christ as his Lord and Savior and was born again!

God faithfully answered the woman's prayers for her husband to turn from his sins and follow Christ.

"In his gospel, Matthew tells of a fish caught with a coin in its mouth for taxes (Matthew 17:27). In West Africa in 2018, a house key in a fish's belly became a key to the kingdom for an abusive husband."

"Our Lord is still a fisher of men."

CHAPTER 45

Identical Twin Studies Prove Homosexuality Is Not Genetic

Eight major studies of identical twins in Australia, the U.S., and Scandinavia during the last two decades all arrive at the same conclusion: gays were not born that way.

"At best genetics is a minor factor," says Dr. Neil Whitehead, PhD. Whitehead worked for the New Zealand government as a scientific researcher for twenty-four years, then spent four years working for the United Nations and International Atomic Energy Agency. Most recently, he serves as a consultant to Japanese universities about the effects of radiation exposure. His PhD is in biochemistry and statistics.

Identical twins have the same genes or DNA. They are nurtured in equal prenatal conditions. If homosexuality is caused by genetics or prenatal conditions and one twin is gay, the co-twin should also be gay.

"Because they have identical DNA, it ought to be 100%," Dr. Whitehead notes. But the studies reveal something else. "If an identical twin has same-sex attraction, the chances the co-twin has it are only about 11% for men and 14% for women."

Because identical twins are always genetically identical, homosexuality cannot be genetically dictated. "No one is born gay," he notes. "The predominant things that create homosexuality in one identical twin and not in the other have to be post-birth factors."

Dr. Whitehead believes same-sex attraction (SSA) is caused by "non-shared factors," things happening to one twin but not the other, or a personal response to an event by one of the twins and not the other.

For example, one twin might have exposure to pornography or sexual abuse, but not the other. One twin may interpret and respond to their family or classroom environment differently than the other. "These individual and idiosyncratic responses to random events and to common environmental factors predominate," he says.

The first very large, reliable study of identical twins was conducted in Australia in 1991, followed by a large U.S. study around 1997. Then Australia and the U.S. conducted more twin studies in 2000, followed by several studies in Scandinavia, according to Dr. Whitehead.

"Twin registers are the foundation of modern twin studies. They are now very large and exist in many countries. A gigantic European twin register with a projected 600,000 members is being organized, but one of the largest in use is in Australia, with more than 25,000 twins on the books."

A significant twin study among adolescents shows an even weaker genetic correlation. In 2002, Bearman and Brueckner studied tens of thousands of adolescent students in the U.S. The same-sex attraction concordance between identical twins was only 7.7% for males and 5.3% for females—lower than the 11% and 14% in the Australian study by Bailey et al conducted in 2000.

In the identical twin studies, Dr. Whitehead has been struck by how fluid and changeable sexual identity can be.

"Neutral academic surveys show there is substantial change. About half of the homosexual/bisexual population (in a non-therapeutic environment) moves towards heterosexuality over a lifetime. About 3% of the present heterosexual population once firmly believed themselves to be homosexual or bisexual."

"Sexual orientation is not set in concrete," he notes.

Even more remarkable, most of the changes occur without counseling or therapy. "These changes are not therapeutically induced, but happen 'naturally' in life, some very quickly," Dr. Whitehead observes. "Most changes in sexual orientation are towards exclusive heterosexuality."

Numbers of people who have changed towards exclusive heterosexuality are greater than current numbers of bisexuals and homosexuals combined. In other words, ex-gays outnumber actual gays.

The fluidity is even more pronounced among adolescents, as Bearman and Brueckner's study demonstrated. "They found that from sixteen to seventeen years old, if a person had a romantic attraction to the same sex, almost all had switched one year later."

"The authors were pro-gay, and they commented that the only stability was among the heterosexuals, who stayed the same year after year. Adolescents are a special case—generally changing their attractions from year to year."

Still, many misconceptions persist in the popular culture. Namely, that homosexuality is genetic—so hardwired into one's identity that it can't be changed. "The academics who work in the field are not happy with the portrayals by the media on the subject," Dr. Whitehead notes. "But they prefer to stick with their academic research and not get involved in the activist side."

Even though same-sex attraction is not genetic, Dr. Whitehead disagrees with those who contend that homosexuals "choose" their orientation. "There can be little informed, responsible choice involved if first attraction is about age ten," he notes. "At that age, no one chooses lifetime sexual orientation or lifestyle in any usual sense. SSA is discovered to exist in oneself rather than chosen."

CHAPTER 46

What Book Was Actor Steve McQueen Holding When He Left Us?

Hollywood icon Steve McQueen, who accepted Christ only a few months before he was diagnosed with an aggressive cancer that proved fatal, died clutching a book close to his chest, according to Greg Laurie's book about the actor.

Laurie released his book, *Steve McQueen: The Salvation of an American Icon*, in 2017.

Laurie offers an in-depth description of McQueen's spiritual journey to Christ in the last months of his life. The book was co-written with Marshall Terrill, who has written five other books on McQueen, according to the Christian Post (CP).

By the late seventies, McQueen's career was fading. He moved from Malibu to Santa Paula, California, and married his third wife, Barbara Minty, in January 1980. For a period, they lived in an airport hangar filled with his motorcycle collection.

He also bought a yellow biplane and took flying lessons from a cantankerous man in his sixties, Sammy Mason.

The two became close friends. McQueen sensed there was something different about Mason and one day asked him directly about his "secret." Mason told him he was a follower of Jesus Christ.

Because McQueen had such respect for Mason, he began to attend his church, Ventura Missionary Church. McQueen mostly sat unobtrusively in the balcony and kept to himself.

After about three months, he finally introduced himself to Pastor Leonard DeWitt and asked to meet him for lunch.

At the lunch meeting, McQueen peppered the minister with spiritual questions.

McQueen wanted to know if the Bible could be trusted. He wanted to know if all his sins could be forgiven. He wanted to know what being a Christian looked like, Laurie recounts in the book. "I think McQueen was trying to wrap his mind around it."

At the end of the meeting, DeWitt asked McQueen if he had accepted Christ as his Lord and Savior. He told DeWitt that one morning, when the pastor had given the invitation, he felt convicted by the Spirit and came forward. "When you invited people to pray with you to receive Christ, I prayed. So yes, I'm a born-again Christian."

McQueen was beginning to grow in his faith when he got the horrible news that he had mesothelioma. He received the news a few days before Christmas, 1979. Some 80% of mesothelioma cases result from asbestos exposure, which may have happened to McQueen when he served with the U.S. Marines as a younger man.

"He blew up a can of beans, and they punished him by making him strip the asbestos off the pipes of a ship," Barbara Minty told attorney Roger Worthington. "That was in the late 1940s. Steve did not talk about it much, but I have a tape recording in which he was asked just before he died what caused his mesothelioma. He said: 'asbestos.'"

He was also an avid race-car driver, and asbestos was also used as an insulating material in racing suits.

McQueen wasn't offered surgery or chemotherapy because doctors at Cedars-Sinai in Los Angeles felt the cancer was too advanced. They told McQueen he had only a few months to live. While the disease started in his lungs, it eventually spread to his abdomen, kidney, and pelvis.

Because doctors in the U.S. could offer no treatment or hope, he sought alternative cancer treatments in Mexico. At the same time, it was clear that he was taking his commitment to Christ seriously.

"Now that he had become a believer, one of the first things he does when he arrives in Mexico at a center where he was going to receive some of these treatments is he starts talking to the lady (Teena Valentino) about his faith in Christ. I thought that was very interesting that he was initiating conversations with people about it," Laurie told CP.

"He had organized a time to feed a lot of the other cancer patients there in the clinic. He wanted to join them. It was a little food that they weren't supposed to eat but he was sort of treating them. He wanted to go spend some time with them, but he wasn't able to do it because he was feeling so sick," Laurie noted. "So, he made a recording that he played for them. In that recording, he prays for them, and he talks about his faith in Christ."

When it was evident his days were numbered, he asked to meet with Billy Graham, one of the most prominent Christian leaders in the country at that time.

According to the book, Graham met with McQueen at least twice during McQueen's final days—once at McQueen's ranch in Santa Paula and before McQueen flew to Mexico for surgery in November 1980.

"I know they had a lengthy meeting where they talked in depth about a lot of things in Steve's life," Laurie told CP. "Billy was really impacted by Steve and felt his conversion was genuine because all Steve wanted to talk about was his faith."

"The ninety-page New Testament Bible that evangelist Billy Graham gave to Steve days before his passing became Steve's proudest possession and was on his chest when he died," according to Steve McQueen's widow Barbara Minty.

McQueen had misplaced his Bible, so Graham personally inscribed his personal Bible and offered it to the dying actor. He stayed by McQueen's side and prayed with him until they reached the airport, then said goodbye as McQueen flew off to Mexico.

McQueen never survived the operation. Four days after the meeting with Graham, he died of a heart attack with the evangelist's Bible resting on his chest. According to the book, McQueen's son, Chad, went to the hospital around 6:00 a.m. that morning and found his father's eyes open, with his hands clutching the Bible that Graham had given him.

"He was holding onto that Bible, and I think he probably was praying," Laurie told CP. "He could tell that his condition was worsening. No one was with him in those final moments of his life in that room because when they came in, he had already died. He probably saw that Bible, or maybe he was already holding and reading it and just held onto it. There it was under the sheet, as I am told. They pulled the sheet back and found the Bible."

Some have reported that McQueen's Bible was opened to John 3:16. However, Laurie told CP that in researching the book, neither he nor Terrill could prove the John 3:16 claim. Multiple sources, however, confirmed he was holding the Bible.

In one of McQueen's last meetings with Pastor DeWitt, he said, "My only regret in life was that I was not able to tell others about what Jesus Christ did for me."

That may be remedied with Laurie's book. He is also making a documentary on McQueen's salvation that will be released soon. The film will be shown at 1,000 theaters in the U.S. for one night only and will also be available on iTunes and other media.

CHAPTER 47

The Day Jesus Invaded a Buddhist Monastery in the Himalayas

Tyler Connell, with the Ekballo Project, is currently in the Himalayan Mountains in one of the most unreached places of the world distributing Bibles, praying for the sick, and preaching the Good News.

"We hope to get a Bible in every home and every village in the next two years," Tyler noted in a recent blog post. "It's exciting to be a small part in changing history in Nepal with God!"

The Ekballo Project uses film as a mobilizing spark on college campuses and churches to send believers into the unreached, unengaged regions of the world.

A month ago, Tyler and his team trekked to a village called Jhong, one of the highest villages in the Tibetan region of Nepal.

"We arrived desperate to hear where the Spirit was wanting us to walk," he recounted. They split into groups of four and prayed for the Holy Spirit to direct their paths.

Tyler's group felt led to walk to the highest point of the village where they observed ancient ruins protruding above them.

At the moment they reached the promontory, a monk appeared, smiling as he approached them. "Hi, I'm Jems," he said in perfect English. "We've been watching you guys; it is rare for anyone foreign to come to our village. Would you like to come inside our monastery?"

Tyler and his teammates looked at each other with wonderment and smiled, sensing it was a God-moment.

They entered the monastery and were met by men and boys of all ages, studying under "the llama of the mountain." They met the llama and proceeded to continue to converse with their new friend, Jems, who studied under the Dalai Lama in Dharmsala, India and learned English there.

"We are followers of Jesus, the man and God greater than any other god," Tyler told the monk.

"Oh, I once heard of Jesus in India, but wasn't able to do any reading on who He was," the man replied.

"Can we introduce you to Him through the power of the Holy Spirit and the presence of Jesus?" one asked.

"He said yes and put out his hands," Tyler recounts, "and suddenly the power and peace of God descended, his eyes got big, he began to take steps back, and began to laugh and shake his head in disbelief."

"He told us he'd never felt a peace or power like this. We proceeded to give him the Gospel and a Bible, and he then INSISTED we come back in the morning to meet his other monk friends."

Twelve hours later, Tyler and his team returned. This time, Jems was coming down the mountain as they were ascending. He said he wasn't able to spend time with them because he had errands to run, but he invited them to meet with the other monks.

They entered the monastery again and were met by a monk in his late twenties. "He invited us into the idol room, the 'holy of holies' for the monastery.

"It was dark, dank, heavy, and strange, perfect ingredients for the lightning of the Gospel to break into!" Tyler recounts.

As they sat down, one of the teammates received a word that someone was injured in the monastery.

"Was anyone injured in the earthquake?" they asked.

The man's eyes widened. "Yes, I myself was injured, and my back is in pain!" he replied.

They asked if they could pray right there in the name of Jesus for healing, and the monk agreed.

As they began to pray, a "sweet, heavy glory filled the idol room."

The man had the same experience as Jems. "I feel a peace and a power like never before!" the monk exclaimed. "It feels as though this major blessing has entered into me."

He tested his back and discovered he was completely healed, saying it felt like a "hot and icy sensation" covered his body.

The monk said he had heard of Jesus fifteen years ago, when a man came to his village and told stories about Jesus, but he couldn't read, so he didn't fully understand who Jesus was.

"Thankfully, we had a translator, and she explained the entire Gospel to him and gave him a Bible. He was grinning from ear to ear, and was so thankful, and told us he wanted to read more, and was going to pray and ask Jesus to reveal Himself to him. We were overjoyed at the kindness of Jesus. We handed out more Bibles to monks and joyfully skipped down the mountain remembering with gratitude the day Jesus invaded a Buddhist monastery!"

Chapter 48

Gay Hollywood Insider Experienced 'Change of Affection'

He grew up in a Christian family in Dallas, the youngest of eight children. At about nine years old, he began to experience same-sex attraction.

"I didn't know where it came from or what to make of it," says Becket Cook, author of A Change of Affection: *A Gay Man's Incredible Story of Redemption.* "It was an odd sensation. I knew I couldn't talk about this. It was a secret I held for many years."

Cook led a double life as a child, "where I pretended I was a normal kid, but on the inside, I was dealing with 'the love that dare not speak its name.'" He thought the feelings would eventually go away.

But, at a Jesuit all-boys school, he met another gay student, and they "came out" to each other. The two teens began exploring the gay culture of Dallas, visiting gay bars.

"It was quite eye-opening. We walked into the Starck Club designed by the famous French designer Philippe Starck. There were straight people, gay people, drag queens, all these different people."

Wow, these are my people, I feel at home for the first time, he thought.

In college, he continued to explore gay culture with another close friend and confidante. God was far removed from his thoughts.

"Even though I was raised in the Catholic Church, God was not an option. The older I got, homosexuality became my identity. Christians were the enemy."

I'm gay and I could never be a part of that club, he thought. *I'm not going to think about God or even consider God. That's off the table.*

After college, Cook went to Tokyo for a year to figure out what he wanted to do with his life. He fell in love for the first time and decided to stop hiding his secret.

When he told his parents he was gay, his mother began to cry. "Mom, it's not a big deal," he told her. "This is who I am. It's normal; it's fine."

"Are you angry about anything from your childhood?" his father wanted to know.

"No, dad, it's fine," he replied.

He says his mother got over the news quickly and both parents treated him with kindness. "My other siblings had their strong opinions but let me live my life."

Cook got accepted to law school, but two weeks before school was scheduled to begin, he abruptly changed his mind and decided to move to L.A. to pursue a career in acting and writing.

He found a like-minded group of friends, mostly from the East Coast that had attended Ivy League schools. "They were whip smart, hilarious, fun, very ambitious, we all just had the same goals, to make it big in Hollywood and find true love. As the years went by, all my friends were selling screenplays and making films that became huge films."

"That whole group of friends now run Hollywood," he says.

Cook was having the time of his life. While initially pursuing writing and acting, he fell into set design for fashion shoots. He attended movie premieres, the Oscars, the Emmys, the Golden Globes, the after-parties, and met many celebrities.

This is what life is about, he thought, *achieving things, and having these amazing experiences.*

He was satisfied with his dreamlike lifestyle for several years. "I went to Cabo San Lucas with Minnie Driver for her birthday. I was going to Nia Vardalos' house and having dinner with Tom Hanks and Meryl Streep. I went to Arianna Huffington's house for cocktails," he recalls.

In 2009, something strange happened at Fashion Week in Paris. Cook went to fashion designer Stella McCartney's after-party. "I was drinking champagne and everyone there was dancing and having the time of their lives," he recounts.

"I looked at them and felt this overwhelming sense of emptiness. *What is going on?* he wondered. *This can't be my life. I can't keep going to parties. This isn't doing it for me anymore.*

Cook quietly left the party without telling anyone. "I went back to my hotel, and I was up all night in a panic about the future. What is the meaning of my life? he asked himself.

"It was not like I hadn't thought about the meaning of life. I had read so many Russian novels and gone to so many plays in New York and London, by serious playwrights like Tom Stoppard, Eugene O'Neill, and Harold Pinter."

These guys are so smart; they will give me some answer to the meaning of life, he thought. "Every time I went to one of these plays, I would get so close to truth and then it would evaporate. I left the theater every time frustrated. I did that for years."

He went back to L.A. in a funk but got busy with work and tried to ignore his feelings of disquiet.

Six months later, Cook was at a coffee shop in Silver Lake with his best friend, also gay. He glanced over at the table next to them and noticed something akin to an extraterrestrial encounter—five young people with Bibles on their table.

"It was strange because I had never seen a Bible in L.A., ever. It was a sighting."

"We just thought it was so odd; we were intrigued. My friend urged me to turn around and talk to them. He liked to stir things up and engage in crazy conversations."

Cook pivoted and asked, "Are you guys, like Christians? What's the deal?"

Several said yes.

"What is your faith?" Cook asked. "I grew up Catholic ... What do you believe? I don't even remember what religion is. Tell me what you believe."

"We are evangelical Christians," one replied. "We go to this church in Hollywood called Reality L.A. This is what we believe, " and proceeded to share about Jesus.

Cook felt compelled to ask the $64 question. "What does your church think about being gay?"

"We believe it's a sin," one said.

"Whoa. OK ... interesting."

Because of his "moment" in Paris where he felt a profound emptiness, he listened to what they said respectfully, instead of erupting in anger, throwing his coffee at them, and leaving.

The Christians invited Cook and his friend to visit their church the following Sunday. "I had the whole week to process and decide if I was going to go ... I wasn't sure when I woke up on Sunday."

He got dressed that Sunday, September 20th, 2009, and began to drive toward the church. *Am I really doing this?* he wondered.

He found Reality L.A. and was surprised to discover it meeting in a public high school auditorium. He was used to stained glass, smoke, and bells.

Cook walked in, heard the worship music, and cringed. *I forgot that Christian music was a thing*, he thought, *Wait, it's not that bad.*

He found a seat by himself, unable to locate the people that invited him.

The pastor was preaching from Romans 7. "The more he preached, the more I was riveted to the sermon," he recounts. "Everything he said, every sentence, started to resonate with my mind and heart as true. Why?"

The pastor finished an hour-long message, then announced there would be an additional thirty minutes of worship music and invited people to come forward for prayer.

Should I go over there and ask someone to pray for me ... I don't know ... that's humiliating, he thought.

Cook finally felt compelled to go forward and told one of

the prayer volunteers: "I don't know what I believe but I'm here."

"Let me pray for you," the man said.

The prayer seemed intense and powerful to Cook. *How could this random stranger love me so much?* he wondered.

"His prayer was so full of love, it was crazy."

Cook went back to his seat and began to process the sermon, the prayer, and the music. Then something amazing happened.

"All of a sudden, the Holy Spirit flooded my mind and body. God in that moment revealed Himself to me. It was a road to Damascus moment."

The still small voice of the Lord impressed on his heart: *I am God and Jesus is My Son. Heaven is real. Hell is real. The Bible is true, and now you're adopted into My kingdom.*

Cook gasped for air, then started bawling, crying uncontrollably. "It was like Isaiah in the Temple when he sees God's holiness and comes undone. I had never cried that hard in my entire life. I don't think I cried that hard as an infant."

"I was crying over my sins. I also felt joy; I was overwhelmed that I had just met the king of the universe, Jesus. I was so overwhelmed by it."

Cook left the church and drove home. "I could hardly see; my eyes were so red," he recounts. "When I got home, I got into bed. I needed a nap; I was so freaked out."

Then the Holy Spirit fell on him again! "It was like Moses in the cleft of the rock. God said, *Here, let me show you a little more of my glory.* He passed by my bed. I jumped out of my bed bawling again.

"Oh my gosh," Cook cried out. "You have my whole life! I'm done! That's it!"

Suddenly, he was a new creature in Christ. "I knew in my heart of hearts that being gay was no longer a part of who I was. That was not part of me anymore. I was not going to live that life anymore. I knew it immediately. I didn't care at all because I had just met Jesus, so I didn't care."

"It all happened in one day. It completely transformed my life, and everything changed."

Cook admits that telling his friends he had become a Christian was a "crazy time."

When he told his best friend from high school the entire story, her first question was, "You're not pro-life now are you?"

"I just met the king of the universe and that's your first question ... what?"

Another friend from high school told him, "That's wonderful for you but don't ever talk to me about it or proselytize me."

"Some people were more supportive, and others were not," he says. "It was a weird period. But a lot of them after seeing me walk in this faith for ten years now are more curious and interested and loving and supportive of it."

Cook grew in his faith at Reality L.A., and then decided to attend Talbot Seminary.

He started writing his book before seminary started, feeling God leading him to help the church better understand the issues related to sexual identity.

"The culture has infiltrated the church," he observes. "Christians don't know what to believe anymore. Is it (homosexuality) a sin or is it not anymore? Lady Gaga tells me it's not. Taylor Swift is saying it's not, so maybe it's not."

"I wrote the book for the church to understand that yes, this is still a sin. It hasn't changed. The culture is lying."

He believes Satan is twisting God's Word in the church. "There are other sins, but this sin is taking over the world and our culture. It is different from other sins in that it is an identity thing. It is so important to understand it and understand how deceptive it is."

Cook has not had a romantic relationship with a woman since his conversion. "It's not that I became suddenly attracted to women, because I still struggle with same sex attraction. Before I got saved, it dominated my thought life, but now it doesn't."

"I am not attracted to women. God created the universe, so he could make me attracted to women. It hasn't happened yet, but it doesn't matter to me, because in Corinthians 7, Paul says it is better to be single."

"I am happy to be single and celibate, happy to be on mission for the kingdom, because that is what God has called me to."

Cook has been sharing his story at churches and Christian universities. "I want people to understand this issue, and understand the Gospel, how it can transform your life."

"It is not to win an argument. My main desire is to get the Gospel to people."

"Jesus is infinitely more important and worth it than this momentary pleasure. Every relationship I ever had before that paled in comparison."

"When I was living that life for twenty years, it was my identity for sure. I thought I would be that way for the rest of my life. I never thought anything would change. When I met God, everything changed."

Chapter 49

Church Caught a Vision to Free Modern-Day Slaves

A church of 400 people in California undertook a big project—to build a school in South Asia. But one thing led to another and on their fourth mission trip to the unnamed country in South Asia, two church members negotiated with a Taliban leader to win the freedom of Christian slaves working at a brick factory.

The man taking the lead on this trip was an unassuming seventy-three-year-old retired barber, businessman, and pastor named Paul Spitz, aka "J.P." He had trouble finding another person in the church to go on the trip with him, but at the last minute, another self-effacing congregant, Mark Williams, agreed to accompany him.

Their Christian connection in South Asia, Pastor Tariq*, is the leader of a sizeable network of house churches in a large city.

A few years ago, "Pastor Tariq had a bounty on his head from the Taliban," J.P. recounts. "His best friend was martyred. The Taliban shot and killed him and burned his body, put it into a fifty-five-gallon drum and took it back to Pastor Tariq, and told him they would do the same to him."

Taking this warning to heart, Pastor Tariq traveled to the U.S. at the behest of his church, and on that visit, made his first connection with the church in California.

"We gave him the second service to preach. He started bawling like a baby. He has a wife and three kids at home and wanted to go back, but his church wouldn't let him. But after a few weeks, a U.S. drone killed the terrorist who put the fatwa on his head," J.P. reports.

After Pastor Tariq returned to his country, the lead pastor at the California church made his first trip to visit Tariq and was impressed by the pastor's vision for Christian education and his desire to free slaves working at brick factories. The pastor visited one of the brick factories and was touched by the sight of an eight-year-old girl named Miriam making bricks.

"Every brick in that country is made by a Christian slave," J.P. notes, because Muslims will not do that kind of work. Pastor Tariq told him there are approximately 56,000 brick factories in that country alone—all functioning with Christian slaves.

"It's been going on for generations," J.P. says. "The slave owner has phony books where he charges them for food and shelter. Not only do they stay enslaved by his books, the debt grows and passes along from generation to generation. They inherit the debt of their parents and grandparents."

While it is against the law to have slaves there, these Christians are considered indentured servants, so their harsh reality becomes a functional enslavement.

It is also against the law for a child under fourteen to work, but the brick factories are full of underage children making bricks. Apparently, the government looks the other way at many of the abuses that go on.

J.P. discovered a typical family of four has a quota to make 2,000 bricks a day, working seven days a week, from sunup to sundown. There are no days off. "They can do it, but they have to work very hard. If they don't meet their quota, they don't eat."

The church in California agreed to partner with Pastor Tariq to start a school and help free some of the slaves. Initially, they inquired about paying the debt of the little girl named Miriam and her family, so they could leave the brick factory.

"It was too late," J.P. laments. "She had already died from the terrible working conditions. She was eight or nine years old."

After the vision to help was planted in the church, one woman gave $40,000 to start the school building project.

After they broke ground, Pastor Tariq informed them he

needed another $36,000 to continue. The lead pastor put the need before the congregation on Sunday and noted the money had to be wired by the following Thursday.

"That's when miraculous things happened," J.P. says. Someone walked up to the pulpit and announced they would give $5,000 and asked if anyone would match it. Another person stood and said they would match the gift. Eleven people raised their hands to say they would give $5,000 each.

On that remarkable Sunday in 2014, between two services, $296,000 was raised. "We built the school and paid for two years operating expenses," J.P. says. The K-12 Christian school accommodates 2,000 students.

J.P. had never wanted to go to South Asia but decided he must see the new school. He got turned down twice for a visa and finally went to the consulate in Los Angeles and shared his heart about the school. A consular official appreciated his compassionate desire to help kids and J.P. got his visa.

After his arrival, the first thing he did was go to a brick factory. He noticed "they treat the Christian slaves worse than animals." He learned the overseers will chop off fingers if a worker is not meeting a quota or tries to run away. "They constantly do things to put fear in these slaves," he notes.

He saw one woman holding a baby while she worked. The baby looked like he was going to die. The baby's father, Simon, had three fingers and his thumb cut off his right hand. He only had one remaining finger on his hand to make bricks.

J.P. told Pastor Tariq he wanted to get that family out. So, they paid the family's debt and set them free.

"That family remains very special to me," J.P. says. "I've seen them every trip." The church bought Simon a donkey and a donkey cart and paid for two months' rent on an apartment. He started picking up trash, then graduated to selling produce on the corner. Then he graduated to supplying restaurants and produce companies. Soon, he was making more than enough to support his family."

After witnessing the joy of setting another human being free, God impressed something on J.P.'s heart: *This is what I want you to do for the rest of your life.*

On that first trip, the church was able to purchase the freedom of forty-eight Christian slaves. On J.P.'s second trip, they delivered sixty people from slavery.

"One brick factory, we got twenty-eight people out for free because we always have a video going and cameras. The owner didn't want us on the property. He said take them and leave. He thought maybe we were from the BBC or some news agency."

The average redemption price is $600 to $700 per family.

The "miraculous" fourth trip in 2016 came together after Pastor Tariq informed the church that a certain Taliban leader, who owned twenty-eight brick factories, was being pressured by the government to close some of them.

"He committed a number of atrocities," J.P. learned. "One of his henchmen threw an eleven-year-old boy down a well and drowned him. The mom and dad were crying and wanted his body. They pulled the body up but wouldn't give it to the family. They doused the boy's body with gasoline and burned him right in front of his parents. They threw the boy's body in the brick kiln."

"There will be no justice for these parents. They (the Taliban owner) consider him just another infidel who has died," J.P. adds.

When word of this and other atrocities leaked to the government, they shut down twelve of the man's brick factories.

In the email sent to the church, Pastor Tariq said there were 584 families they could free from slavery at the factories, approximately 4,500 people. He thought they could get them out for $250 per family.

In a short time, the church raised $96,000 to free 384 families. The remaining 200 families would be released for free, due to pressure from the government.

J.P. questioned whether they could accomplish everything on a one-week trip. After wrestling with the logistics, J.P. decided to go.

"I was going to go by myself," J.P. notes. "I couldn't get

anybody to go with me. It was short notice. At the last minute, Mark went, and he was a major godsend."

When J.P. and Mark arrived in South Asia, the first day they went to see the 200 families who had already been freed. They were living in a Christian neighborhood and found housing through Pastor Tariq's network of 150 house church pastors.

The church sent enough money with J.P. and Mark for one month's supply of food for all the redeemed slaves. The church always works to provide transitional food, housing, and jobs for the families they rescue.

The second day, J.P. went to the brick factory and told them they were going to be freed. "We are planning on getting you out tomorrow," he declared. "You made your last brick."

But there was some degree of faith behind his announcement because they had not cemented their final deal with the Taliban leader.

Immediately, they went to the brick factory to see the Taliban owner. "I don't want to talk here," he told them. "I want you to come to my farmhouse at 6:00 tonight."

It was Ramadan, the month-long period of fasting by Muslims that commemorates the revelation of the Koran to Muhammad. At a little after 6:00, the Taliban owner called and said he couldn't make it but would call when he was ready. At 9:00, they started to get nervous.

"I'm afraid to go over there," J.P. admitted to Pastor Tariq. "This guy is evil." Pastor Tariq said he wanted to get the deal done that night.

Finally, the Taliban leader called at 9:30 and told them to come to his farmhouse. J.P. said it was pitch black as they approached the man's home. A guard came out to the gate with a 57-magnum pistol.

"In our car, it was Pastor Tariq, Mark, and me with our security guard carrying an AK-47."

A second car followed with three pastors on Pastor Tariq's board and another security guard. A third car was filled with four security guards equipped with AK-47s.

As they pulled up, a porch light revealed the house was heavily guarded by other Taliban with AK-47s. They were ushered into a room that had one door, two windows without glass, and a desk. The night air was heavy.

"Mark and I sat down, and Pastor Tariq stood at the end of the desk. The three pastors were standing against the wall." The Taliban leader and his secretary sat on the other side of the desk.

"Their guards and our guards were standing around. The guy guarding the door was very evil looking. The secretary looked very evil," J.P. recounts.

Immediately, the Taliban leader declared he wanted $1,000 per family—a dramatic increase over the agreed terms. The secretary asked if Pastor Tariq brought cash with them.

"No, it's in the bank," Pastor Tariq replied.

The secretary turned red and pounded the table. "We want cash, cash, cash," he roared.

"You ought to give them to us for free because of all the money they've made for you over the years," Mark blurted out.

One of the Taliban leader's guards started shouting, then got up and stuck the barrel of his AK-47 against one of the pastor's throats.

This is going to be a blood bath, J.P. thought to himself. He waited for the room to erupt in gunfire.

"Somehow, some way, nobody said anything else, and it calmed down. I have no explanation. A lot of prayer went into the meeting, and we were praying under our breath," J.P. recalls.

Pastor Tariq turned to J.P. and said, "Do you have anything to say?"

"How old are you?" J.P. improbably asked the Taliban leader.

"Seventy-three," he said.

"I'm seventy-three." They stared at each other for a moment. "I am an honorable man," J.P. said. "I came from

America, but I really was sent by God. God sent me over here to get His children free. You made an agreement with Pastor Tariq for $96,000. I'm not trying to get them out for $76,000. I'm keeping the commitment that he made to you to get God's people out of slavery."

"I will have to stand before God someday, and I will have to give an account of how I've lived my life," J.P. continued, sensing God's presence in the moment.

J.P. pointed directly at the Taliban leader. "You will have to stand before God some day and give an account of how you lived your life. I'm asking you right now to honor the commitment. We will write a check for $96,000, and you can go in the morning and cash it."

The Taliban leader studied J.P. carefully, then nodded his head in approval.

To their great shock, he stood up abruptly, looked at J.P., and said, "Will you pray for me?" He put his hands next to his kidneys and said, "My kidneys are failing."

J.P. stood up and placed his hand on the man's back and prayed an audacious prayer: "God, will You convict this man of all the horrible things he has done to Your people? Would You convict him of his sins? Would You through the power of the Holy Spirit reveal Yourself to him and save this man from all the things he has done, and save his soul, and heal his kidneys?"

They wrote out the check to free the slaves and began hugging one other.

The following day, they brought all the newly freed slaves together in one place, under a massive shade tarp. Pastor Tariq drove up in a Honda with J.P. and Mark in the back.

"It was like we were rock stars," J.P. recounts. "They were touching the car. Old women were crying, wanting to shake our hands, little kids hugging us at the knees, and everybody got food."

"It was the happiest day of my life. The magnitude of it—it's hard to explain. To see that many slaves set free ... I couldn't even fathom it. I went to bed that night and said, 'God, nothing could top this.'"

At noon the next day, Pastor Tariq spontaneously decided to organize an evangelistic outreach for 9:00 that night.

"I didn't think he would get anybody there. At 8:00 p.m., there were 200 people. Then cable TV showed up and a guy with a drone. By 9:00, the crowd had grown to 600 or 700. Then the band fired up and amazingly, the crowd grew tenfold—to 6,000 people!"

J.P.'s eyes widened when the worship stopped, and eleven Muslim clerics walked in. "Pastor Tariq had invited them to come. He allows the Shiites to use his church for their prayers on Friday."

The worship was very demonstrative, with people raising their arms and some were dancing. "The Muslim clerics were not participating. They were watching this," J.P. notes.

Then Mark got up to preach. He had never preached before. "Mark started talking about how to hear God's voice. His wife went to India a year ago, and they were her notes. He didn't realize it would be twice as long with a translator. He went fifty minutes, and it was close to midnight when he finished."

J.P. was set to speak next. Pastor Tariq turned to him and said, "Make it short."

J.P. only spoke for a few minutes, presenting the Gospel in a simple, straightforward way. He talked about Jesus living inside a person.

"Jesus can come in and change your life," he declared. "You can talk to Him and pray to Him, and He answers your prayers and you can have this incredible relationship."

J.P. gave an opportunity for people to raise their hands and receive Christ. To the glory of God, several hundred raised their hands! Paul turned his head slightly and watched a Shiite cleric raise his hand. *What's going on?* he wondered.

Then Paul prayed for the sick. A woman came onto the stage asking for prayer because she was blind. When she still could not see after two rounds of prayer, she was persistent, and asked for a third round of prayer. After the third prayer for healing, the woman cried out, "I can see! I can see!" She was miraculously healed!

The Shiite Muslim cleric who raised his hand came up to close the evening in prayer. "He started preaching up a storm (declaring Jesus as the Messiah). Then Pastor Tariq tugged on his robe and whispered to him, 'You're on TV and shouldn't be saying this.' The man had received Jesus and wanted to tell the whole world!"

The next morning, Pastor Tariq received a phone call. One of the Muslim clerics wanted to come over to meet the American visitors. After he hung up the phone, Pastor Tariq explained that this man was a known terrorist, responsible for a plane going down.

"On the internet, he is identified as a terrorist," Pastor Tariq said. "I don't want him to come over," he informed them.

"But if he wants to kill us, he wouldn't call first, he would just come over and do it," Mark reasoned. Pastor Tariq changed his mind, called the man back, and invited him to come.

When the man arrived and J.P. saw him, he was stunned. "I looked at him, and I thought, *this isn't the same guy I saw last night*. He was grinning and crying at the same time, tears coming down his cheek. It wasn't the same guy."

Then the Muslim cleric shared an amazing story with them. For the last couple years, it became apparent that he had serious heart problems and needed a transplant. He was on the list for a heart transplant.

The cleric watched and listened attentively to everything that happened at the evangelistic meeting. Nothing that was said or done seemed to penetrate his hard heart.

But after he went home and went to sleep, something remarkable happened. He had a startling vision of Jesus—the Man in White—who came to his bed as the Great Physician. Jesus began to do surgery on the cleric's heart.

When he awakened the next morning, he felt better than he had in years. He raced over to see his cardiologist, who performed some tests and came back with his head shaking, completely mystified.

"Your heart is normal!" the doctor declared.

Overwhelmed by the vision and the healing at the hands of the Great Physician, the Muslim cleric prayed to receive Jesus with Pastor Tariq, J.P., and Mark. "He was crying, like a big old ball of jelly. He grabbed me and hugged me," J.P. recounts.

After J.P. returned to California, he called Pastor Tariq. He said he was going to meet the former Muslim cleric that night. "He wants 1,000 Bibles in Urdu," Pastor Tariq said. "His wife has received Christ as her Savior; she saw such a difference in him."

"It is clear to see how God was showing His favor and protection over our ambassadors as they ministered," says J.P.'s wife, Diana. "God is moving in powerful ways amidst a country that desperately needs Him."

CHAPTER 50

Former Muslim Raised from the Dead Shocked Her Neighbors

Her Muslim neighbors and relatives grieved the loss of this relatively young mother of nine children. But after mourning her death for twelve hours, God brought a miracle that touched many lives.

"This is one of the most unusual and dramatic testimonies we've ever recorded in our AIMS ministry," says Dr. Howard Foltz, president and founder of AIMS. "It all started when a man named Warsa got saved, and then God spoke to him that he would be used by God to see the dead raised."

Trained as a missionary by AIMS, Warsa was already reaching many Muslims with the Good News about Jesus Christ. Then one of women in his village became ill.

"For two months, I was very seriously sick," says Fatuma Shubisa. Fatuma grew up in a Muslim home, but she and her husband converted to Christianity.

One day, Fatuma's mother came to visit her ailing daughter and was shocked to find her lying motionless and unresponsive. She searched in vain for a pulse or heartbeat, but Fatuma's body was already cold.

She closed Fatuma's eyes and straightened her leg. Unable to control her grief, she began to wail, and her shrieks aroused many of her Muslim neighbors who gathered in and around the home. They, too, began to grieve.

At the moment Fatuma died, her soul left her body, and she was drawn up to heaven. The first person she met was her brother-in-law, who died two years earlier.

"That brother of my husband took my hand and led me away," she recalls. As her former home on earth receded like "an open ditch," heaven opened to her.

"I went to a place where everyone was dressed in gold,"

Fatuma says. "I looked at the earth as very dirty." In heaven, she felt "free and clean."

Fatuma also met her mother-in-law in heaven. "She was begging them to send me back so I could raise my children," she recalls.

Meanwhile, a missionary named Warsa Buta was walking nearby and saw the crowd gathered around Fatuma's home. When he learned of her passing, he went inside and began to pray.

Some wondered why he prayed, since she had already been dead twelve hours. When he heard the murmuring, he persisted in prayer, because he remembered the promise God gave him as a young believer, that he would be used in such a time as this. *Could this be the day?* he wondered.

"I had faith the Lord would work through me," Warsa says. "I prayed as Peter prayed, 'Fatuma, be raised ... I ask you in the name of the Lord, come to life.'"

"Fatuma, be raised in the name of Jesus!"

Suddenly, Fatuma sat up in the bed, as everyone gasped in astonishment.

"I found myself in my body," Fatuma recalls. "I said, 'What is this? What's happening? What is going on?'"

Most of those around her were speechless. "Can he call back a dead person—a dead soul to a body?" someone asked.

"If this is real, we will all become Christians," one man said. "Your God is a very powerful God!" another shouted.

Many believed in the Lord Jesus that day, and there was great rejoicing in Fatuma's village. She is convinced she knows the reason for her return.

"I came back because it was the will of God for me to live with my children, but I would be very happy to go back there," she notes. "Now I have seen when a Christian dies, he goes to a better place, and his body goes back to dust. For a nonbeliever, that (hell) is a place of sadness. But when a Christian dies, he goes to a place where everything is good, where everyone is happy."

Dr. Howard Foltz believes God will use powerful testimonies like Fatuma's to provide breakthroughs among unreached people groups. "Our goal is to see all the remaining thirty-five unreached people groups of Ethiopia reached with the Gospel of Jesus Christ," he says. Dr. Foltz notes that Fatuma's miracle was also reported on by *The 700 Club*.

CHAPTER 51

Heavy Metal Satanist Rescued by Christ

If there was any man seemingly beyond redemption, Kirk Martin personified that man. Full of violence and hate—having made a pact with the devil himself—only God could fashion the creative strategy to pull his feet away from the fiery abyss.

"I always thought God loved some people, just not me," says Martin. He was the adopted fourth child of a loving family that prayed at dinner. Confirmed at his church in Livonia, Michigan, he quickly began to stray from his godly roots.

At seven years old, two older boys that "went to church" held him down and sexually assaulted him. "God doesn't love you," they said after the attack. "God will hate you if you tell anyone. You better not tell your mom and dad because they'll hate you too." He bled for days because of the assault, but never told his parents.

A couple years later, a friend introduced him to marijuana on the school bus. "There were signs showing up of me getting in trouble," Martin admits. "I was always lying, stealing, and beating other kids up," he says.

His father's response was swift and severe. "I remember cowering in the corner of the room and him bashing the snot out of me."

"We hit you because we love you," his mother told him, although she was never aware of how heavy-handed Kirk's father was. "I remember hearing all the time that God loves you ... so I put two and two together at a young age and figured that every bad thing happening was because God loved me, and I didn't want that kind of love. So, that is what really started pushing me away."

When Martin was eleven, authorities charged his minister with embezzling $175,000 from their church over a ten-year period. "One week later, he dropped dead from a heart attack. I thought God got him because he was bad, and God must have loved him too."

He joined the military at seventeen but only lasted six weeks. "I quickly learned I had a hair-trigger temper like my father," he confesses. "I was picking fights with everybody." He could hit "like a freight train" so his fights were brief—often a man would fall after only one punch.

But he met his match with a tough, southern boy from Georgia, who refused to go down. "He had a jaw of steel," Martin recounts. "I told him the first chance I get on the rifle range with live ammunition, I'd put a bullet through his head."

"They told me I was no longer able to touch weapons," he says. Then superiors ordered a psychiatric evaluation.

As he sat in the hospital rubber room, a military doctor confronted him. "What's up, private?" the man asked.

"I hate people," Martin replied. "I would like to kill people."

"That's not good, because wherever you go, there's going to be people," the doctor advised.

Martin returned home to Michigan briefly, experienced some trouble with the law, and then he ran off to Virginia Beach, where he was homeless for several months. He let "astute-looking businessmen" take him to their hotel rooms for gay sex. "I would give them whatever they wanted, and then I would beat the life out of them and take all their money and credit cards. Back in that era, they didn't go to the police. It was when being gay was not okay."

"I went to New York City and got involved in some dark, dark things," he recalls. "If I got caught, I would have lost my freedom for a long time."

"There was more than one time I snapped if someone said the wrong thing to me," Martin says. "Friends would pull me off someone who was lying there in a bloody mess."

Afraid for his life because of something he had done within the "brutal" company that he kept, he left New York and returned to Michigan. "I took a step back and calmed down," he says. He cut his hair and went to work at a grocery store to keep a low profile.

Martin had always nurtured a musical gift. At twenty-three, he joined some friends in a heavy metal band they called, "Frigid B****." During this period, immediately before and after he got into the band, Martin did some soul searching.

"I thought there was something wrong in my head," he says. "Dying didn't scare me. Being beaten up didn't mean anything to me." He cried out to God a few times, looking for a sign.

In the silence, he arrived at a troubling conclusion. "You ignored me, so now I hate you," he told God. "You don't love me, and this is who I am. I'm destined for darkness and there's no way to fight it."

"I turned into quite the freak," he confesses. "I got heavily into acid and cocaine and selling drugs to kids."

As the lead guitarist and principal songwriter for the band, he derived a certain measure of status from his performances on stage. "Everywhere I went, people wanted to give drugs to me," Martin says. "Finding young ladies to fulfill my evil, perverted desires was very easy. They were practically throwing themselves at me." Sadly, girls as young as fourteen were hanging around his group.

Martin admits that every cop in his county wanted to take him to jail at one time or another. Ironically, the band practiced in a basement studio next door to the police station. Years later, he asked a police officer why they never arrested him.

"We busted people for drugs, but they wouldn't turn on you because people were afraid of you," the officer told him.

Martin returned home to visit his parents before his group went on tour along the East Coast. "I had my head shaved and tattoos all over my body," he recalls.

"We're going to tour the world and screw everyone's f—ing heads up," he announced defiantly to his parents. "What do you think about that?"

They didn't know what to say.

Martin's band bought a handicap bus, converted it, and

traveled south seeking fame and notoriety. As the band toured in Florida, the bus broke down. After playing all over Florida, two of the founding members of the group told Martin they were leaving. "They realized I was a complete fruit loop, and they were sick of me. They thought I would do something to piss people off and someone would do a drive-by on us."

Martin broke down because of the setbacks. "I thought it was God picking on me again," he says. He went out on a deserted baseball field and fell down on his face.

"I hate you, God," he announced. "Jesus, I spit on Your name. I hate Christians and everything about Christianity," he declared.

Then, as he clawed the field with his fingers, he made his pact with the devil. "Satan, give me what I want, and I will twist as many young people as I can get my hands on. I will send people to hell with music."

A few days later, his manager called to say he had a recording contract for the group, something Martin sought for years. His pact with the devil seemed to be paying off! Martin changed the name of the group to "Hate Plow" and quickly replaced the two missing members.

His ability to play seemed to deepen as his lyrics grew darker. "God is a liar; your parents are liars; everybody is a liar except me," he sang. He started seeing two attractive strippers who were bisexual.

Martin felt on top of the world, completely fulfilled in his own twisted way. But in the depths of his darkness and hatred toward God and all things Christian, God sent the most unlikely messenger to get his attention.

One morning, Martin sat in a McDonald's restaurant at a table in the corner. He was one of only a few customers in the restaurant until another man came in and unexpectedly sat down at his table. It seemed odd, because Martin's intimidating façade did not ordinarily draw strangers.

"The guy was short, fat, with a funky tie, a yellow sweater vest, and bushy white beard," Martin recalls. He looked a bit like Santa Claus but wore a yarmulke. His tie had "a million different weird designs" on it.

"What's up, pops?" Martin asked, somewhat surprised by the stranger's approach.

"What's up, pops?" the funny-looking man aped as he stirred his coffee.

"Hey, what's happening dad," Martin said.

"Hey, what's happening dad," the man repeated.

Infuriated by the man's apparent mockery, Martin jumped to his feet, bent over, and put his nose next to the man's face. "I cursed him. I called him every foul thing I could think of."

The man didn't repeat the string of invectives, but the ice was broken. "Look, God sent me to tell you He loves you," the man began.

This statement really infuriated Martin—he wanted to pull the man's face off, but before he could lash out, the man said, "God wasn't responsible for you being abused when you were a little boy. He didn't make that happen."

"Your dad really loves you," the man continued, "he just doesn't understand how to love you. He did what his father did to him."

After more revealing conversation and some small talk, the man concluded by saying, "God is waiting for you to turn your face toward home." Then the mysterious man abruptly stood up and left the restaurant.

Martin chased after him. "He was fifteen-feet ahead of me, and we went around a row of hedges, and he disappeared. He was only out of my sight for five seconds."

Despite the strange encounter with a person Martin now believes may have been an angelic messenger, he went back to business as usual. He didn't tell anyone about what happened.

A month later, at 3:30 a.m., Martin was lying in the bus sound asleep when he felt the bus shake for a moment. He awakened to a powerful encounter with his Creator. "God came into the bus, tapped me on the shoulder, and allowed me to see what I had become. I hated what I saw."

His life flashed before him in a matter of moments. "I felt like a little boy in a big department store who lost his family and lost my way."

He lay there, sobbing and crying for hours. "God, please kill me or change me, because I don't want to be this anymore," he sang like a lost boy. Then he fell into a deep sleep.

When he awakened at 2:00 in the afternoon, he walked outside, and everything seemed different. "The clouds were a little fluffier, the grass greener, the birds chirpier."

The next morning, he was struck by a change in his normal routine. Normally, he would get high, grab his guitar, and start working on his music. Inexplicably, he had no desire for those things anymore.

Even the longing for a record contract—something he worked toward for years—left him. "I didn't want anything to do with it anymore," he says. "The whole thing stunk."

Ten days after God's rescue operation ushered in a profound change in his heart, he developed kidney stones. "I decided I would go back to Michigan to get surgery. I told the guys I would come back, but I never went back. I didn't want to go back."

After his surgery, an old friend came to visit him. His friend shared some recent challenges in his life. "My wife left me, and I was going to kill myself," the man confided. "But God came to me and changed my life. Now I'm serving Him. I believe God told me to give you this Bible."

He invited Martin to church, something for which he never had any previous interest. Later, Pastor Bill Tulip began to mentor him and became a spiritual father. "He spent a lot of time with me and refused to let me go," Martin says. "It took a lot of years. I had to work through a lot of major issues."

As Martin looks back, he realizes he wasn't seeking God or salvation when he was born again. "The light came into the darkness and the darkness comprehended it not," he says, quoting the Apostle John.

"A light bulb came on, and I was alive," he says. "I was no longer blind to who He was and why He was there. I realized God wasn't the bad guy."

"He opened my eyes and let me become like a little boy again. I was totally awakened to who He is. Everything changed instantly. All of a sudden, I was thinking different, feeling different. If that's what born again means, then that's what happened to me," he proclaims.

After growing in his faith, Martin began traveling, ministering, leading worship, and sharing his story throughout North America. In 2002, while ministering in northeastern Ontario, Canada, Martin met "the most beautiful woman I had ever seen." Six months later, he married Lesley, an accomplished piano player and worshiper. They travel and minister together, touching many lives.

God has blessed them with three beautiful children, and they continue to serve God and write worship music. More recently, God placed a new desire on Martin's heart "to be a light in a dark community." He sensed God's leading to start a new kind of heavy metal band. His new group, "Mercyhammer," will not be a "Christian band," but a band of Christians, who write music not about Christ but more about what Christ did for him personally.

"I'm in love with God, and He's in love with me, and that's never going to change," says Martin. "I was a mess, and He turned me into a miracle."

CHAPTER 52

The Kundalini Yoga Instructor Who Found Jesus

After a near-death experience in his freshman year at Florida State, he embarked on a quest for the "true light" and ultimately became a yoga instructor at four universities—until a hitchhiking encounter left him changed.

"I had been a rock musician in my latter high school years, but the alcohol, the drugs, and the absence of moral boundaries took its toll," says Mike Shreve, the founder of Deeper Revelation Books and Shreve Ministries.

Mike nearly died after ingesting a bad batch of LSD shortly after he entered college.

"I was not a heavy drug user, but I had a bad trip," he explains. "I lost control of my body, was convulsing, couldn't get up. I felt like my soul left my body and went into a dark void."

The experience frightened him enough to quit drugs, and he began to explore nearly every new philosophy or belief system that crossed his path. While raised a Roman Catholic, he thought the insistence on one way to God seemed narrow-minded.

He studied Ayn Rand, Herman Hess, Meher Baba, and other books by gurus and out-of-the-box thinkers. He joined an Edgar Cayce meditation group in Orlando, which used "The Lord's Prayer" as a basis for meditation but reinterpreted the prayer to promote metaphysical concepts.

Yogi Bhajan, a guru from India, who arrived in America to help the flower children find their way spiritually, became a big influence. "He taught us about yoga. The emphasis was not on obtaining a relationship with God, but rather, on attaining a realization of our inherent oneness with God (actually, an understanding that we are God)," Mike notes.

In every free moment between his college classes, Mike pursued the goal of reaching enlightenment.

But then, he unexpectedly dropped out of Florida State. He thought his conventional studies could lead him toward a mundane existence where he might become "a stale crumb to be eaten by the tiger of time," to quote one of his favorite Hindu poets.

After he left school, he helped start an ashram in Daytona Beach, a commune where yoga votaries lived and practiced their spiritual disciplines together. As he studied the Bhagavad-Gita and the Vedas (ancient Hindu Scriptures), he felt he was beginning to blend into oneness with the "oversoul," and experience out-of-body excursions into the astral realm and vivid spiritual dreams.

Because he felt a zeal to help the dawning of the "Age of Aquarius," he moved to Tampa, Florida, where four universities in the area opened their doors to him to teach Kundalini Yoga.

As a following developed around him and his classes, the Tampa Tribune newspaper published a story about Mike. He was thrilled by the free publicity as his classes continued to grow.

But little did he know, the news story also alerted a Christian group in Tampa to clip the article, pin it to their prayer board, and assign people to fast and pray for him every hour of every day until his conversion!

Several weeks after the article appeared, he received a letter from a college friend named Larry, who had also been devoted to yoga and meditation. But Larry happened to walk into a church one day and heard an audible voice say, "Jesus is the only way." At that moment, the Holy Spirit opened his heart to believe, and Larry was born again.

When Mike read Larry's letter, he thought the term 'born again' must be synonymous with Nirvana, Samadhi, or Christ consciousness, but Larry insisted it was different.

"Mike, you'll never find ultimate peace through yoga and meditation," Larry wrote. "You have to go through the cross.

You have to be spiritually reborn. Jesus really is the way to eternal life."

Mike wrote back a respectful letter, explaining he was happy his friend found a path that was right for him, but noted that he thought Christianity seemed illogical and the claims of Jesus too exclusive.

Unexpectedly however, a few weeks later, Mike's heart began to soften. He thought he shouldn't dismiss Jesus out-of-hand, but give him a chance. So, one morning, instead of following his usual yoga routine, he decided to dedicate one day to Jesus.

"Lord Jesus," he prayed. "I commit this day to You. I believe if You are real and if You're the Savior of the world, You will show me today."

Mike opened up a Bible and began to read through the gospel of John and the book of Revelation until the afternoon, when he left for the University of South Florida.

That same afternoon, Kent Sullivan, a member of the student prayer group that had been praying for Mike (and a former follower of an Indian guru named Yogananda), was on the way to wash his dirty clothes. He got halfway through the door of a laundromat when God impressed this on his heart:

Don't go in there. I have something else for you to do. Get back in your van and drive where I lead you.

Kent made several distinct turns as directed by the Holy Spirit until he was on a road behind Busch Gardens. He had no idea the yoga teacher he had been praying for in the last few weeks was hitchhiking, trying to get a ride to the University.

Suddenly, Kent spied a young man with long curly brown hair, a long beard, and Indian-style clothing hitchhiking on the side of the road. Kent felt compelled to pull over and pick him up, but had no idea who it was.

As Mike stepped into the van, he immediately noticed a picture of Jesus taped to the ceiling, and his heart began to race.

"Can I ask you a question," Kent asked.

"Yes."

Kent was very direct. "Have you ever experienced Jesus coming into your heart?"

"No," Mike replied, "but when can I? I've been praying about the experience all day long."

Kent's eyes widened with surprise. He didn't expect such a quick response. "You can come to our prayer meeting tonight."

"I don't want to wait for a prayer meeting," Mike said. "I want to experience Jesus right now."

Excitedly, Kent pulled his van off the road into the first parking lot he could find. Within a few minutes, he realized Mike was the one he had been praying about during the last four weeks!

As Kent went through the Scripture and explained the Good News of the Gospel, Mike peppered him with a myriad of questions, but Kent kept replying: "Don't concern yourself with those things. Just try Jesus."

Finally, Mike's heart was ready to receive the gift of salvation. With the motor idling, the two young men bowed their heads together in the back of the van and Mike prayed:

"Lord Jesus, come into my heart. I repent of all my sins. Forgive me. Wash me in Your blood. By faith, I receive Your gift of eternal life. I acknowledge that You died for the sins of the world and that You arose from the dead. I accept You now as Lord of my life."

Mike felt a warm sensation wash through his heart that brought cleansing beyond any laundry soap. "The peace of God settled like fresh dew on my soul. I was changed, and I knew it," he recalls.

"God generated a brand-new spirit in me, and I had truly become a new person—a 'new creation.'"

Mike Shreve's story is shared in greater detail in his book *In Search of the True Light* and in a free download on his comparative religion website titled *The Highest Adventure: Encountering God.* www.thetruelight.net

CHAPTER 53

Stage Four Lung Cancer Went into Her Brain

Messianic Jewish believer Bobbie Barsky likes to identify herself as a completed Jew. When she went through a horrific health battle with metastasizing cancer, the God of Abraham, Isaac, and Jacob gave her assurance every step of the way.

"God made the difference!" Barsky exclaims three times to emphasize her gratitude. Barsky and her husband, Rabbi Dr. David Barsky, oversee Congregation Beth Hillel in Coral Springs, Florida, a messianic synagogue.

Long before her cancer diagnosis, she received a vision that helped prepare her for what was coming. "It wasn't my imagination, because I couldn't turn off what I was seeing," she notes in her book, *The Silver Lining* (Gazelle Press). In the vision, she sat in a hospital bed but appeared healthy, as if a crisis had passed, and many people were lined up to see her.

After the vision, she shared her concern with husband, David. "Something is going to happen," she told him.

"We have to pray against it," he said.

When the crisis hit, none of her symptoms conveyed anything serious. But a stubborn case of bronchitis didn't respond to antibiotics, so her doctor ordered a chest x-ray. "I was never sick a day in my life," Barsky says. She wasn't concerned.

He called a few days later to deliver the stunning news: she had a large mass in her right lung. Later, it was identified as adenocarcinoma, one of the deadliest and most aggressive forms of lung cancer. Over 90% of sufferers die within eight months.

"I thought he made a horrible goof," Barsky says.

God doesn't have to get my attention, she thought, because

I'm already serving Him. I'm leading all these people to the Lord. What are you doing, God?

Barsky confesses she was angry with God for several weeks, then a Matt Redman song, "You Never Let Go," ministered a spiritual breakthrough in her soul.

Surgeons wanted to remove one-third of her lung, but the surgery was cancelled when it was discovered the cancer had spread to her lymph nodes. Her doctor warned her the cancer was so aggressive, it might also spread to her brain, so he ordered a brain scan.

Four days later, he called with an urgent tone in his voice. "Bobbie and David, you must come to my office right away."

After they arrived, he delivered more bad news. He informed Bobbie she had a large metastatic brain tumor.

David began to quietly sob, as both wondered whether they should plan for brain surgery or a funeral. But then something unusual happened in the doctor's office.

"The Holy Spirit moved in like the fourth man in the fire," she recalls, referring to the story of Meshach, Shadrach, and Abednego in the fiery furnace. "He was in the room, and I felt His arms around me and this peace flooded me from my head to my toes. It swam all over me."

In the midst of devastating news, she was suddenly and inexplicably smiling from ear to ear. Barsky had felt God's love like this only two other times in her life. She exchanged a knowing glance with her husband and nodded at him. He instantly knew she had heard from God.

"I'm going to be fine," she told a surprised Dr. David Khan. "I'm going to live and not die and proclaim the works of the Lord," she said with assurance.

Dr. Khan looked down at his papers, not sure how to respond.

Even though Barsky was certain of God's presence in the depths of her struggle, she also had faith that God would work through her doctors. Five days later, she had brain surgery.

"I had no fear going into the surgery," she recalls. "I was laughing and kibitzing with the nurses." Most of her congregation were in the waiting room praying for her, another powerful reminder of God's love.

Barsky also endured chemotherapy and radiation treatments. "The worst part was the radiation," she notes. "It was horrendous."

She had the last of thirty-five radiation treatments in July, 2011. Eight weeks later, Barsky's radiation oncologist, Dr. Ana Botero, scheduled a nuclear PET scan to view the results of the treatment.

Dr. Botero shared the remarkable news in a phone call: her lung tumor was completely gone. When the two met face-to-face, Dr. Botero choked up, and her eyes filled with tears.

"I didn't do this," Dr. Botero said, with emotion in her voice. "He did. If I could do this for all my patients, I would, but He did this," referring to God.

Dr. Botero led Barsky down the hall to meet the two techs who had given her the radiation treatments. "It's Bobbie! It's Bobbie!" she exclaimed. "She's cancer free!"

Barsky believes God brought a miracle, but he also used the doctors. "If I didn't go to doctors, I would be dead," she insists. "But I know I'm healed, and God healed me. I didn't get instantly healed. I had to go through the horror (of radiation)."

"The difference is God," she says. "God orchestrated everything. God still heals!"

Chapter 54

Computer Scientist-Engineer Experienced Vision of Hell

He was a computer scientist-engineer working on the F-22 stealth fighter project in 2002, when he had a massive automobile crash in which he nearly died. As his car flew through the air, he lost consciousness, and God gave him a frightening vision of hell.

In his vision, his chained body hurtled downward toward the lake of fire, and he heard awful screams and felt choking smoke and heat. He also saw three scriptures that convicted him about his double life. He had been attending church regularly but visiting prostitutes on the weekend.

As the roar of hell's fiery flames rose to meet him, suddenly everything went dark for a second, and he found himself 3,000 miles above the earth.

"The first thing I said was, 'I got out, I don't know how I escaped, how I got out.'"

Then Rathbun had a personal encounter with God the Father. Rathbun says the Father was obscured so he could not see Him.

My son, you have an important decision to make, and I'm going to let you make the decision and give you all the time you need to make it, the Father began.

Rathbun was struck by His authority. "His voice had so much authority the universe would shake. You couldn't get any more authority than that voice. It was the authority that said, 'Let there be light,' and it was done. I had never heard that kind of authority my whole life."

Then the Father said something that surprised him: *I trust you my son.*

"I hadn't heard my own earthly dad say that in fifty-one

years. My own dad didn't trust me. Here was the person with the most authority telling me He trusted me."

Rathbun tried to argue with Him. "This doesn't make any sense at all. I was almost in hell. I almost hit the lake of fire. I did everything to disobey you. I went against your Word. How could you trust me?"

I know all that, and I have put all that on My own Son, He said. Rathbun knew that all his sins had been placed on Jesus on the cross, but now, it became much more real. It was only by the precious blood of Jesus shed on the cross that atoned for his sins and allowed him to escape the judgment he deserved in hell.

Then the Father told Rathbun He would let him see areas of heaven. *After you are done sampling these areas of heaven, you can decide where you want to go and be.*

Then Rathbun went on the tour of his life. The first thing that struck him was the immensity of heaven. "It is huge. It is a very joyous place. Everywhere I looked was praise and worship. All of heaven was permeated with wonderful joy, very harmonious. It was the opposite of hell with people screaming and yelling. I went from night into day, darkness into light. Now I could see how good the good really was," he recounts.

The first area of heaven Rathbun visited involved education. "I had been a magna summa cum laude graduate from college. I was valedictorian of my high school and college. The Father let me know there are universities of learning in heaven."

"He reminded me that all knowledge comes from Himself." Rathbun was startled to find areas in heaven with colleges similar to his earthly experience. However, one difference is that none of the books and none of the instruction contain anything in error, only truth.

The Father told him he could continue to grow in his understanding of mathematics. "Math is not an earthly invention; it is something God overlaid on all creation," Rathbun notes. "Mathematics is how God puts things together. God is a lawful God, and mathematics is a pure description of God's law."

In the second area he visited, he saw people engaged in artistic activities, making crafts and other things with their own hands. "I had finished carpentry for five years and had done well. The Father knew I had a carpentry talent. He showed me the place where you take your gifts. He knows the gifts and talents He gave you," and encourages you to further develop them in heaven.

You can be a carpenter here like My Son, the Father told him.

"I saw women working with embroidery, making the most incredible tapestries for the homes in heaven. They were using transparent but shiny cloth. It vastly exceeded anything on earth. The women did it out of love. One of the joys of heaven is to continue to make things like this—fine furniture, jewelry, and gifts to give to each other."

Then God placed Rathbun in the middle of an apricot orchard. "There are vast orchards in heaven," he reports. "John writes about the Tree of Life and the twelve fruits." Rathbun inspected ripe apricots on the trees. "Everything glows with light up there and is transparent. You can actually see through the stuff. It is not like matter down here. It is like looking at glass but they are living things, glowing with the light of God."

"The flowers were blooming and fruitful at the same time," he notes. "I could smell the apricot fragrance, and it was indescribable, with a slight hint of almond. Then I saw orange groves, pears, all perfect fruit, no blemishes, no yellow leaves. It was very alive."

Then God showed him a social center in heaven. Rathbun had always wanted to develop his speaking abilities. "Things didn't work out in high school, and I didn't get on the debate team," he recalls.

"Perhaps you would like to learn how to share the truth of heaven," the Father told him.

Then Rathbun saw crowds learning how to speak "with heaven's standards."

"There were also groups meeting together, having fellowship with one another, social centers, areas all over where people could gather for talking and fellowship."

"Then He took me to two other areas that had to do with heaven itself. He would not allow me to remember this part. It was like a very special treasure waiting for God to unwrap and show you. It is not in my conscious memory," he says.

The ultimate was saved for last, when God gave him a glimpse of the throne room. "The Father had masked out Himself in the center, because the light was so bright, it would have instantly blinded me. What was going on above the throne was what He wanted me to fully taste and experience. Right above the throne, there is a rainbow, and that rainbow is multicolored."

"The part I focused in on was absolutely incredible, gorgeous violet, a deep purple color. The seraphim were immersed in that flame. It was a fire, very hot; it was very pure. The seraphim were in there singing, and they were going back and forth in a semicircular pattern in that rainbow." It seemed to Rathbun they actually passed through each other, with one group traveling clockwise and another group moving counterclockwise. "Their singing and worship was absolutely the most incredible worship you have ever had a chance to hear."

"Isaiah said he was undone when he heard the seraphim singing. When I heard them sing, I was totally melted down instantly on the spot from the beauty and purity and the holiness of that worship. It was in sixteen-or-more-part harmony. They were unified in this incredible, holy worship. I was pulled right into that."

"I told the Father, 'Here is where I want to be for eternity. This is the best part of heaven.'"

Then God pulled him away from the throne room. He said, *No, I want you to make a fair decision. If I allowed you to stay longer with the seraphim, it would have fixed things for all eternity.*

Rathbun was "miffed" that he was pulled away from such an incredible scene of beauty, purity, and holiness. He sat for a moment, trying to take it all in.

Have you made up your mind yet? the Father asked.

How could I answer the Father? he thought. *All heaven is so wonderful, beyond imagination.* "I don't know what to say or do. I need Your help," Rathbun replied.

Gladly, my son, I will help you, the Father said.

Then God unfolded a tapestry "like an excel spreadsheet" that described Rathbun's life. "I saw the beginning where I was born. The eighteen years until I was born again were grayed out. After that, the things counted. It was a beautiful tapestry."

Rathbun peered with curiosity at one section of the tapestry and asked, "What is that?"

Those are your eternal rewards. I have planned (rewards for) everyone's life. If they are obedient to My will, their tapestry is filled in with My divine works.

"This is different from salvation," Rathbun notes. "No one can earn salvation. But there are rewards that come from co-operating with God. He showed me the tapestry up to the automobile accident. He showed me the tapestry into the future, and I had thirty to thirty-five years to go."

As a result of his vision, Rathbun thinks he will live to be eighty to eighty-five.

"Why are there are more rewards after the accident?" he asked God.

Because you have decided to more fully obey Me.

Then Rathbun remembered he had just been rescued from hell, and the Father had offered him the very best of heaven. "I realized God had purely loved me with totally unselfish motives, and He had not said one thing about what He wanted."

So, he turned to God and said, "Wait a second, Father, You just gave me the very best You had. You haven't said one thing about what You want. Heaven is about love, and I should be loving You. So, I'm going to ask You, what do You want? What is Your will?"

Rathbun could feel the Father smiling after he said that.

"He made me know He wanted me to come back to earth and talk about Him. He told me what was going to happen in the auto accident very lovingly and caringly. It was like He said there would be broken bones and lacerations, blood all over and contusions, and much pain."

"I want to go back," he told the Father.

Are you sure?

"If I can hold Your hand, I can get through anything."

The Father beamed when he said that. You have made a wise decision, He said.

Instantly, Rathbun was back in the car flying through the air as it hit a eucalyptus tree. "I was screaming in pain. It was just as bad as He told me."

Rathbun cried out, "No, no, I want to go back to heaven."

The Holy Spirit reminded him, *Randall, you made your decision, and it is final.*

When paramedics arrived at the horrific crash scene, they intubated him. "I had a tube put down my throat for breathing, and I choked on that tube for several hours. My body thrashed around, and they finally duct-taped me to the gurney."

"I had to hold on to God with all my faith. I was fully conscious."

Rathbun had many broken bones, contusions, and almost broke his back in half. "They had to bleach the car there was so much blood. When I came home, I was in a body cast. It took me eight months to recover."

After he recovered, he got his clearance back from the government. He is currently self-employed, involved with software development.

As a result of his experience, Rathbun has been profoundly touched by the Father's love. "Men don't know who the Father is. When you see Him for who He really is, it will change you."

"At the point of the accident, I didn't have a father. The Father in heaven believes in us. He rescued me right before I hit the lake of fire. It was all grace on His part. He wants to reveal

Himself to us, particularly His purity and His holiness."

Rathbun's double life is over. His desire for obedience is a response to the love he found in God. "The Father has been increasing His holiness in me. It is the vital factor that will keep us from wandering off, looking for love in the wrong places. You want to stay pure for the Father because you feel special, you feel treasured by Him; He is very loving. He has to be sought out with one hundred percent of your heart."

"A passion for God has to be birthed in a man's spirit, so that his spirit comes afire and is lit with passion for the Father's purity and holiness. If we can get a glimpse of that holiness, it will be crucial towards setting us men free."

CHAPTER 55

Mickey Rooney's Encounter with Unusual Busboy

Legendary actor Mickey Rooney, one of Hollywood's last surviving stars of its classic era, passed away in 2014 of natural causes, at the age of ninety-three.

The award-winning actor became the biggest star in the world in his teens when he played the character Andy Hardy in *A Family Affair*.

The son of vaudevillians, his career started even earlier—as a mere babe. On a lunch break when he filmed the Mickey McGuire comedies, five-year-old Rooney walked into an office at Warner Bros. and introduced himself to a cartoonist named Walt Disney.

"Come over, and sit on my lap," Disney told the youngster.

When he sat on his lap, Disney held up a mouse he had drawn. "That's a good-looking mouse, Mr. Disney," Rooney blurted out.

"It sure is, Mickey," he said, and then paused for a moment. "Mickey, Mickey," he said with a gleam in his eye. "Tell me something, how would you like me to name this mouse after you?"

"I sure would like that, but right now, I got to go and get a tuna sandwich," Rooney replied, and he jumped off Disney's lap.

"It's a true story," Rooney told Kira Albin, in a 1995 interview.

Sadly, Rooney's private life was turbulent, and his eight marriages became the fodder for late-night comedians' jokes. But the challenges he survived, including elder abuse more recently, left him with an uncommon depth of wisdom.

After the deaths of his mother and fifth wife in 1966, he battled substance abuse and financial problems. In the depths of the valley, Rooney had an unusual encounter that he said changed his life, according to the same interview with Albin.

Over breakfast at a Lake Tahoe casino coffee shop, Rooney was greeted by a busboy with "blond curls, a white-rose complexion, and shining teeth," he recounted.

When the young man called his name, Rooney started to stand, thinking he had a telephone call. But the busboy leaned toward him and whispered in his ear, "Mr. Rooney, Jesus Christ loves you very much." Then the mysterious busboy vanished.

When Rooney looked for the young man and gave his description to the manager of the establishment, he was told that no such person worked there. Rooney believed he was visited by an angel.

Even though Rooney veered into the Church of Religious Science, which many evangelicals would label a cult, by the 1990s, Rooney boldly proclaimed a very orthodox faith centered on Jesus Christ as his Savior.

In 1995, Albin described Rooney as an "unabashed Christian."

"I've given my life to God," he told Albin, "and I try and do the right thing, but inevitably, and unfortunately, I do the wrong thing. I suffer from being human."

Rooney's oldest child, Mickey Jr., is a born-again Christian and has been involved in evangelical ministry. It may be due to his son's influence that Rooney found the Truth.

"You should take your children to church and teach them about Jesus Christ and about God, who makes the sunshine and the moon glow and gives us so many blessings," Rooney said in 2011.

"I talked before the House and Senate about (elder) abuse. No one had more abuse than Jesus Christ."

"If you go with God and with Jesus Christ as your personal Savior, and leave the troubles and everything to God, everything will work out for you."

Chapter 56

Paul Harvey's Amazing Prediction About the Future of America

Some will remember the homespun, conservative ABC radio commentator Paul Harvey. Millions of Americans listened to his news and commentary broadcast over 1,200 radio stations nationwide during his lengthy career.

In one famous broadcast, first delivered April 3, 1965, he considered how the devil might undermine the United States over time, using a subtle and not-so-subtle, yet diabolical strategy.

"If I were the devil, if I were the prince of darkness, I would want to engulf the whole world in darkness," Harvey began, "and I would have a third of its real estate and three-fourths of its population, but I wouldn't be happy until I had seized the ripest apple on the tree, thee, so I would set about however necessary to take over the United States."

Harvey predicted the devil would begin by undermining religious institutions. "I'd subvert the churches first. I'd begin with a campaign of whispers. With the wisdom of a serpent, I'd whisper to you as I whispered to Eve, 'Do as you please.'"

"To the young, I would whisper that the Bible is a myth. I would convince them that man created God, instead of the other way around. I would confide that what is bad is good and what is good is 'square.'"

He would cause seniors to believe that solutions to their problems lie with the federal government. "And the old I would teach to pray after me, 'Our Father, which art in Washington.'"

After this, the devil's media campaign would begin. "Then I would get organized. I'd educate authors in how to make lurid literature exciting so that anything else would appear dull and uninteresting. I'd threaten TV with dirtier movies and vice versa."

"I'd peddle narcotics to whom I could. I'd sell alcohol to ladies and gentlemen of distinction. I'd tranquilize the rest with pills."

"If I were the devil, I'd soon have families at war with themselves, churches at war with themselves, and nations at war with themselves until each in its turn was consumed. And with promises of higher ratings, I'd have mesmerizing media fanning the flames."

Then he would set his sights on the school system. "If I were the devil, I would encourage schools to refine young intellects, but neglect to discipline emotions—just let those run wild, until before you knew it, you'd have to have drug-sniffing dogs and metal detectors at every schoolhouse door."

"Within a decade, I'd have prisons overflowing. I'd have judges promoting pornography. Soon, I could evict God from the courthouse, and then from the schoolhouse, and then from the houses of Congress."

"And in His own churches, I would substitute psychology for religion and deify science. I would lure priests and pastors into misusing boys and girls and church money."

Even Christian holidays would lose their meaning. "If I were the devil, I would make the symbol of Easter an egg and the symbol of Christmas a bottle."

"If I were the devil, I would take from those who have and give to those who wanted, until I had killed the incentive of the ambitious. And what do you bet I couldn't get whole states to promote gambling as a way to get rich."

"I would caution against extremes in hard work, in patriotism, in moral conduct."

Fewer young people would decide to get married. "I would convince the young that marriage is old fashioned, that swinging is more fun, that what you see on TV is the way to be, and thus I could undress you in public, and I could lure you into bed with diseases for which there is no cure."

"In other words, if I were the devil, I'd just keep right on doing what he's been doing ...

Paul Harvey, good day."

CHAPTER 57

Jesus Miraculously Healed Woman's 'Incurable' Cancer

She was diagnosed with multiple myeloma, a cancer of the plasma cells in the bone marrow, which is considered incurable. But with Jesus-centered faith, prayer, and a powerful dream, God brought a miraculous healing that confounded her doctors.

"They said I had three to five years to live," says Tecla Miceli. "It was dreadful, and I was scared to death," she says. Tecla grew up in Sicily and came to the U.S. as a sixteen-year-old with her parents.

Fortunately, she caught the cancer at an early stage. Tecla was opposed to chemotherapy, so doctors agreed to monitor the progression of the cancer with bone surveys and blood tests every sixty days.

"The oncologist did a spinal, and it came out at 17 blood plasma level and the threshold is 5," says Gary LaFerla, her son, who accompanied his mother to the doctor visits. At 17%, doctors were willing to wait on the chemo.

But after three years of monitoring Tecla, doctors noticed an alarming increase in cancer cells. "It was full blown cancer, at least 27% in her blood," Gary says.

Raised as a nominal Catholic, Tecla was born again through the influence of Gary and his sister, Laura, who were involved at Calvary Chapel in Costa Mesa, California.

Nicky Cruz, the former gang member, was speaking when Tecla visited Calvary Chapel for the first time. Moved by his message, she felt compelled to go forward. "I felt a big flame in my heart literally pushing me to go up there," she recounts.

"I accepted Christ, but I didn't know what I was doing. I drove home, and I felt different. I never wanted to sin again.

The next morning, I woke up with a smile on my face, and I felt so peaceful."

Tecla finally grasped her daughter's previous words. "For the first time, I really understood what Laura meant when she told me about the peace of the Lord that fills the heart of a new believer and how the sky looks bluer and the grass greener."

"Throughout my illness, Laura prayed with me daily and gave me positive and encouraging words of faith in Jesus."

Tecla's faith became a vital component as she faced a potentially deadly health crisis. "This cancer eats the bones from the inside and they will collapse," Gary noted. "It can be very painful."

After thirty-six months, the scan of Tecla's head now revealed cancerous lesions covering her skull. "She was weak all the time, sleeping a lot, not able to move much," Gary recalls. "She had blood splots all over her arms and legs. She was very anemic."

"It's a horrible type of cancer."

Tecla's doctors wanted a bone marrow biopsy from her spine before they started chemotherapy.

"I had a whole week to think and pray and was petrified all the while," Tecla recounts. "I didn't know if I wanted chemo or if I should just die naturally. I was crying all the time."

One evening, son Gary had dinner with his mother. After their meal he said, "Mom, let's kneel down and pray." They both knelt down together. "Mom, the psalms are full of God's promises. I want you to read all of them and stand on God's promises. We will be praying for you."

Tecla spent the entire week in her patio reading the psalms and praying. "That's all I did. I prayed that God would heal me."

She poured out her heart to God: I know I have done it all, I've been married, have children, grandchildren, finished college, but I'm not ready to die yet. If you heal me, I will tell of Your miracle to anyone that wants to listen, she told God.

That night, shortly before her bone marrow test, she had a remarkable dream.

"I was outside a market and noticed I had a cart filled to the brim with long loaves of bread. I tried to give some away but only some would take it."

Then she found herself dangling from a foot-wide ledge, thirty feet above the ground. "I looked down, thinking I'm going to fall. All these people were looking up. I was hanging from a ledge, but my hand was holding a big thick nail with my right hand."

She thought she was going to fall and would surely die. "Then I realized the nail I'm holding is slowly creating a crevice and is sliding down. It was slowly bringing me down to the floor. When I reached the floor, I cried because it was a miracle."

"It's a miracle, don't you know it's a miracle," she cried out when she landed safely. "God is real. Don't you believe me?" She took her shopping cart and started offering bread to people. Some took the bread and others did not.

Tecla awakened the next morning feeling perfect peace. "I understood the bread to be the bread of life," she says.

Then Jesus declared, "I am the bread of life. Whoever comes to me will never go hungry, and whoever believes in me will never be thirsty." (John 6:35)

A few days later, Tecla had the bone marrow test, a painful procedure that required a strong sedative, but she woke up peacefully and surprisingly had no pain after the test.

Gary and Tecla went to meet with the doctor to go over the results. Her first chemotherapy was set to begin the following Monday.

The oncologist had an unusual expression on his face as their appointment began. "You know how problematic this industry has become," he began. "Look at this. I'm curious. I already know we're at 27-32, so she's at full-blown cancer."

"But look at this test I took from the spine ... this came back at 5 or 6. That's impossible. Blood plasma never retracts.

It is an axiom of medicine. They must have made a mistake at the lab," he said, shaking his head in disbelief.

One of Tecla's students happened to be a radiologist, who was convinced a more recent scan of Tecla's skull was a mistake.

The two doctors managed to connect by phone during the appointment. The oncologist hung up the phone and said, "Well, this is completely stupefying to me ... I don't agree but I don't know what to say."

"Do you believe in God?" Tecla asked.

"Yes," he replied.

Then Tecla proceeded to tell the doctor about her dream and the prayers for her healing.

The doctor looked at them both with curious amazement and then said, "In twenty-five years of practice, I have never seen anything like this before."

The doctor finally admitted that all her numbers were down, lower than when she first got diagnosed. Tecla began to cry, and Gary was amazed.

"The doctor called it an anomaly—his way of explaining away a miracle," Gary recalls. "But he, too, started crying because he was really moved by it."

When the doctor regained his composure, he said, "You are free to go and live your life ... I will continue to monitor your blood tests."

From that point forward, her tests were all clean.

"It was a miracle," Tecla exclaims. "Both my son and daughter and their families had each of their churches praying for me all that time, and I want to thank them all."

"Prayer works, and God does hear!"

CHAPTER 58

He Preached the Gospel as Hijacked Plane Hit the Water

After hijackers commandeered an Ethiopian Airlines flight in 1996, and it eventually ran out of fuel, one man stood to give passengers one last chance to hear a life-saving message—the Gospel of Jesus Christ.

About twenty minutes after Flight 961 took off from Ethiopia's capital, Addis Ababa, on a flight to Abidjan, three hijackers stormed the cabin and demanded to be flown to Australia.

"The stewardesses started looking scared and upset," British passenger Katherine Hayes told the Daily Record. "Then this man came on the intercom. He said he had hijacked the plane and had a bomb."

Hayes says she was surprised that most people remained calm. "It was almost surreal," she reported.

A man nearby borrowed Hayes' book, as a dreamlike normalcy prevailed for a while. "This went on for four hours without food or drink, but we were OK," Hayes told the Daily Record.

The pilots knew, however, there was not enough jet fuel to get to Australia. As the precious fuel drained away, Pilot Leul Abate spoke directly and firmly to the lead hijacker.

"Guy, we have thirty minutes to live. Unless you allow me to land and refuel, we cannot make it to Australia. The only option we have is to die in the sea," Captain Abate later told The History Channel.

The hijackers didn't seem to care and refused his request to land at Moroni, capital of the Comoros Islands.

Then the inevitable happened. One of the engines sputtered and stopped.

Shortly after that, Captain Abate came on the intercom and gave passengers the grim news: "We have no fuel," he said evenly. "We have lost the left engine, and we are about to lose the right. Prepare for a crash landing. That's all I can say."

People began yelling, screaming, and crying and some became nauseous. After the adults got upset, children began to cry.

"They'd been blissfully unaware anything was wrong. But as soon as the adults got upset, so did they," Hayes told The Daily Record.

At 21,000 feet, the second engine failed. The 150-ton plane was still gliding, however, falling out of the sky at 2,000 feet per minute. They would hit the water in about forty miles at that rate.

Andy Meakins, forty-three, from Beckenham, Kent, who worked with the Christian charity Tear Fund in Addis Ababa, was on the flight, seated next to his wife.

Franklin Graham met Meakins in Ethiopia in the eighties and recounted the next critical moments as retold to him. "Andy Meakins was a gentle giant of the faith, an Englishman who loved Jesus Christ and served Him in Africa for many years," Graham recounted.

With a courage and boldness supplied by the Holy Spirit, Meakins felt compelled to do the unexpected. "Andy's wife heard the snap of a seatbelt being unbuckled and turned to see her husband stand up," Graham reported.

"Many of us might die in this crash," Andy called out, "so there's something you need to know."

Andy then began to explain the Gospel message with urgency but simplicity. He moved to each part of the cabin so that everyone would hear.

"He invited people to place their trust in Jesus Christ in repentance and faith," Graham recounted.

"A flight attendant heard Andy's words, bowed her head, and asked Jesus to forgive her sins and come into her heart. She watched many more respond and, along with another survivor, later told the story."

"Of the 175 people on board, 125 died, including Andy, who was still on his feet preaching the Gospel as the plane hit the water."

"Every day, tens of thousands of people slip from this world into eternity—the vast majority unprepared, *'dead in the trespasses and sins.'* (Ephesians 2:1, ESV) We need to take every opportunity to share the love of Jesus Christ and the truth of the Gospel, the only message that will make a difference to a lost soul. Just like an airplane going down, time is running out."

CHAPTER 59

When God Sends Signs in the Natural World after the Death of a Loved One

Could the appearance of a hummingbird, a flock of geese, or a beautiful sunset bring comfort and peace to grieving loved ones following an untimely loss? Does God send such signs to His beloved to help the process of mending their hearts?

Recently, our dear friend, Kathy Buskirk, passed into the waiting arms of the Lord after a valiant battle with cancer. At the relatively young age of sixty, her loss was devastating to her friends and family.

In the days leading up to her passing, family members noticed a hummingbird had constructed a nest in a palm bush next to their front door, something that had never happened.

"I would jokingly refer to Kathy as my 'hummingbird,'" says husband David, "as she had so much energy and was always busily doing so much. In fact, to commemorate this reference, she bought a metal hummingbird for our kitchen wall. Later, she attached a cross to the bottom, how ironic!"

The appearance of the nest by the front door struck several as unusual. "It was very strange that a hummingbird would nest in such a busy location," David thought. "She would sit on her eggs and allow us in and out throughout the days of Kathy's passing. She was always there watching us, allowing us to watch her, and giving us comfort."

After Kathy's memorial service, a reception was held in the backyard of Kathy's brother's house. As friends and family stood in the backyard, several miles away from Kathy and David's house, they noticed a hummingbird perched in the branch of a tree that overlooked the gathering.

"We were there for hours, and the hummingbird stayed perched looking down on us for most of the time," David notes. "Hummingbird sightings are relatively rare, and certainly they rarely just perch as they are usually moving, rushing from here to there. This bird seemed to just be watching, listening, and comforting us."

Two weeks after Kathy's passing, the eggs hatched next to the Buskirk's front door, as David continued to watch in wonder. "She's back and forth feeding her babies," David says. "I am alone now in the house, and she continues to give me comfort." His departed wife was very nurturing—a woman who always seemed to be focused on meeting her family's needs.

Shortly after the babies hatched, David took their golden retriever, Gracie, on a walk to the park. "I sat on the bench while throwing Gracie a ball. I felt a little sad and alone," he recalls.

"Right in front of me appears a hummingbird, it hovers, then floats to the sky out of sight. Then out of the blue another one—or the same one—hovers in front of me, then floats to the sky out of sight." As David watched in amazement, the bird appeared and reappeared five times.

"I don't think Mom likes it when I'm sad," he says.

David sees the hummingbird as a symbol of love, joy, and beauty. His spirit-filled wife gave off these same qualities because of her close walk with Jesus.

"The hummingbird is also able to fly backwards, teaching us that we can look back on our past," he notes. "But this bird also teaches that we must not dwell on our past; we need to move forward."

As the Apostle Paul said in the book of Philippians 3:13-14, "But one thing I do: Forgetting what is behind and straining toward what is ahead, I press on toward the goal to win the prize for which God has called me heavenward in Christ Jesus."

"When the hummingbird hovers over flowers while drinking nectar, we learn that we should savor each moment, and appreciate the things we love," David says.

David also notes that in the South American Andes, the hummingbird is considered a symbol of resurrection. "It seems to die on cold nights but comes back to life again at sunrise."

When Jesus went to the tomb of Lazarus, He said, *"I am the resurrection and the life. The one who believes in me will live, even though they die; and whoever lives by believing in me will never die. Do you believe this?"* (John 11:25-26)

David doesn't believe these unusual signs after his wife's passing could simply be by chance. "We are at peace that her spirit lives on."

CHAPTER 60

Dying Farmer Left Civil War Bible Behind for New Age Homebuyer

Dale Walker grew up unchurched in Montpelier, Vermont and doesn't recall meeting a Christian during his formative years. His parents attended church twice a year, but were not followers of Jesus.

His small, picturesque New England city had such an exceptional quality of life that he never heard a single person speak about having a need for God or desiring to have a personal relationship with God. He didn't know such a thing existed.

In high school, he considered himself an atheist and refused to say, "One nation under God," when the Pledge of Allegiance was recited.

When he went off to college at Wesleyan University in Connecticut, profound cultural changes were afoot. "The hippie revolution started, and I became a sixties, 'turn on, tune in, drop out,' psychedelic, free love person. Then I started to get into Eastern religion. I was trying to find something."

"I graduated from Wesleyan University without knowing who John Wesley was, or who Jesus Christ was. And I never really met a single person that knew God or could tell me about God."

"Becoming a Bible-believing Christian was near the very top of things that I hoped would never happen to me."

During graduate school at Michigan State University, he became active in the civil rights movement. "I was around a whole bunch of people that were trying to find some meaning to life, but I had no idea of any meaning or purpose to life whatsoever," he recalls.

As the Vietnam War raged, Walker was granted Conscientious Objector status by the Presidential Appeal Board and was allowed to serve two years at a psychiatric hospital in Vermont. This was followed by three years as a social worker for the Vermont Welfare Department. "In both of these venues, I found the world to be filled with many problems and no viable solutions," he notes.

Someone gave him a book about "The Farm"—a spiritual commune founded by a hippie guru named Stephen Gaskin who mixed Eastern religion, Christianity, and New Age ideas together. While Walker still didn't believe in God, he found Gaskin's ideas about spirituality to be intriguing.

"I was heavily impacted by one teaching in the book which I later discovered to be a quotation from the Bible. It was: 'Seek, and ye shall find.' Gaskin proposed that if a person honestly searches to find the meaning of life, 'the Universe' would guide them and direct them to it."

In 1971, Walker left his job at the Welfare Department on a quest to find greater meaning. He bought a red Dodge van, equipped it with a camper, and put $2,000 in cash under the mattress as a possible down payment for a house. He headed for Nova Scotia, along with a book about the Communist Revolution in Russia, another about E.S.P., and Gaskin's book about his New Age commune.

His reading subsequently began to explore the "unknown forces" which might explain the universe. "I bought book after book on mysticism, Eastern religion, U.F.O.s, and psychic phenomena of every kind. Each one of them opened my mind a little more to the spiritual realm in some way."

After failing to find what he wanted in Nova Scotia, he decided to explore nearby Prince Edward Island, continuing to ask the Universe to guide him.

In the village of Montague (population 2,400), he dropped by a small real estate office where a clerk showed him photos of available properties. "And then we have this one," she said, "for $1,500."

"Hardly believing my ears, I asked for directions and within minutes was standing in a large field looking at a two-story, gray-shingled farmhouse, ten miles out in the country which was to become my home for the next three years."

The asking price was supposed to be $2,500, but the clerk mistakenly read the "lowest acceptable price" instead of the asking price.

Walker and the owner, a dying farmer in a nursing home, settled on a sales price of $1,750. The house had electricity, no running water, and sat half a mile back from a dirt road—an ideal place for Walker to live close to nature.

Furnished with antiques, the small farmhouse had one bookcase containing three books the farmer left behind: a large, eight-inch-thick 1865 family Bible, a book on Bible prophecy, and a biography of the evangelist, Dwight L. Moody.

Walker didn't want anything to do with those three books, so he promptly stowed them in the attic. Over the next couple years, he filled the empty bookshelves with books about meditation, the occult, reincarnation, and the search for enlightenment. "I even ordered esoteric books from a New Age publishing house, the Lucis Trust (formerly the Lucifer Trust), which promised to reveal 'the secret wisdom of the ages.'"

Over a three-year search for meaning, he held onto a New Age meme that says: "When the student is ready, the teacher will appear."

Walker often took long walks in the woods and fields around his house and would sit quietly, observing nature. One day, he sat on an old tree stump and noticed it was a "ladybug factory."

"As I watched, I noticed hundreds of the beautiful, little red-and-black-spotted creatures coming and going from their colony inside the rotting stump. The more that I studied nature, the more it astounded me, and, in this case, I sat wondering who had given these little Volkswagen-like bugs their perfect paint jobs. What artist had so delicately hand-painted each of these creatures?"

"I had a similar awe for the whole natural world—the swirling galaxies, the brightly-colored flowers, the beautiful lace-like designs of snowflakes ... While I had no explanation for this wondrous universe, I began to feel that it reflected a brilliant and creative Mind of some sort. I longed to somehow merge with this Creative Force, to blend in with it, find my role to play in its drama."

Even practicing Eastern meditation, his inner emptiness wouldn't go away. "At the same time, my personal life was tangled into a series of knots which I didn't know how to untie. I had come to Prince Edward Island on a search for a life and hadn't been able to find it. At the age of thirty-one, I was empty, at war within myself, and losing hope that I would ever find what I was looking for."

Feelings of desperation began to overwhelm him. "I felt that if something didn't happen very soon, I was going to lose my mind, kill myself, or perhaps just die from the implosion of the emptiness and meaninglessness of my life."

One day on a walk, Walker did something unusual, something he had never done before. "I got down on my knees in the red Prince Edward Island soil, looked up at the sky above me, and prayed the first prayer I had ever uttered in my life. Since I didn't know 'Whom' or 'What' to pray to, I desperately intoned: 'IF THERE'S ANYBODY UP THERE, PLEASE HELP ME!'"

It was the heartsick prayer of a despairing atheist.

A few days later, God answered his prayer. As he meditated in the middle of a 200-acre field surrounding his house, an inaudible, but loud, inner voice impressed these words on his heart and mind:

The Lord is my shepherd.

Remarkably, the meaning of these words suddenly flashed into his mind. "Just as these farm animals had a master who fed them, cared for them, and provided for them, I, too, had a master somewhere up above who was watching over me. This master was called, 'The Lord,' and He had been looking down upon me as I searched for the truth and was trying to find the path which I should take with my life," he recognized.

Suddenly, it hit him that those words came from the Bible.

Walker got up from the place he had been meditating, and began running across the field toward his house, flew through the front door, and raced up to the attic where he found the old farmer's 1865 family Bible, now covered with dust. "I brought it downstairs and started searching for the Psalms where, despite my almost total ignorance of the Bible, I thought the verse could be found. I finally located the 23rd Psalm and read with rapt attention the rest of the message which had come to me while I was sitting in the green pasture."

The truth he discovered in the 23rd Psalm thrilled his soul. "It spoke of a loving God who cared for, led, and protected His people as a shepherd cares for his sheep and a farmer does for his livestock. It spoke of a path on which He would lead His people until they could find still waters and green pastures which would restore their souls. These words were like a medicine to my soul and struck me as the greatest truth which I had found in my long search for spiritual reality. I finally had what seemed to be the beginning of an answer to my search—and my prayer!"

The Bible stood in stark contrast to the books he had been reading. "I had two bookshelves of New Age gobbledygook, ascending to twelve levels of spiritual reality, and that kind of gunk. And I started Matthew, and I started reading the Sermon on the Mount, and it was like the words were unlike anything I've ever read before in my life; I was riveted by it."

He stayed up until 3:30 in the morning reading the Bible and decided the Sermon on the Mount was the greatest teaching he ever encountered. Moved by the powerful truth, he took an old typewriter and typed the Sermon in red ink on gold paper and placed it in the middle of his dining room table.

He found that Jesus spoke with a wisdom and authority he had not encountered anywhere else in his search for the truth and the words of Jesus "arrested him" like nothing else he had ever read.

Walker went upstairs to retire, and happened to turn on the TV, stumbling upon a program about Roy Campanella, the Brooklyn Dodgers catcher seriously injured in a car accident. Before his accident, Campanella was considered one of the greatest catchers in the game.

While driving home one night, Campanella's rented 1957

Chevy sedan hit a patch of ice, careened into a telephone pole, and overturned, breaking his neck. He fractured the fifth and sixth cervical vertebrae and compressed his spinal cord, which left Campanella paralyzed from the shoulders down.

The program dramatically depicted Campanella in the emergency room, not knowing if he was going to live or die. "It flashed back to him as a little boy about ten years old and his mom, saying prayers by the bedside. And she turns to him, and says, 'I want to teach you something you may need someday.' And she said: 'The Lord is my shepherd. I shall not want. He maketh me to lie down in green pastures ... '"

"At this point, the camera flashes forward to Roy in the hospital emergency room where the doctors were desperately trying to save his life. Beads of perspiration had formed on his brow, and he appeared to be semiconscious, but his lips were moving. I suddenly realized that in the most desperate moment of his life, he was mouthing the same words that his mother had taught him: 'THE LORD IS MY SHEPHERD.'"

"I almost fell off my chair. He's racing to the hospital, and his lips are moving, and he's saying, 'The Lord is my shepherd.'"

"As I sat there in astonished silence that night, I knew one thing, and one thing only, that my prayer for help and search for a teacher or a guide for my life was being answered. My teacher had appeared, and to my surprise, it was not some far out swami, mystic, or guru master—it was the God of the Bible!"

Walker began reading the Bible regularly, but he still considered himself a materialist, so he was put off by the miracles of Jesus. "I still didn't believe in miracles," he recalls.

He stopped reading the Bible for a while. "The next time I went to my New Age bookstore, where I was getting all my New Age books, I pulled one out that was written by Kathryn Kuhlman, the Christian faith healer, and the name of the book was, *I Believe in Miracles.*"

Wanting to know more about miracles, Walker began reading her book. "It was all about people that got supernaturally healed at her healing services."

"Down the lane from me, and where I was living, was a lady, Mildred Macdonald, who had cancer. And she was told by the doctor that she was going to die very soon. The cancer had spread from her breast into her lymph nodes and into her lungs. They took muscles out, and they couldn't stop it. The doctors told her husband to prepare for the funeral."

"At the same time, I'm reading a book about a man with cancer that went to a Kathryn Kuhlman service. He went there, and she prayed for him. He felt this warm feeling going through his body and was totally healed of cancer. And ten years later, when I was reading the book, he was still healed."

Walker gazed out the window of his farmhouse and thought, *I would like to take Mildred to see Kathryn Kuhlman. But I don't even know if I believe this stuff. No, I'm not gonna run down the lane and say, "Hey, listen, you can be healed," because I'm not even sure about it.*

Walker thought about driving Mildred to see Kuhlman in Pittsburgh, but it was a fifteen-hour drive. *I don't have the money to take her down there*, he thought.

The next day, Walker was eating lunch at the end of a dock when his girlfriend came by. "Guess what," she said excitedly.

"What?"

"Mildred got healed ... "

Walker was incredulous. "What?"

"Mildred has a daughter in Toronto who flew her there for a visit. While she was there, Kathryn Kuhlman just happened to be in town conducting a healing meeting and Mildred's daughter brought her. When Mildred came forward for healing and was prayed for in the name of Jesus, she felt a warm sensation through her body. After that, she was able to run up and down the stairs which only minutes before she could hardly drag herself up."

"Mildred flew back to the Island full of life, and x-rays later confirmed that the cancer had entirely left her body. All that remained was a tiny scar on her lungs showing where it had once been!"

The miraculous healing took place at the same time Walker was reading Kuhlman's book. "I realized how utterly faithful God had been to me, and what great lengths He had gone through to prove Himself to my skeptical mind. Looking up at the big blue Prince Edward Island sky over my head, I inwardly said to Him, 'I can't ask anything more of You. You have been more than fair to me. YOU'VE GOT ME!'"

"At that moment, I decided that God was real, and that Jesus was real, that He had undeniably revealed Himself to me, and that I wanted to know Him. I wanted the kind of personal relationship with Him that the people in the Christian testimony books had described and that Kathryn Kuhlman had spoken about in her book."

"*Somewhere,* I thought, *there must be a church where there are people who know God in this way and can tell me how to find it.* I told some of my hippie friends about this and, together, we decided that we would attend a different church every week until we found such a church."

It was on the third try that Walker and his friends met the pastor of a small church in a fishing village down the road. "He invited my girlfriend and me to dinner at his house. That night, after dinner, he and his wife explained the Gospel (or Good News) of Jesus Christ, his offer of forgiveness and eternal life, and we both bowed our heads and prayed to receive Him as our Savior."

"Driving home that night, I experienced the beautiful, personal presence of God in my heart which has been my life, my strength, my guide, and my joy ever since. I remarked to my girlfriend: 'I feel like there's someone in the car with us!' And, indeed, there was! For Jesus had promised His followers in Matthew 18:20, KJV, *'For where two or three are gathered together in my name, there am I in the midst of them.'* And, even better, He had come into our hearts to live."

When Walker was buying the farmhouse from the old farmer, he went by the nursing home where the man had been living. "I walked by his room, and he was down on his knees, and the nurse said, 'He's in there every single day praying for God to take him.'"

One day, he needed to have some medical tests, and the staff said they were going to take him to the hospital for the tests. "He turned to everybody in the nursing home and said, 'I'll see you; it's been nice knowing you.' He said goodbye to everybody like he was not coming back. He went in and had his medical test. And he died. And the tests came back, and they said there was nothing wrong with him."

Walker believes there was divine purpose in the farmer leaving behind the three books on his bookshelf. "I think about that, because Dwight L. Moody became one of my all-time heroes."

He not only got a furnished farmhouse; he got three books that God used to change his life. "I was waiting for my teacher to appear, and I looked up at the sky out there, it was Jesus that appeared. I found my teacher."

After these life-changing events, Walker went to Bible school for three years, then started an inner-city church in New York. He also became a drug counselor and was hired full time as a drug counselor at a mission, where he worked for twenty-eight years. Walker also served as chaplain to the New York State Legislature for five years.

The transformation was immense. "The changes which He has brought into my life: the joy, the peace, the supernatural guidance, the beautiful presence, the help in times of trouble, the answered prayers, the miracles He has done for others—all of these things and more have made His ever-present reality so strong that I seldom think about the path by which I got here."

"If you want to know God, if you want your sins to be forgiven, if you want your life to be changed, and if you want to know that when you die, you will go to heaven, you can ask God for these amazing blessings at any time. You can even do this right now just by praying a prayer like this":

Lord Jesus, thank You for dying on the cross to pay for my sins. Please forgive all my sins and come into my heart to live. Help me to live a life which glorifies You and to become the person You want me to be. I accept You as my personal Lord and Savior. Amen.

www.ingramcontent.com/pod-product-compliance
Lightning Source LLC
Chambersburg PA
CBHW031309150426
43191CB00005B/150